# THEATRE ODYSSEY

**Ten-Minute Play Festival**

**2014 - 2017**

# Nigel Publishing

Published by Nigel Publishing, LLC

Bradenton, FL 34209

nigelpublishing@gmail.com

Copyright © 2018 by Nigel Publishing

All rights reserved.

CAUTION: Professionals and amateurs are hereby warned that the plays represented in this book are subject to a royalty. They are fully protected under the copyright laws of the United States of America, and of all countries covered by the International Copyright Union (including the Dominion of Canada and the rest of the British Commonwealth), and of all countries covered by the Pan-American Copyright Convention and the Universal Copyright Convention, and of all countries with which the United States has reciprocal copyright relations. All rights, including professional, amateur, motion picture, recitation, lecturing, public reading, radio broadcasting, television, video or sound taping, all other forms of mechanical or electronic reproduction such as CD-ROM and CD-I, information storage and retrieval systems and photocopying, and the rights of translation into foreign languages, are strictly reserved. For any such reserved use, permission must be secured in writing from the author or the author's agent. Pages 273-274 constitute an extension of this page.

First Edition, March 2018

No part of this book may be reproduced, scanned, or distributed in any printed or electronic form without permission. Please do not participate in or encourage piracy of copyrighted materials in violation of the author's rights. Purchase only authorized editions.

Printed in the United States of America.

Cover photos courtesy of Cliff Roles (http://cliffroles.smugmug.com)
    Ann Gundersheimer and Fredric Sirasky in *Clarinet Licks* by Fredric Sirasky
    Joshua Brin and Nicole Cunningham in *Hands* by Sylvia Reed
    Andrea Dovner and Chuck Conlon in *The Clown* by Larry Hamm
    Cover and logo design by Brooke Wagstaff, original logo by Daniel Greene

ISBN-10: 0-9841984-7-4/ ISBN-13: 978-0-9841984-7-4

# CONTENTS

## The 2014 Ten-Minute Play Festival ...... 1

*A Bottle of Vodka by Connie Schindewolf ...... 2

**Smart Bra by Sylvia Reed ...... 9

***Visiting Grandpa by Ron Pantello ...... 16

Fancy Seeing You Here by Marvin Albert ...... 23

For Art's Sake by Bernard Yanelli ...... 30

I'll Be Home for Christmas by Dale E. Moore ...... 37

Just Fooling by Verna Safran ...... 47

School for Wives by Arthur Keyser ...... 54

#Elevate My Life by Joseph Grosso ...... 62

## The 2015 Ten-Minute Play Festival ...... 72

*High School Reunion by Arthur Keyser ...... 73

**The Coward by Dylan Jones ...... 82

Dream On, Merry May by Bernard Yanelli ...... 90

It's Time to Move by Ron Pantello ...... 98

Nimby by Robert Kinast ...... 104

The Dancing Lessons by Connie Schindewolf ...... 111

The Locket by Mark E. Leib ...... 117

Why by Marvin Albert ...... 123

#As Long as the Moon Shines by Julien Freij ...... 130

*Best Play Award

**Runner-up/Honorable Mention

***Audience Favorite

#Winner, Annual Student Ten-Minute Play Writing Festival

## The 2016 Ten-Minute Play Festival..........137

*Hands by Sylvia Reed..........138

**Clarinet Licks by Fredric Sirasky..........145

A Tender Moment by Frank Motz..........153

Call These Delicate Creatures Ours, and Not Their Appetites by Peter A. Balaskas..........160

Chopping Celery by Connie Schindewolf..........169

Miss O'Hara, I Have a Confession to Make by Bernard Yanelli..........175

Silences by Mark E. Leib..........183

The Clown by Larry Hamm..........189

#Brothers in Arms by Julien Freij..........197

## The 2017 Ten-Minute Play Festival..........205

*The Best Ten Minutes Ever by Dylan Jones..........206

**Always by Stephen Cooper..........215

***I'm Dead When I Say I'm Dead by Ron Pantello..........223

A Big Wave by Connie Schindewolf..........231

Kennedy's Acolytes by Jack Gilhooley..........238

Secret's Out by Greg Burdick..........245

The Call by Frank Motz..........252

Wheelchair Chicken by Jason Cannon..........259

#Amazing Grace by Luke Valadie..........266

*Best Play Award

**Runner-up/Honorable Mention

***Audience Favorite

#Winner, Annual Student Ten-Minute Play Writing Festival

# Prologue

In December of 2005, Tom Aposporos and Larry Hamm met with a local playwright who wished to have his play read by skilled actors in a formal setting in front of an audience. In the course of their discussion, they began to talk about the tremendous amount of artistic energy and talent in the region, and, subsequently, plans were made to schedule a festival of ten-minute plays on a date approximately a month after the reading. In January 2006, Theatre Odyssey was created with these immediate goals in sight.

Both the reading of Robert Lipkin's <u>Sweeter than Justice</u> and the initial festival took place at the Arts Center Sarasota, and both, directed by Thomas Griffin, exceeded expectations in terms of audience. The first festival was performed only for one evening and to a capacity crowd of one hundred and twenty.

In the following years, Theatre Odyssey's Ten-Minute Play Festival became an annual event and was performed at multiple venues until first repeating a venue with the West Coast Black Theatre Troupe from 2011 through 2013, and finally finding a more permanent home at the Asolo's Cook Theatre in 2014. Over the course of its existence, the festival has introduced Sarasota audiences to a number of new works, many of which have gone on to be recognized in national publications and with international performances.

The philosophical purpose of Theatre Odyssey remains unchanged: to encourage and promote the efforts of local playwrights and actors. For actors, Theatre Odyssey shares profits from productions so that some compensation is provided for an actor's time commitment. For playwrights, Theatre Odyssey offers a potential means of play production and a fair source for feedback on a given work. Plays for the Ten-Minute Play Festival are chosen by an anonymous group of three readers and judged in competition by three adjudicators.

# Ten-Minute Play Festival

# 2014

**Dates:** May 2nd, 3rd, and 4th, 2014

**Location:** Jane B. Cook Theatre, Asolo/FSU Center for the Performing Arts, Sarasota

**Best Play Award**

    A Bottle of Vodka by Connie Schindewolf

**Runner-Up/Honorable Mention**

    Smart Bra by Sylvia Reed

**Audience Favorite**

    Visiting Grandpa by Ronnie Pantello

**Student Playwriting Festival Winner**

    Elevate My Life by Joseph Grosso,
                Lakewood Ranch High School

# *2014 Best Play*

# A Bottle of Vodka

### by

### Connie Schindewolf

Directed by Preston Boyd

with

Don Walker as Will

Jenny Aldrich as Judy

CHARACTERS
WILL, a man, 30 to 60, alcoholic.

JUDY, a woman, 30 to 60, alcoholic.

SETTING
A room with no doors somewhere in the Universe or beyond. CENTER is a small table with a large bottle of vodka on it. RIGHT is a chair and LEFT is a chair.

TIME
The present.

> *As lights come up, the sound of a car crash precedes a pause, and then, the sound of an ambulance. WILL is seemingly thrown on stage from the RIGHT. Looking confused, he walks around trying to figure out where he is. He spots the bottle of vodka, smiles, and approaches it. He looks around to see if anyone is watching and reaches for the bottle but his hand is stopped by some invisible shield. (Every time WILL and JUDY touch the invisible shield, an electrifying zapping sound is heard.) He walks to the other side and tries again but is blocked from getting the vodka. He sits in the chair RIGHT and puts his head in hands. He then laughs out loud. LEFT JUDY is seemingly thrown onto stage and stumbles in her high heels to gain her balance. She walks around confused, and WILL stands and takes a couple of steps.*

JUDY: Stop right there. (*She takes one of her high heels as a weapon.*) Don't come any closer or I'll scream!

WILL: Scream away. (*He sits again.*)

JUDY: Where am I? *(Hiccups.)* Is this some kind of joke?

WILL: Yeah, it's real funny. An empty room with no doors and a bottle of vodka.

JUDY: I must be hallucinating again. (*She slaps herself.*) I'm awake. Are you going to tell me where I am?

WILL: Look lady, I just got here myself.

JUDY: You did?

WILL: Yep.

JUDY (*Walks to bottle of vodka.*): Grey Goose? Nice brand. I'm impressed. I'm used to Absolute, if I'm lucky. This situation calls for a drink.

WILL: Good luck with that.

JUDY (*She reaches for the bottle but her hand is stopped by invisible shield.*): What the hell!

WILL: Now you're getting close.

JUDY: What? You think this is hell? (*She walks with one shoe on and one off.*)

WILL: Where else?

JUDY: Well I was just in the hospital, that... terrible accident. Three people were around me doing the defibrillator thing with the paddles and saying "clear" and all that. They must have zapped me three or four times. Only I was looking down from above... I guess an out of body experience. I kept thinking, jeez, my roots look bad. I really need a dye job. But I wasn't wearing these shoes on that bed. Strange.

WILL: So did you see a bright light or something? Walk down a tunnel, see loved ones?

JUDY: No, *(Hiccups.)* not at all.

WILL: Me either, that's why I think this is hell.

JUDY: I'm looking down at myself, from above, and all of a sudden I'm hit by something big... like maybe a baseball bat and here I am.

WILL: Last I remember was the crash...that loud crash and the feel of glass going through my body, then, wham! I'm here, in my own personal hell.

JUDY: Could I really be dead? I mean I know I shouldn't have been driving, but I never had an accident like that before. Was it the same crash?

WILL: Maybe. I was driving on state road 54 going east. How about you?

JUDY: I was going west.

JUDY AND WILL: Head-on!

WILL: You dozed off and came into my lane, didn't you?

JUDY: No, I mean I don't remember that.

WILL: But you were drunk weren't you?

JUDY: Why would you say that?

WILL: Because it all makes sense. Two alcoholics are drunk, hit head on, they croak, and their hell is this!

JUDY: No. I can't believe God would be that cruel... I mean I didn't mean to hurt anybody. *(Seems to be sobering up now.)* Oh my God, did we hit anyone else?

WILL: I don't know, but I don't remember another car around so probably not.

JUDY: Whew! Least I didn't take somebody's child with me. This must just be a weigh station or something, you know, like in the movie Heaven Can Wait.

WILL: Think what you want. My name is Will. We might be here together for eternity so it might be helpful for us to be on a first name basis.

JUDY: Judy.

WILL: Judy, I'd rather have met you in my earthly life, but hi.

   *WILL offers his hand and they shake.*

JUDY: I'm really getting scared now because I'm starting to believe you. *(Tries unsuccessfully to get to the bottle again.)* How can we get this bottle open? Help me, will you?

WILL: I will repeat once more, this is our hell; we'll never be able to drink that vodka! We'll go through the DT's, everything, and be here for eternity.

JUDY *(Sarcastically.)*: Hey, don't try to gloss it over for me or anything here. I don't deserve this. *(Sits, pauses.)* Yes I do!

WILL: You couldn't have been as bad as me, really. I am such a low life.

JUDY: I'm a drunk. Is that what you want to hear? Is this a test maybe, trying to get me to repent. *(Rises, looks around and yells.)* I repent, do you hear me, I repent!

WILL: Who are you yelling at?

JUDY: I don't know... God, Satan, anyone who can get me out of here. I need to get home and... and... dye my hair.

WILL: Have no one to go home to, do you?

JUDY: Not really. My cat even left me. Found someone who'd feed her regularly I guess.

WILL: Let me say this. No matter how bad you think you are, you can't begin to compare to me.

JUDY: Oh yes I can. (*Sits and starts to cry as she speaks.*) I am so bad my children won't even speak to me. Even if my X let me see them, they wouldn't want to see me.

WILL (*Walking over to her to give comfort.*): Judy, you don't strike me as being a bad person. Alcoholism is a disease you know. Don't be so hard on yourself. I've blown every opportunity for recover… all because my dear old Dad. I got this from him, being a drunk I mean. It's genetic you know. We can't help it.

JUDY: I could help it. Doesn't run in my family at all… my brother's as sober as they come, and my Mom and Dad never had a problem with booze. It's me… I'm just a worthless human being… one with a very bad hangover (*Grabs her head.*) Couldn't God or Satan or whoever have had pity and left some aspirin around?

WILL: I don't deserve pity. I used to hide bottles in my desk at work.

*They try to outdo one another with their confessions.*

JUDY: Well, I hid them in my linen closet. I changed sheets a lot.

WILL: I always had one in the garbage can, except on Thursdays—that was garbage day.

JUDY: No one in my family liked tomato juice so I'd just put vodka in there and drank it when I wanted… they never knew!

WILL: Had it under the seat in my car.

JUDY: I had this pair of pants with an elastic waistband. Put the bottle there like it was a pouch on a frickin kangaroo.

WILL: You know those carpenter pants? The bottom pocket.

JUDY: I'd empty out little bottles of shampoo and put it in there. They're great to have in your purse. Once I blew bubbles after a swig.

WILL: I didn't need a purse. I'd use little mouthwash bottles and keep them in my pocket. Everyone thought I had the freshest breath!

JUDY: Well, I went through AA three times.

WILL: Four for me.

JUDY: Step 9.

WILL: Make amends?

JUDY: That's all the farther I get... to 9. All three times I've tried to make amends with my daughter, and she won't talk to me. Never made it to 10. And the last time... I really thought I could get her to forgive me.... I don't even remember what step 10 is.

WILL: Oh I've made it through the steps all right. I even go early to meetings twice a week to make the coffee. On the way I stop at this fish place out in the country. Believe it or not, they still have a phone booth outside. I wouldn't exactly call it a booth, but I act like I'm on the phone... while I'm drinking my vodka. I'm skunked at the AA meeting- now that's pathetic.

JUDY: That is bad, but I've gotten two DUI's.

WILL: Three for me.

*They are really trying to outdo one another now.*

JUDY: I once picked my kids and my neighbor's kids up from Bible school, toasted!

WILL: I slept in a park and was beaten and mugged!

JUDY: I stole from my daughter's piggybank <u>and</u> from a passed out homeless man!

WILL: I <u>was</u> a passed out homeless man! Was that you?

*JUDY shrugs her shoulders.*

JUDY: I sent my kids to school with no lunch money... just some crackers!

WILL: I lied to my sponsor a gazillion times!

JUDY: I left my sponsor at a Starbucks and she thought I just went to pee!

WILL: I lost my license for 6 months!

JUDY: I still don't have my license back!

WILL: I've drunk mouthwash!

JUDY: I taught Sunday school with a buzz on!

WILL: I let my nephew walk out on thin ice!

JUDY (*Yelling, slowly, and emphatically.*): I got plastered at my niece's wedding and slept with my husband's brother!

WILL (*His demeanor has changed now, and he's not trying to outdo her anymore. Very serious.*): I was too afraid to have kids.

JUDY (*Also very serious.*): I lost mine.

WILL (*Going to JUDY.*): Seems to me as if we have a lot in common. Like you might be able to understand me because you've been there.

JUDY: I feel like I know you better than people I've spent years with. Are you married?

WILL: Are you kidding? Who could live with me?

JUDY: Will, will you hold me for a minute?

WILL: Sure. (*Holding her.*)

JUDY: Thanks.

> WILL *kisses her and she responds favorably. There's obviously a physical attraction.*

WILL: Whew! I haven't felt like that in a long time.

JUDY: I haven't felt anything for so long.

WILL (*In thought, walking RIGHT, leaving JUDY LEFT.*) You know, maybe I was all wrong... maybe this is not hell.

JUDY: Maybe this is our heaven?

WILL: Yes, someone to be with who totally understands me.

JUDY: Someone who can hold me and comfort me.

WILL: Someone I can make mad passionate love to!

> *They walk towards each other, about to touch, when an invisible shield stops them from touching and they are zapped. They try again with no luck. Then they try for the bottle with no luck. In desperation they look at each other, unable to touch.*

JUDY: Will?

WILL: Judy?

*Lights fade.*

*Blackout.*

## END OF PLAY

## *2014 Runner Up*

# Smart Bra

### by

### Sylvia Reed

Directed by Carole Kleinberg

with

Brianna Larson as Jane

Mitchael Pearl as John

CHARACTERS
JANE, a woman, in her 20s.

JOHN, a man, in his 20s.

SETTING
A coffee/wine bar. A table and two chairs.

TIME
The present.

*As the lights come up, JOHN is looking at his phone, checking for messages, etc., as JANE enters and approaches him cautiously.*

JANE: Ummmm... Are you...?

JOHN: Jane?

JANE: I'm Jane.

JOHN: Of course. I wasn't saying I'm Jane. You're Jane. I'm John.

*They shake hands.*

JANE: Nice to meet you.

JOHN: Yes. Face to face. Please sit down.

JANE: So.

JOHN: Yes.

*Awkward silence, then finally—*

JOHN (*Cont.*): Your voice is different than I thought it would be.

JANE: Really?

JOHN: Yeah.

JANE: Different... in a good way?

JOHN: Yeah. I mean, it's not like I thought you'd have a bad voice or anything, but your texts were really, really clever, and I was kind of picturing Tina Fey when I read them and my god, I love her, even though she's older than me, but I love her and the way her voice is – not her doing Sarah Palin – but actually kind of like that because when I see her now all I can think of is Sarah Palin.

JANE: I hate Sarah Palin.

JOHN: Oh. Well... I don't really have an opinion of her one way or the other but...

JANE: You don't?

JOHN: No.

JANE: I don't think I've ever met anyone who doesn't have an opinion one way or the other about her.

JOHN: She's kind of irrelevant these days so...

*The sound of a soft buzzing noise.*

JOHN (*Cont.*): What's that?

JANE: It's my bra.

JOHN: Your... bra?

JANE: It's sensing something.

JOHN: Like what?

JANE: It's telling me I don't believe you.

JOHN: Believe me? About what?

JANE: About Sarah Palin.

JOHN: What about Sarah Palin?

JANE: It's telling me to be skeptical about your statement you have no opinion of her.

JOHN: Your bra can tell you that?

JANE: I guess my heart started beating a little faster and my heart-rate fell into the category of Proceed With Caution/Don't Trust What's Happening Around You, and I took this to mean maybe I shouldn't believe what you just said.

JOHN: A bra can do that?

JANE: It's a Smart Bra.

JOHN: Do you... want to order something? Coffee? Glass of wine?

*JANE'S bra starts to buzz again.*

JOHN (*Cont.*): Is that... your bra... again?

JANE: It's warning me I'm about to eat comfort food. (*Speaking to her chest.*) You are really clever. (*To JOHN.*) This thing knows me. It knew I was about to get a cookie.

JOHN: So it's like a diet thing.

JANE: I guess. I still don't know the extent of what this bra can do because I'm just getting to know it. An Amazon drone dropped it at my front door yesterday.

JOHN: Oh.

JANE: And it came with this link to a website where you program in all this stuff about yourself and you synch it to your bra like what time of day are you most likely to crave junk food and when you crave it do you go for chips or do you go for cookies and cake – salty versus sweet, I guess – 'cause maybe the heart beats differently depending on how you like to binge? (*Shakes her head as if "this stuff eludes me."*) I don't know. Technology.

JOHN: Wow.

JANE: Right? And the manual says you have to be really honest about it or it won't work properly and quite frankly it was kind of hard for me to program in just how much I love wine because I know it's gonna be buzzing like crazy every time I get the idea I want a pinot grigio and that's gonna suck because it's like I've got the Alcohol Police strapped to my chest.

JOHN: Huh. That's... wow. Maybe that's why it buzzed then. 'Cause I mentioned wine.

JANE: I was really feeling chocolate chips when it buzzed.

JOHN: I never would have gotten this... from your texts.

JANE: I didn't have it when we started texting. And of course I had to program it and that took For. Ev. Er.

JOHN: I suppose if I would have called you we could have had some talks and maybe I would have learned you are a sweet versus salty eater and you like white wine more than red. I could have learned some things about you. Heard your voice.

JANE: That might have been awkward.

JOHN: What?

JANE: Talking? On the phone? Who does that?

JOHN: What about this?

JANE: What?

JOHN: You don't think this is awkward?

JANE: What?

JOHN: You think this is going well?

JANE: What's wrong with it?

JOHN: Well your bra called me a liar for one thing.

JANE: My bra doesn't call people out like that.

JOHN: Yes, it did.

JANE: It simply indicated I might not want to believe you that you have no opinion of Sarah Palin. It was just a... red flag. An advisory sort of thing.

*The bra buzzes again.*

JOHN: What's happening now?

JANE: I guess I'm nervous.

JOHN: Because …

JANE: Because you're making me feel uncomfortable.

JOHN: Can we start over?

JANE: I guess.

JOHN: I think we should just sit here and be silent for a moment and erase all the stuff that's just gone on, okay?

JANE: Like just sit here and not say anything?

JOHN: Yeah.

JANE: And just look at each other?

JOHN: Or look wherever you want. Just breathe. Just... be in the moment.

*They breathe. After a moment, the bra makes a loud noise like a zap.*

JANE: Ouch!

JOHN: What happened?

*JANE gets up. She jogs around the table as she talks to JOHN. He follows her with his eyes round and round.*

JANE: My god that hurts.

JOHN: What did it do?

JANE: It shocked me.

JOHN: The bra?

JANE: Yeah. I need to adjust that setting, holy crap.

JOHN: Are you okay?

JANE: Yeah, I'm okay. It's just when you sit for too long it gives you a jolt and makes you get up and get moving. It actually counts your steps and if it looks like you aren't going to get 10,000 steps in by the end of the day it goes full-on bitch-mode and gives you a jolt.

JOHN: That sounds awful.

*JANE does some jumping jacks. JOHN watches. She finally sits back down.*

JANE (*Practically out of breath.*): Okay... I think it's safe to sit down... I was counting in my head as I jogged and I got about 25 steps in. And then... when I did the jumping jacks... that really helped because it dumps that activity into a savings account sort of thing that lets you sit for a little longer. And the bra massaged me like, Good job, Jane! It's supportive like that. (*To her chest.*) Thanks for the props, Bra. (*To JOHN.*) I guess I've appeased it for the time being. So where were we?

JOHN: I... have no idea.

*JOHN looks at his phone.*

JANE: What are you doing?

JOHN: Ummm. Nothing.

JANE: You're checking your phone. (*Pause.*) Are you with me or are you with your phone?

*The bra buzzes again.*

JANE (*Continuing, looking down at her chest.*) I know, I know, I'm getting it loud and clear you don't have to tell me.

JOHN: What? What are you getting loud and clear?

JANE: I'm getting that your phone is more important to you than being here with me.

JOHN: You're getting that?

JANE: Yes I am.

JOHN: Well you want to know what I'm getting?

JANE: What are you getting?

*The sound of crickets chirping.*

JOHN (*Looks down at his lap.*): Nothing.

JANE: What are you looking at?

JOHN: Let's just say they make similar technologies for men.

JANE: Like a Smart...?

JOHN: Yep.

JANE: And you get nothing from me?

JOHN: Crickets.

JANE: Like... you don't think I'm attractive?

JOHN: I actually find you attractive. On the surface.

*JANE is very hurt. Her bra buzzes along with the crickets. Then the noises finally stop.*

JANE and JOHN: What just happened?

JANE: It stopped. I don't know what I feel. If I had to guess, I think I feel like maybe I blew it with you.

JOHN: I think maybe I was a little too harsh. (*Pause.*) What if we tried something new?

JANE: Like what?

JOHN: What if you took off your bra?

JANE: I suppose I could do that.

*JANE reaches under her shirt and unhooks her bra. She shoots it off like a sling shot.*

JANE: Your turn.

JOHN: Okay.

JANE: I guess you'll need to go to the bathroom.

JOHN: There's an app on my phone.

*JOHN turns off the app. He looks at JANE. After a moment—*

JOHN (*Holds out his hand.*): I'm John.

JANE: I'm Jane. Nice to finally meet you.

*Blackout.*

### END OF PLAY

*2014 Audience Favorite*

## Visiting Grandpa

**by**

**Ronnie Pantello**

Directed by Carole Kleinberg

with

Don Walker as Vinny

Anthony Chase as Brad

Mary Jo Johnson as Beth

Ren Pearson as Robert

CHARACTERS
VINNY, a man, mid– to late-70s, the Grandfather.

BRAD, a man, around 45, VINNY's son and ROBERT's father.

BETH, a woman, 40s, ROBERT's mother.

ROBERT, a young man, 16, BRAD and BETH's son.

SETTING
VINNY's home, located in a Florida retirement community and a room in BRAD and BETH's home.

TIME
The present.

*Lights up on BRAD and BETH in the room on the RIGHT. VINNY's living room, dining room, and kitchen are CENTER and dark.*

BETH: I can't believe there's no one to keep Robert.

BRAD (*With reluctance.*): I'm out of ideas... we could ask Dad.

BETH: Great, we leave our only son with a lecherous old man with dementia.

BRAD: He's not that bad.

BETH: Really? He eighty going on eighteen. He can't remember what he did yesterday. I can't believe you let him move all the way to Florida.

BRAD: What do you mean "let him." He moved himself. Frankly, he had enough of us butting into his life.

BETH: Butting in! We were trying to save him from himself.

BRAD: We should have never taken his car.

BETH: He was dangerous to himself and others.

BRAD: He's our only option.

BETH: Fine. But I'm calling everyday.

*BRAD picks up the phone and calls VINNY. Lights up on center stage. Phone rings at VINNY's home. VINNY is wearing a Tommy Bahama shirt, hair slicked back with gold chains. He answers the phone center stage.*

VINNY: This is Vinny, make it good.

BRAD: Hey Dad.

VINNY: How "U doin?"

BRAD: Everything is fine.

VINNY: Really... a mid week call? What's up?

BRAD: I got promoted, a big promotion. But I have to go to Hong Kong and I have to take Beth...

VINNY: Promoted to what?

BRAD: Executive Vice President Operations...

VINNY: Wow! I'm really proud of you. Congratulations.

BRAD: Thanks. But this Hong Kong trip was a surprise and I... I mean we were wondering if you could take Robert for a week?

VINNY: Did I hear you right... we?

BRAD: Yes... We.

VINNY: You must be desperate. Beth's parents out of town?

BRAD: As a matter of fact...

VINNY: Not to worry, I'm happy to do it. You sure this is okay with Beth?

BRAD: Absolutely.

VINNY: That confirms it, you're desperate.

BRAD: And Dad, I'm sorry about the car thing... you were getting too old to drive. It's just...

VINNY: I know you had my best interest at heart. No problem. We have a car service here, I'll arrange a pick up for Robert. Email me his flight information.

BRAD: I really appreciate this...

VINNY: Does Beth want to say hi? It's a joke. Take care.

*Phone call ends. Lights dim. Lights up, a few days later. Enter ROBERT and VINNY.*

ROBERT (*Very excited.*): Wow! That was some ride. I've never gone a hundred miles an hour. Isn't that against the law?

VINNY: Not in Florida, they got special laws for grandfathers. We can drive as fast as we want.

ROBERT: I didn't know that.

VINNY: You got a lot to learn and I got a lot to teach.

ROBERT: Mom said you didn't drive.

VINNY: Well I do. And that's the first of a lot of things you're <u>not</u> going to tell your parents. You've heard the saying "What happens in Vegas stays in Vegas"?

ROBERT: Not really.

VINNY: We got a saying in Florida, "What happens in Florida, stays in Florida." In other words, your parents don't need to know everything we do down here. Got it?

ROBERT: I suppose. I was surprised… I mean… Dad said he took your car.

VINNY: He took that car. This is another car.

ROBERT: But…you're not exactly telling the truth.

VINNY: I'm telling the truth. It's a different car. You get it? "What happens in Florida, stays in Florida." You got a lot to learn kid and I only got seven days.

ROBERT: Okay, but Mom's not going to like it.

VINNY: What did I just tell you?

ROBERT: The staying in Florida thing…

VINNY: That's between us. If you're going to be a teenager you gotta learn about sins of omission. Your parents don't need to know everything… trust me… they don't want to know everything. And that's why you have grandfathers. We tell you what your parents won't.

ROBERT: I guess.

VINNY: We're going to have some fun this week.

ROBERT: What's with all the golf carts?

VINNY: Want to see mine? It has a Roll Royce grill. Look here…

*They move to the window and look out.*

ROBERT: That's really cool.

VINNY: That's how we get around this community. And, guess what, you can drive it.

ROBERT: Really?

VINNY: Yep. Can't wait to send your mother a picture of you driving my cart. That should flip her out.

ROBERT: Maybe we should keep it between us.

VINNY: Now you're learning. Too much information causes problems.

ROBERT: I'm starting to understand. So I shouldn't tell Mom you picked me up in a Corvette.

VINNY: And it's none of your father's business either. Got it?

ROBERT: Got it.

VINNY: That's your room. Unpack. We need to plan our week.

*ROBERT exits. Phone rings. Lights up RIGHT on BETH. VINNY picks up.*

VINNY: This is Vinny, but you know that.

BETH (*Cautious.*): This is Beth... Everything okay? How's Robert?

VINNY: He's fine. He just got here.

BETH: May I speak with him?

VINNY: Sure. (*Yells to ROBERT.*) Yo... "Bobster." It's your Mom.

BETH (*To VINNY.*): Vincent, his name is Robert.

VINNY: Not here. His Florida name is "The Bobster."

BETH: That's so reassuring.

*ROBERT enters.*

VINNY: It's your Mom. (*Hands the phone to ROBERT.*)

ROBERT: Hi Mom. Everything is fine.

BETH: The car pick-up worked?

ROBERT: The car was fine. Grandpa was there, it was... (*Looking at VINNY smiling.*) a very fast ride to his house.

*VINNY pushes back in his seat, smiles giving ROBERT the thumbs up.*

BETH: Remember your homework... and don't forget to study your SAT workbook.

ROBERT: Yes-ma'am.

BETH: Let me speak with your grandfather.

*ROBERT hands phone to VINNY and moves offstage.*

BETH (*CONT.*): Vincent, Robert should spend at least three hours a day studying. He knows what to study.

VINNY: I can help with his homework...

BETH: That won't be necessary. He has his assignments.

VINNY: Then I'll be in charge of entertainment...

BETH: He does not need entertainment. He needs to study. You do know he wants Harvard.

VINNY: I did not know that. You know I wanted Harvard.

BETH: Really?

VINNY: But my SAT scores screwed me.

BETH: Put so poetically. Well, that's one family tradition we want to avoid. Let me say goodbye to Robert.

VINNY: "Bobster," your mother wants to say goodbye. (*Hands phone to ROBERT.*)

BETH (*Muttering to herself.*): "Bobster" (*To ROBERT.*) Have fun darling. Study. Keep an eye on your grandfather. He's old and forgetful. You have our number.

ROBERT (*ROBERT looks over at VINNY, who's pouring himself a drink.*): I think grandpa is fine. Have fun, I love you.

BETH: I love you too.

   *Lights dim CENTER. BRAD enters RIGHT and stands next to BETH.*

BRAD: Everything okay?

BETH: Something's not right... I can't put my finger on it.

BRAD: Stop worrying. He can learn a lot from Dad.

BETH (*Disbelieving look.*): That's what I'm worried about.

   *Lights dim RIGHT. Lights up CENTER. ROBERT enters from LEFT and approaches VINNY who's seated, drinking.*

ROBERT (*Holding a pair of sexy female panties with a coy smile.*): Grandpa, I found these by the night table.

VINNY: Oh, those... you see... I... they're my friend's... sometimes friends... sleep over... yea, that's it.

ROBERT: Grandpa, I'm sixteen. I know all about these things.

VINNY: Oh yea. How much do you know? You got a girl?

ROBERT: I know about sex... well... at least in theory. And no, I don't have a girl... too much studying. (*A little sad.*) I wish I had a girl. It's just... well hard.

VINNY: What? What's so hard?

ROBERT: Girls! I don't know what to say. If I do say something it will most likely be wrong.

VINNY: Baloney. Girls are easy. In fact, your grandpa is an expert on girls, I spent a life studying the subject. Maybe that's a subject we can study together. My friend, you know... the one who owns those panties...

ROBERT (*With a coy smile.*): Your sleep over friend.

VINNY: Yea, that's the one. She has a granddaughter your age. I was thinking maybe we should... you know get together...

ROBERT: You mean double date?

VINNY: Why not? It's a start. We'll get you two together. If you like each other you could have a regular... uh... study group.

ROBERT: I see... a study group? I suppose that's what you plan to tell Mom. We formed a study group.

VINNY: You're catching on kid. Remember, what happens in Florida, stays in Florida.

ROBERT: I think I'm going to like Florida.

VINNY (*Playful smile.*): When I'm done with you you'll have a Masters degree in fun.

   *Lights fade.*

   *Blackout.*

END OF PLAY

# Fancy Seeing You Here

by

## Marvin Albert

Directed by Richard LeVene

with

Chuck Conlon as Stan

Linda MacCluggage as Claire

Lucinda Schlotterback as Louise

Richard Caldwell as Len

Mitcheal Pearl as Ben

Characters
STAN, a man, early 40s.

CLAIRE, a woman, early 40s.

LEN, a man, early 40s.

LOUISE, a woman, early 40s.

WAITER, a man of indeterminate age.

Setting
An upscale restaurant, with two tables.

Time
The present.

*Lights up on STAN and CLARE, seated at one of the tables.*

WAITER (*Handing them menus.*): My name is Ben. I will be serving you this evening. Would you care for a drink, some wine perhaps.

STAN: The lady will have white wine and I will have a very dry Rob Roy up with a twist. Make that very, very dry. Make sure they use dry vermouth, not sweet.

WAITER: Very good, Sir. (*Exits.*)

STAN: Would you believe it, our third date and all in one week.

CLAIRE: Why did you order me a white wine?

STAN (*Apologetic.*): Well that's what you always ordered.

CLAIRE: Well, tonight, I wanted something else.

STAN: I'm sorry. I'll get the waiter and...

CLAIRE (*Slightly annoyed.*): No, that's all right. I'll have the wine.

STAN: Are you sure?

CLAIRE: I'm sure.

STAN: It's just that...

CLAIRE: I know. It's all right. We still have a lot to learn about each other. Like, tell me more about your divorce.

STAN: Oh? It's just that it got to the point that we fought all the time. She thought I was too domineering and insensitive.

CLAIRE: Really. Hmm.

*Just then the WAITER brings another couple to the empty table next to them. The woman, LOUISE, is seated with her back to STAN. Her date is LEN. STAN looks at her.*

STAN: Oh God.

CLAIRE: What?

STAN: That's her.

CLAIRE: Who?

STAN: Her. My ex-wife.

CLAIRE: You're kidding. This should be interesting.

*The WAITER returns with their drinks.*

STAN: Could we change our table?

WAITER: Is something wrong?

STAN: That couple, I'd rather not...

WAITER: I believe we are fully booked tonight.

CLAIRE: Not a problem. This is fine.

WAITER: Very well. Are you ready to order?

CLAIRE: Give us a few more minutes.

WAITER: Very well.

STAN: This is not good.

CLAIRE: Relax. I'm sure it will be fine. (*To the other table.*) YooHoo.

STAN: What are you doing!?

CLAIRE: We may as well say hello now. She'll see you eventually. YooHoo.

*LOUISE turns around and is shocked to see STAN.*

LOUISE: Oh my God.

CLAIRE (*To LOUISE.*): That's what he said. Hi, I'm Claire.

LOUISE (*To LEN.*): That's him. That's Stan.

*LEN nods.*

CLAIRE: Won't you join us?

STAN: No! What are you doing?

CLAIRE: I think we should meet.

STAN: Are you crazy? No! This is really not good.

LOUISE: You want us to join you? I think not. I wouldn't eat with him if I were starving.

STAN: Good. Now turn around and forget I'm here.

CLAIRE (*To LEN.*): Hi, I'm Claire.

STAN: Why are you doing this.

LEN: Len.

CLAIRE: Pleased to meet you.

LEN: Likewise.

STAN: You seem to be enjoying this. I don't see the humor here. I've lost my appetite.

CLAIRE: You're bound to run into her from time to time, it would be nice to be civil.

LOUISE: He doesn't know how to be civil.

STAN: You stay out of this.

LOUISE: You can't tell me what to do anymore.

STAN: I never could.

LOUISE: But boy, did you try.

CLAIRE (*To LEN.*): I think they did the right thing getting a divorce.

LEN: Oh, they're not divorced.

CLAIRE: I don't understand. He told me...

LEN: They haven't agreed on the details. I'm her lawyer.

CLAIRE: He led me to believe... Son-of-a-bitch. (*To STAN.*)You weren't honest with me.

CLAIRE: It's just a formality. As far as I'm concerned, we're divorced.

LEN: That's not the way the law looks at it

CLAIRE: That's not the way I look at it either.

STAN: This is a nightmare.

LOUISE: He cheated on me!

STAN: Oh, for...

CLAIRE: A liar and a cheat. Wow.

*The WAITER returns.*

WAITER: The other customers are complaining about the noise. Would you please keep it down.

CLAIRE: Sorry. Louise would you change seats with me while I talk to Len?

LOUISE: What!? I, I...

CLAIRE: We don't want to disturb all of other people who are trying to enjoy their dinner, now would we.

*CLAIRE takes LOUISE's arm.*

LOUISE: I can get up without your help.

*LOUISE, totally confused, sits at STAN's table while CLAIRE joins LEN.*

CLAIRE: I actually think they make a cute couple.

*LEN rises, chuckling, as CLAIRE sits.*

LEN: You are really something.

*As the dialogue continues, we hear each table while the other table is visible talking and/or arguing.*

CLAIRE: What does that mean?

LEN: You're turning this into a game.

CLAIRE: I went out tonight to have fun. I didn't (*Beat.*) and now I am.

STAN: For the ten-thousandth time, I did not cheat on you.

LOUISE: Still deny, deny, deny? We're getting divorced, you don't have to keep lying anymore.

STAN: Oh, what's the use. Look even if I did cheat, which I didn't, people forgive and try to save their marriage.

*The WAITER returns to the other table with drinks.*

LEN: Thank you. No, I am definitely not married.

CLAIRE: Are you sure?

LEN: I'm sure

CLAIRE: Good.

LEN: I see the bad side of marriage every day.

CLAIRE: Oh, so now you are a cynic. Being a divorce lawyer has its drawbacks.

LEN: It started earlier than that. My folks were divorced when I was twelve.

CLAIRE: Poor boy. Not all marriages are bad.

STAN: Of course I was happy.

LOUISE: I always saw the way you looked at other women...

STAN: I won't deny, I looked. But that's all. I just looked. All men look.

CLAIRE: Well, they're still talking.

LEN: Hard to believe. I really tried to get them help. She was so pissed off at him. You know what, I kinda believed him.

CLAIRE: Taking the man's side?

LEN: Hey, I'm a man.

CLAIRE (*Flirtatiously.*): So I noticed.

LEN: Are you flirting with me.

CLAIRE: Does it show? Maybe I'm just trying to have fun. (*Laughs.*) Let's say I'm trying to make the best of a very strange night.

LEN: It's not over yet. The night's still young.

STAN: You could have given me the benefit of the doubt.

LOUISE: I was so sure.

STAN: And now?

LOUISE: I don't know. I'm confused.

CLAIRE: They're still talking. Hey, is that a smile on her face?.

LEN: Looks like a smile. Maybe there is still hope.

CLAIRE: You'll be losing a fee.

LEN: No problem. I got a retainer. We're just about even. (*Beat.*) Do you want to order?

CLAIRE: You know what, I just want to get out of here.

LEN: Me too. (*Beat.*) Do you like jazz?

CLAIRE: I love jazz.

LEN: I know this little place where...

CLAIRE: Lead me to it.

*STAN and LOUISE are smiling and talking as LEN leaves money for the waiter and they leave, arm in arm, unseen by the other couple.*

LEN: This has been a most interesting evening.

CLAIRE: And the night is still young.

*Lights fade.*

*Blackout.*

END OF PLAY

# For Art's Sake

by

**Bernard Yanelli**

Directed by Richard LeVene
with
Tom Aposporos as Tom Musante
David Meyersburg as Sid Horowitz
Chuck Conlon as Stanley Bergman

CHARACTERS
TOM MUSANTE, a man, 55, a writer.

SID HORWITZ, a man, 75, a theater patron.

STANLEY BERGMAN, a man, 53, a theater patron.

SETTING
The lobby of a theater in New York City. A large poster hangs in the background reading "Now Playing, <u>Denial or Deceit</u> by Tom Musante."

TIME
1983

> *Lights up on TOM MUSANTE, dressed in a white shirt, blue blazer, and jeans. He stands by himself. SID HORWITZ approaches. Dressed in an expensive suit and tie, he has distinguished-looking grey hair and a grey beard. As they speak, STANLEY BERGMAN approaches. Dressed casually, he stands a few feet away, but close enough to hear the conversation.*

SID: Congratulations on your remarkable play.

TOM: You're too kind.

SID: My name is Sid Horowitz. (*He shakes hands with TOM.*) You should know that I've seen well over two hundred plays on and off Broadway, and only a few better than this one.

TOM: Thank you. It wasn't an easy play to write.

SID: I know. I was there.

TOM: You... you were at Auschwitz?

SID: No. Treblinka. Maybe you heard of it?

TOM (*Nods.*): Poland. 1942-43. Over 500,000 dead.

SID (*Somberly.*): Oh, more than that. Many more than that.

TOM: It's a great honor that you came to see my play.

SID: Sorry for such a direct question, but you're not Jewish, are you?

TOM (*Shakes his head.*): Italian Catholic. 100% Wop.

SID: Then how did you come to write such a poignant play about such a traitorous Jew? (*STANLEY slowly leans in.*)

TOM: I married a nice Jewish girl. She lost her maternal grandparents to such a scoundrel at Auschwitz, so she asked me to write a play in their honor.

SID: Good for you. Jews and Italians, we have a lot in common.

TOM: Of course we do. Our lives all revolve around the big three: Food. Family. Fighting.

SID (*Chuckling.*): If only we saw God the same way, who could tell us apart?

TOM: My wife Rachel has such a volatile temper that sometimes I forget she's not Italian.

SID: My Gilda used to be the same way. When she got angry, I'd run like hell from the kitchen before she could clank me over the head with one of her pots.

*Clearly agitated, STANLEY tries unsuccessfully to get TOM's attention, then he walks away and exits.*

TOM: You lost her?

SID: (*Grimly.*) September 25, 1943. A day before our tenth anniversary. Gone these forty years. Gone, but never forgotten.

TOM: I'm so sorry.

SID: Don't be. You honored her and the other six million with your magnificent play.

TOM: If you don't mind my asking, what do you do for a living?

SID: These days? I read, go to the theater, and talk to my Gilda through my dreams.

TOM: And before that?

SID: I taught Russian literature at Columbia for thirty-three years. As a connoisseur of good literature, I was impressed by your lyrical use of language.

TOM: You wouldn't be if you had read the first dozen drafts or so.

SID: Tell me, how did you come up with the specific details for your story?

TOM: Didn't you read the playbill?

SID: I never read the playbill. If the writing's good, there's no need. If the writing's bad, well, a playbill won't help much—unless, of course, I go home and burn it. Why? What did yours say?

*STANLEY reenters, looking much more anxious than he did before.*

TOM: That my play is based on a true story.

SID: Where did you learn about it?

TOM: An article I read in The Chicago Tribune a few years back.

SID: I see.

TOM: I also read the court case, but when I write a play about a real person, I don't let the details of someone's life get in the way. They can interrupt the emotional arc of the story.

SID: Interesting.

TOM: The rest of his life—after he left Auschwitz—was just as sad. The state of Israel hunted down this turncoat Jew for 35 years before he finally got caught and was forced to confess. (*Shrugs.*) The guy sold insurance. Had a family. Lived in a dumpy apartment in South Chicago. In his whole life, he never did anything noteworthy other than betray his own people.

SID: That is sad.

TOM: From what I could tell, he seemed like a good man... an honorable man. In fact, I still don't know why he did such an awful thing.

SID: So even though you gave him a motive in your play, you don't actually know what compelled him to commit such an atrocity in real life?

TOM: No. The odd thing is, even though I read his confession, I still have my doubts about his guilt.

SID (*With a tinge of anger.*): Then, I'm confused. Why did your play have him send a hundred men to the ovens in exchange for a cartoon of cigarettes?

TOM: Well, I... I thought the story would seem more tragic if his payoff was so cheap.

SID (*With rising anger.*): Then perhaps I misjudged you. Didn't you just say that you had doubts about this man's guilt? (*TOM nods.*) If that's the case, then it's your writing that's cheap! You're dealing with the life of an actual human being here, are you not? Did you even think about that before you...?

TOM (*Getting angry.*): Hold on for a second. You're looking at this all wrong.

SID: Am I? How? (*TOM gestures but doesn't speak.*) Well, I obviously misjudged you. And I now regret this entire conversation... this entire evening. (*Frustrated, he exits.*)

*As soon as SID leaves, STANLEY bursts forward.*

STANLEY (*Shouting.*): You son-of-a-bitch! How could you write such a pack of lies?

TOM (*Still stunned.*): Who the hell are you?

STANLEY: Stanley Bergman. Art Bergman's son. (*Pleading.*) How could you do this to my father?

TOM: What are you talking about?

STANLEY: I'm talking about the way you poured salt into a dead man's wounds.

TOM: But I changed his name. I even changed some of the circumstances in the camp so that no one would know it was him.

STANLEY: Bullshit! Anyone who knew my father will know. I've spent the last two years trying to clear his reputation—and now this! You bastard! You cold, cold-hearted bastard.

TOM: Hey! You have no right to make that kind of accusation.

STANLEY: Go to hell! Don't you writers have some type of standard to live up to, some obligation to tell the truth?

TOM: No! I mean, I... I can interpret a story any way I want, as long as I'm not being willfully malicious.

STANLEY: So you're saying you had a free pass to ruin my father's name without any consequences at all?

TOM: Let's get something straight, pal. Your father dug his own grave, not me.

*STANLEY turns as if he is going to walk away, then he quickly turns back and takes a wild swing at TOM. After he misses, TOM punches STANLEY in the gut, causing him to briefly lose his wind.*

TOM: I'm sorry. I didn't mean to hurt you.

STANLEY: My father's innocent. He never betrayed anyone.

TOM: But I read the article in the Tribune... the court case... his confession.

STANLEY: He was a dying man, confined to a hospital bed. The Israelis forced that confession out of him under duress.

TOM: What's your proof?

STANLEY: I don't have any proof. I just believe that's the truth.

TOM: So why the hell did you just attack me if all you have is your opinion?

STANLEY: Because I overheard you say that you had doubts yourself.

TOM: What does that have to do with anything?

STANLEY: You're ruining my chance to restore the only thing my father ever cared about: his name. My name.

TOM: I don't know what you want me to say. I was moved by your father's story, but I had to give him a motive. And I decided on one that seemed the most dramatic.

STANLEY: You should have come and found me. I would have told you everything that I knew.

TOM: But you just said that you didn't know his motive, either.

STANLEY: I have a pretty good idea, though. On the day he died, he pulled me close and whispered that the only reason he confessed was to protect someone else.

TOM: Who? Who was he trying to protect?

STANLEY: He wouldn't say. I begged him, but he wouldn't tell me. He just grew silent, then a few minutes later he was dead.

TOM (*After an awkward silence.*): I... I apologize. I didn't intend for my play to bring back such obvious pain. But you still haven't told me why you're so sure he was innocent.

STANLEY: Because he had no reason to lie to me. We hadn't spoken in almost twenty years. He was furious when I decided to become a cop. Told me I was throwing my life away. I hated him right back for not providing a better life for my mother or me. And he knew it.

TOM: If what you're telling me is true, then why are you so concerned about his legacy?

STANLEY: Because he thought he was protecting me. He thought I was the one who collaborated with the Nazis.

TOM: I don't understand.

STANLEY: There was a rumor going round the camp that a young boy had just turned in an entire barracks after he found out that they were digging a tunnel. When my father confronted me, he made me swear that I didn't do it. But even after I did, I could tell by the look in his eyes that he didn't believe me. A week later, the Allies arrived at our camp. He and I never spoke of the incident again.

TOM: Stanley, I don't know what to say except to apologize—again. You were right. I should have spoken with you. I should've done that before I wrote the story. There's no excuse.

STANLEY (*Emotionally.*): Thank you. Your apology is all I wanted to hear. You're the first person who's actually taken the time to listen to me.

TOM (*Deep sigh.*): I was also wrong about something else.

STANLEY: What's that?

TOM: Before, when I was talking with that other gentleman, I told him that as far as I was concerned Art Bergman had never done anything important in his entire life.

STANLEY: I hate to say this, but you were probably right.

TOM: No. He did the most important thing of all.

STANLEY: What's that?

TOM: He raised a good son.

*Lights fade.*

*Blackout.*

## END OF PLAY

# I'll be Home for Chrismas

by

Dale E. Moore

Directed by Rosalind Cramer

with

Amanda Heisey as Millicent

Donna Gerdes as Mother

CHARACTERS
MILLICENT, a woman, 30ish, professional.

MOTHER, a woman, 60, society type, MILLICENT's mother.

SETTING
LEFT is MILLICENT's home office. RIGHT is a poolside setting at MOTHER's retirement center.

TIME
The present: August 17th

*MILLICENT and MOTHER sit on opposite sides of the stage. There is a poolside lounge chair, and table on MOTHER's side. MILLICENT is seated at a desk in her home office.*

*A phone rings.*

MILLICENT (*Pin spot on MILLICENT.*): Hello. (*Pin spot off.*)

MOTHER (*Pin spot on MOTHER as she shouts orgasamatically*): I'm coming! Oh! I can't believe I'm coming... (*Pin spot off.*)

MILLICENT (*Pin spot on MILLICENT.*): Who is this? *(Slams down phone. Spot out. Pause. In the dark we hear the phone ringing several times.)*

MILLICENT (*Pin spot on MILLICENT.*): Hello?

MOTHER (*Pin spot on MOTHER* ): Millicent, you hung up, Dear. Why'd you...

*Spots open on both women.*

MILLICENT: Who is...? Mother?

MOTHER: Yes, Dear.

MILLICENT: Mother?

MOTHER: Yes. Who were you expecting?

MILLICENT: Well, not you, that's for sure.

MOTHER: I'm so excited. I'm coming...

MILLICENT: Yes, I heard that.

MOTHER: I had to tell you right away.

MILLICENT: TMI

MOTHER: TMI?

MILLICENT: Too much information. Been a while has it?

MOTHER: I think it's been two, maybe even three, years. Well, you should know.

MILLICENT: No, I really had no idea. And I need to know this why?

MOTHER: I thought you'd be thrilled.

MILLICENT: Oh, I am… I am. I think.

MOTHER: I arrive on the twentieth.

MILLICENT: Arrive?

MOTHER: Flight 2071. O'Hare.

MILLICENT: Oh, you're saying… you're just telling me you're coming to Chicago?

MOTHER: Yes, I'm so excited. I just had to let you know right away that I'm coming.

MILLICENT: Coming… ah, arriving, and in three days.

MOTHER: Three days? What are you talking about?

MILLICENT: Well, the last time I looked, this is the seventeenth of August. You're arriving on the twentieth. That's three days the last time I could count… though at this moment, I'm not really sure of anything. Could we just hang up, let me call you back, and start this whole conversation over?

MOTHER: What's wrong with you?

MILLICENT: What's wrong with me?

MOTHER: Have you been drinking? Millicent, it's two o'clock in the afternoon, much too early to start happy hour.

MILLICENT: Happy hour? I feel more like I'm at the Mad Hatter's Tea Party. You're arriving on the twentieth. For how long?

MOTHER: Ten days. I plan to arrive a few days early because I want to do my shopping there.

MILLICENT: Shopping?

MOTHER: I know the stores there better and I don't want to have to lug all those gift wrapped boxes on the plane.

MILLICENT: Mother, whoa! Hold it! You're arriving on the twentieth for ten days. Are you talking about coming for Christmas?

MOTHER: That's what I said.

MILLICENT: No, actually, you didn't mention that.

MOTHER: They charge for everything now.

MILLICENT: Mother.

MOTHER: And it just infuriates me. Pay $400 for a plane ticket and then...

MILLICENT: MOTHER!

MOTHER: What, Dear? Don't yell at me. It's unbecoming. I did not raise you...

MILLICENT: Mother.

MOTHER: What is it?

MILLICENT: Have you mentioned this to Fredrick?

MOTHER: No, why would I?

MILLICENT: Well, it might have been good to check with one of us. I'll talk to him tonight and see what he may be planning for... for then.

MOTHER: Don't be silly. Freddy never plans anything except to sit in his chair there in the bay window and listen to classical music. Now you know I love classical music. I've always been a patron of the arts. When I lived in Chicago...

MILLICENT: I know! I know! You had season tickets to the Symphony.

MOTHER: I had season tickets to the Symphony. But honestly, Millicent there is a limit and Freddy...

MILLICENT: Fredrick, mother. Fredrick. So you just decided, without checking with either of us, to come back for Christmas?

MOTHER: Well, I didn't think I needed to make an appointment. I am your mother. Anyway the tickets are non-refundable and non-exchangable. Is that a word, "non-exchangable." Whatever! I arrive at 11:30 in the morning, but don't you take time off work to come get me. I'll just get a cab. I'll unpack and then have dinner ready by the time you and Freddy get home.

MILLICENT: Mother, it is <u>Fredrick</u>! Let's just plan to eat out that night. Actually, now that I think about it, we were talking about flying out to Palm Springs for the holiday.

MOTHER: Not over Christmas. Millicent, no one goes to Palm Spring over Christmas. Christmas is about family. Of course you and Fre... him... don't seem in any hurry in that regard.

MILLICENT: Don't go there.

MOTHER: I was just going to say...

MILLICENT: I know what you were going to say and please don't.

MOTHER: The most wonderful Christmas present I could hope to receive would be to learn that I'm going to be a Grandmother. But then that's you and Freddy's business.

MILLICENT: Yes, mother, it is <u>Fredrick</u>'s and my business.

MOTHER: So I'll just keep my feelings to myself. There isn't anything wrong with him, is there? I mean...

MILLICENT: No, mother.

MOTHER: His sperm count is high enough, I suppose.

MILLICENT: Mother!

MOTHER: He certainly can't suffer from ED at his age... though you know the old saying...

MILLICENT: He's fine.

MOTHER: ...if you don't use it, you lose it.

MILLICENT: Oh, Gawd, mother.

MOTHER: Maybe he should see a doctor, a specialist, a urologist. Well, that's your business, I suppose.

MILLICENT: So you keep saying. Yes, thank you.

MOTHER: I told your father we should have more than one child, then I'd be sure to be a grandmother and not be all alone. Anyway, I'll do my shopping on the twenty-first and twenty-second. Is Stein's Jewelry store having their big Christmas sale this year? Well, of course they are. They've had it every year since I was a little girl. I always thought it was funny that a Jewish store would have a Christmas sale.

MILLICENT: I assume so, but I haven't seen an ad yet. Maybe it's because it is only August?

MOTHER: Would you mind calling them for me? Oh never mind! I'm coming anyway. My ticket is...

MILLICENT: Non-refundable and non-exchangable. Yes, I know!

MOTHER: Oh, Millicent, I need you to get the makings for Grandma's date nut loaf. I'll mail you the list of...

MILLICENT: Mother, there'll only be the four of us and that recipe makes enough for the...

MOTHER: Four?

MILLICENT: At most.

MOTHER: Who else is coming?

MILLICENT: This is August. I really don't know.

MOTHER: Well, you said four pretty definitely for not knowing.

MIILLICENT: I think Fredrick might invite his father again.

MOTHER: Again? Was he there last year?

MILLICENT: Yes.

MOTHER: You didn't tell me.

MILLICENT: It must have slipped my mind.

MOTHER: I see. Where does he sleep?

MILLICENT: What?

MOTHER: Where does he sleep? I'll sleep in the front bedroom, of course. I hope you didn't...

MILLICENT: Mother that's...

MOTHER: That was my bedroom... and your father's, of course. I couldn't possibly sleep anywhere else. It just wouldn't seem right.

MILLICENT: That's the master bedroom.

MOTHER: We shared that room forty-four years.

MILLICENT: That's...

MOTHER: You were conceived in that room.

MILLICENT: Yes, I know, though why it's important at this moment escapes me.

MOTHER: And it has a private bath. I cannot, cannot, share a bathroom with anyone. Even your father used the other bathroom.

MILLICENT: I know, mother. And you remember that you and Daddy slept there because it is the master bedroom?

MOTHER: Of course I know it's the master bedroom. Millicent, I'm not senile. Why is he coming anyway?

MILLICENT: Who?

MOTHER: Freddy's Father.

MILLICENT: Maybe because he's Fredrick's father? You did say Christmas was for family.

MOTHER: Well, I didn't mean...

MILLICENT: Whatever you meant.

MOTHER: In-laws. He's an in-law for Gawd's sake, Millicent.

MILLICENT: Not to Fredrick.

MOTHER: In my house he's an in-law... or outlaw. I never did understand what he did for a living. I hate to say this, but I was always suspicious.

MILLICENT: Mother, we've had this conversation. And you do also remember Fredrick and I bought and paid for this house seven years ago?

MOTHER: Yes, but if I'd known you were never going to have a family, I wouldn't have sold that big house to you. It's far more than you and Freddy need.

MILLICENT: Fredrick, mother.

MOTHER: Whatever! Now, Sweetie, what would you like for Christmas? Why don't you leave a list on the dresser in my bedroom before I get there? Put down several things so, whatever I decide to get you will be a surprise.

MILLICENT: Not nearly as big a surprise as your coming. What in the world made you decide to come back this year?

MOTHER: Oh, I'm glad you're so pleased.

MILLICENT: I said surprise. I don't think I used the word...

MOTHER: Just leave a list.

MILLICENT: All right. And I'll also put down some ideas for Fredrick.

MOTHER: Oh, I suppose. A couple of things but nothing too expensive. Remember, I'm on a fixed income. I should have done it last year but I had just moved...

MILLICENT: Done what?

MOTHER: Here and there were so many parties, and oh that reminds me, I'm planning to send a few things on ahead so...

MILLICENT: Define "a few things."

MOTHER: ...please hang them in my closet so they don't get too wrinkled. Actually, maybe you should send them out to be pressed. I always use Johnny Cleaners over on Fourth St. I trust them. I'll mail them early so...

MILLICENT: Do you think there's still time for you to "mail them early?"

MOTHER: I'll send my gold evening dress to wear to church Christmas Eve. I wore it to the Robinson's party last year and everyone commented on how elegant it looked on me.

MILLICENT: Mother...

MOTHER: I'll just put in a couple of other dresses. Well I should probably send the bag I carried with that dress. I shouldn't tell you this but...

MILLICENT: But you will.

MOTHER: ...I paid $250 for that bag. But it was so perfect with that dress and my white fox stole.

MILLICENT: You were right. You shouldn't have. Must have been a real sacrifice "being on a fixed income" and all.

MOTHER: Oh, and my blue velvet dress for Christmas day.

MILLICENT: Mother, there's something I need to tell...

MOTHER: Not now! Don't tell me now. I'll forget.

MILLICENT: I seriously doubt you will.

MOTHER: Oh, I know I will. Just put your list on my dresser and I'll see if I can surprise you. See, now you've interrupted me and... where was I? Oh yes, what do I need to Fed EX? If I don't have to bother with the suitcase, it is so much less hassle, and would you believe it is cheaper to Fed Ex it? I pay $400 for a ticket and then have to pay for my luggage. What do they think I'm going to wear for ten days?

MILLICENT: Mother!

MOTHER: Millicent, I asked you not to yell at me. I am not deaf.

MILLICENT: We're not going to church Christmas Eve.

MOTHER: What!

MILLICENT: I said...

MOTHER: I heard what you said. What do you mean? This is all because of Freddy's father coming, isn't it? I knew it. I knew it.

MILLICENT: No. Well, yes, in a way.

MOTHER: Young lady, our family's gone to church Christmas Eve at Main Street Presbyterian every year since your great-grandfather gave the first $100 to build it back in...

MILLICENT: You do remember Fredrick is Jewish?

MOTHER: A fact I try to forget. But are you sure? I thought Jewish people believed in having big families. Maybe his Dad can help him.

MILLICENT: That's enough.

MOTHER: He could go with you to your church once a year. It wouldn't hurt him if he really loved you.

MILLICENT: I don't expect him to.

MOTHER: Well, I do. If he can't get you pregnant, he could at least get you to church once a year.

MILLICENT: I'm sorry, but I'm having a little trouble with that logic.

MOTHER: Sounds to me like that's not all you're having trouble with.

MILLICENT: You said your tickets are non-refundable?

MOTHER: And non-exchangable. I've got to look that word up when we're done.

MILLICENT: I'll tell you what. Fredrick and I'll refund the price of your ticket.

MOTHER: Of course not.

MILLICENT: I insist

MOTHER: But why on earth would you?

MILLICENT: Well, when we send you the refund, you send the ticket to us, and then I'll explain.

MOTHER: And what do I use to get on the plane?

MILLICENT: Ummm

MOTHER: Millicent?

MILLICENT: Mother, okay! Okay... here goes! Just please do not interrupt.

MOTHER: Interrupt! When have I ever interrupted you? That would be so rude. Honestly, Millicent, you act as though I've had no upbringing at all.

MILLICENT: If you want to hear what I have to say, you need to be quiet because I am going say this only once and if you try to talk over me you're going to miss it. I am not going to repeat it.

MOTHER: All right! All right! Go ahead!

MILLICENT: Mother, after a lot of very careful prayer and serious contemplation, I decided...

*The following lines are said simultaneously. MOTHER's should be softer so we hear MILLICENT clearly.*

MILLICENT (*Simultaneously, over MOTHER's voice.*): ...that I love Fredrick the way you loved/Daddy and that when, not if, but when/ there are children, it would be less/confusing to them if the family were/all of one faith, so I decided to take/instruction and I have converted to/Judism. That's why we're not going/to Main Street Presbyterian on the twenty-fourth of December.

MOTHER (*Simultaneously.*): Talking about deciding... I need to remember/to take Grandma Webster's pearl and diamond /necklace to the jeweler's. I was going to give it /to you for Christmas, but I decided it was a/family heirloom that should just be passed/down not given as a Christmas gift, though I/don't know who you will pass it down to if/ Fred... if Fredrick doesn't get his... well if it doesn't get fixed

MOTHER: What'd you say? I didn't get it.

MILLICENT: I warned you to listen. Mother, you're welcome to come visit the family for the holidays. Did I really just say that?

MOTHER: Before! What were you saying before?

MILLICENT: Happy Hanukkah, mother.

*Lights fade.*

*Blackout.*

END OF PLAY

# Just Fooling

## by

## Verna Safran

Directed by Rosalind Cramer

with

Alan Kitty as Armin

Joe Kerata as Shakespeare

David Meyersburg as Burbage

CHARACTERS
ROBERT ARMIN, a man, mid– to late 30s.

WILLIAM SHAKESPEARE, a man, mid– to late 30s.

RICHARD BURBAGE, a man, mid-30s.

SETTING
Scene 1, a tavern and Scene 2, a theatre in England.

TIME
1602

> SCENE 1: Lights up on ARMIN and SHAKESPEARE having a tankard at the tavern.

ARMIN: I appreciate everything you've done for me, Will, but –

SHAKESPEARE: But! Every joke has a butt—it's the person or entity which gets kicked in the butt by the jester's barb!

ARMIN: I invited you here in order to ask you something, Will.

SHAKESPEARE: Ah, yes. You appreciate everything I've done for you, but—you'd like a raise in salary. I can't do that, Robin. It would antagonize the rest of the company. Burbage in particular.

ARMIN: No, it's not that. I mean, I'd like a raise in salary, but that's not foremost on my mind.

SHAKESPEARE: You are foremost on my mind, Robin, my friend. For most of every piece, you play the fool, and play him to perfection.

ARMIN: Exactly. That's what I want to talk with you about. I would so appreciate it if you gave me the chance to...

SHAKESPEARE: You want to direct. I'm sorry, the answer is no. I am the director. There can only be one director in a stage production. The theatre is not a democracy, it is a monarchy, and the director is king.

ARMIN: I know that, Will, you are the king of the Globe, and I'm happy to be one of your subjects.

SHAKESPEARE: Flattery will get you everywhere. Well, what is it you want?

ARMIN: I want the chance to... to be a leading man.

SHAKESPEARE: You mean a romantic hero?

ARMIN: Yes, if you put it that way. I can be as romantic as the next fellow.

SHAKESPEARE: Robert Armin! You can't be serious!

ARMIN: I'd like to prove to you that I can. Be serious.

SHAKESPEARE: But I don't see you as a Hamlet or a Romeo. You are Feste in <u>Twelfth Night</u>, you are <u>Touchstone</u>. You are <u>Bottom</u>. You are the porter in <u>MacBeth</u>. You and you alone, Robert Armin, have changed the art of clowning—from mere slapstick to that of a witty philosopher.

ARMIN: Thank you.

SHAKESPEARE: You are to Comedy what my leading man Dick Burbage is to Drama. I can't see you in motley proposing love and fidelity to a young maiden.

ARMIN: But can't you just give me a chance? I'd be willing to audition.

SHAKESPEARE: Nonsense. No need to audition. All the straight parts are already taken.

ARMIN: Then write me a new one.

SHAKESPEARE: A new romantic lead... but who?

ARMIN: Think of all the lovers of history: Antony and Cleopatra...

SHAKESPEARE: Been there, done that.

ARMIN: Arthur and Guenevere...

SHAKESPEARE: Camelot? It would work better as a musical.

ARMIN: Dido and Aeneas...

SHAKESPEARE: Our audiences would never sit still when they hear the name Dido. It sounds too much like "dildo." Anyway, I think Marlowe's working on that one.

ARMIN: He's writing a play about a dildo?

SHAKESPEARE: No, Dido. Calling it <u>The Queen of Carthage</u>.

ARMIN: Some other famous lovers, then. How about Layla and Majnun, the star-crossed lovers from Persia? Or Heloise and Abelard --

SHAKESPEARE: Heloise and Abelard. Mmm. That has possibilities. I've got to run now. Rehearsing the musicians for <u>As You Like It</u>. Meet you here tomorrow, and I might have something for you.

ARMIN: Tomorrow? You mean it would take you only one day to come up with a script?

SHAKESPEARE: Just one scene, of course. Geniuses always work fast. And in case you haven't heard, I'm a bloody genius. I put on plays with no scenery, with men playing the women's parts, with history twisted every which way from Sunday, and the audience believes these characters are real. If that's not genius, what is?

ARMIN: Time will tell.

SHAKESPEARE: Time always does. Can't keep a secret, that nasty Father Time. Until tomorrow, then! I'll bring a few buskers along, just so we get a reaction. A play is not a play on the page.

ARMIN: And a page is not a page until he is paged for a purpose. Au revoir!

*Blackout*

*SCENE 2: In the theatre, there's a long table behind which sit SHAKESPEARE and BURBAGE. ARMIN stands in front of them with a script in hand.*

SHAKESPEARE: Just relax and pretend you are a star-struck lover. You don't mind if Burbage sits in on the reading, do you?

ARMIN (*Minds, but tries not to show it.*): I... um... no, no, of course not. (*Clears throat.*) Are you ready?

SHAKESPEARE: Whenever you are.

ARMIN (*Clears throat.*): Hell-oh-weez, Oh, Hell-oh-weez...

SHAKESPEARE: It's pronounced "ELL-oh-weez." The "H" is silent.

ARMIN: Oh. Sorry. ELL-oh-weez, Oh, ELL-oh-weez, I would swim the ELLS-pont, to be close to you.

SHAKESPEARE: That's pronounced "HELLS-pont." The "H" is aspirated.

ARMIN: Are you sure?

SHAKESPEARE: Honest. (*He aspirates the H.*) Quite sure. Anyhow, it wasn't Abelard who swam the Hellespont, it was Leander.

ARMIN: I knew that. (*Aside.*) Leander?

SHAKESPEARE: Do me a favor, sweetheart. Don't improvise. Just read the lines as they are written. I'm told I have a way with words.

ARMIN: Okay. "Although you're a nun in the convent of St. DENN-is, I will woo you although I do not have a PENN-is."

SHAKESPEARE: That's PEE-nis. You were castrated.

ARMIN: I was castrated?

SHAKESPEARE: Yes. That's what makes the story so romantic. He went to live at the house of this young and very intelligent young lady, ostensibly to be her tutor, but he seduced her, she got pregnant, and to teach him a lesson his friends practiced a rather crude sort of birth control.

ARMIN: But if he was without... How did they...?

SHAKESPEARE: They wrote letters to each other.

ARMIN: Ah. (*Returning to the script, he reads this with forced emphasis on the iambic pentameter beat.*)

> "Let me tutor you, you tutor me
>
> Teaching me to live and love, and speak
>
> A language far more eloquent than Greek."

SHAKESPEARE: No, no, no!

ARMIN: What's wrong now?

SHAKESPEARE: It's true I write in iambic pentameter, but not so's you'd notice. Just speak the speech, I pray you. Let the words fall trippingly on the tongue...

ARMIN: Trippingly?

SHAKESPEARE: Yes. Don't emphasize the beat; emphasize the meaning. Listen. (*Reads the same speech, pausing so as not to emphasize the beat.*)

> "Let me tutor you (*Pause.*) You tutor me (*No pause.*)
>
> Teaching me to Live (*Punch.*), to Love (*Punch.*), to speak
>
> A language far more eloquent (*Roll the word around on your lips.*) than Greek.

ARMIN: I see what you mean. (*Puzzled.*) So, when did she join a nunnery?

SHAKESPEARE: Do you mean a convent or a whorehouse? The word has a double entendre.

ARMIN: A convent. She became a religieuse.

SHAKESPEARE: Some say that Abelard stuck her there to get rid of her. But anyhow, he was so embarrassed at losing his manhood, he became a monk. He might have had some back door romances at the monastery; history doesn't tell us about that, but you wanted a love story, not an exercise in sodomy. Go on, try that speech again.

ARMIN (*This time performing with wild, flailing gestures.*): Let me tutor you (*Falls on his knees.*); You tutor me (*Waving his arms from her to his heart.*) in life (*Marches up and down.*), in love (*Sighs and blows kisses.*), in languages more eloquent than Greek. (*Does a Zorba the Greek-type dance.*)

SHAKESPEARE: No, no, no! Stop waving your arms about and parading around like a new recruit in the Queen's guards! We're not in an ancient amphitheatre, where people sat so far away they didn't always hear the words and had to figure out what was going on through gesture and movement. Our groundlings are right there, practically on the stage. If you throw in so many gestures, you'll scare them to death and give them nightmares.

ARMIN (*To BURBAGE.*): Did you think I moved too much?

BURBAGE (*Solemnly.*): Yes. But I was not moved.

ARMIN (*Rips up the script.*): I give up. I hate being the romantic lead. You never know what the audience is thinking. When you're a comic, you can hear them laugh.

SHAKESPEARE: That's all right. No harm done. Everybody likes to step out of character every once in awhile, and become somebody completely different. That's the secret of Hamlet's success. He was so many things to so many people. Soldier, statesman, scholar—madman, lover, detective, actor... You're entitled to weary of Robert Armin's garments.

ARMIN: Forgive me, Will. I feel like such a fool.

SHAKESPEARE: You are such a fool. Such a fool as there never was before and never will be again. I think I have a new role for you, Robin. I'm working on a very important play. I know it's important because when I work on it, the hairs on the back of my hands stand on end. It's a tragedy called <u>King Lear</u>—about an old man who foolishly gives his property away before it's time and in the end he—he goes mad.

ARMIN: Surely you don't want me to play the king!

SHAKESPEARE: No, this role is almost as good. The king's fool is wiser than he.

ARMIN: Are you sure you don't want Will Kempe to play it?

SHAKESPEARE: Will Kempe can dance a jig. He's a clown. He makes people laugh. This fool will make people cry. It's a role that was made for you. Literally. Made just for you.

ARMIN: Break out the jester's cap and the motley garb! I'll play it to perfection!

SHAKESPEARE: Then I shall go home and write it this afternoon!

*The men get up and leave, putting their arms around each other's shoulders singing.*

SHAKESPEARE, ARMIN and BURBAGE (*Singing.*): Hey, ho! Nobody home. No meat, nor drink, nor money do I own.

Yet will I be merry! Hey, ho! Nobody home!

*Lights fade.*

*Blackout.*

END OF PLAY

# School for Wives**

## by

## Arthur Keyser

**School For Wives is fully protected under the Copyright Laws of the United States of America, Canada and all other countries of the Universal Copyright Convention. Under an agreement between the playwright and ArtAge Senior Theatre Resource Center ("ArtAge"), any use of this play including, without limitation, any performance, requires advance written permission from ArtAge and the payment of any royalties in accordance with the royalty schedule then in effect, ArtAge may be contacted by phone at (800) 858-4998 or through its website at www.seniortheatre.com.

Directed by Bob Trisolini

with

Donna Gerdes as Penny

Betty Robinson as Carla

Jenny Aldrich as Maggie

Noel Nichols as Waitress

Donna DeFant as Dee

CHARACTERS

PENNY, a woman, mid-60s, very thin, dressed in a designer pants' suit and wearing a faux diamond necklace and matching earrings.

CARLA, a woman, mid-60s, plump, dressed in light colored slacks and blouse, long colorful earrings and several large bracelets.

MAGGIE, a woman, mid-50s, dressed in blue jeans and a tee shirt with a photo of Che Guevera on the front and a peace sign on the back. She wears no make-up, lipstick or jewelry.

WAITRESS, a woman of indeterminate age.

DEE, a woman, late-40s, slim, wearing a black dress and modest jewelry.

BRADLEY, a man, mid-60s, dressed spiffily in a tailored suit.

SETTING

An outdoor patio area of a restaurant.

TIME

Two-thirty in the afternoon on an early fall day.

*Lights up on PENNY and CARLA walking into the patio area and sitting down at a table set for six. WAITRESS approaches.*

WAITRESS: If it's just the two of you, may I suggest a smaller, more comfortable table?

PENNY: We're expecting others.

WAITRESS: May I take your drink orders, while you're waiting?

CARLA: I'll have a diet coke.

PENNY: Vodka martini... a double... no ice. I don't want it diluted. Fill it to the very brim in the largest glass you can find.

WAITRESS: Would you like to see the menu?

CARLA: I shouldn't. I've just had lunch. But maybe I'll just sneak a peak at your dessert menu.

PENNY: I never eat anything between my morning coffee and dinner. It interferes with my martini schedule.

*WAITRESS leaves the table.*

CARLA: Bradley always said you were a world-class drinker.

PENNY: I never even smelled alcohol until I met him. Three years of marriage changed that. After we split, it took me seven years and two more husbands to cut down to four double martinis a day.

CARLA: I wish I had turned to drink instead of chocolate. When I became Bradley's second, I was almost as skinny as you. I went up five sizes in the first two years.

PENNY: Plumpness suits you. It fills out the wrinkles. Have you thought about Jenny Craig?

CARLA: It's crossed my mind. But if I lost too much weight, my skin might hang. Of course, I could always ask you for the name of your plastic surgeon... if you don't mind sharing.

> Before PENNY can respond, MAGGIE arrives at the table. She hugs PENNY, and then CARLA, and sits down at one of the empty chairs.

MAGGIE: I'm sorry. I couldn't break away from my Origami class. My days are always so full. I don't know how I'd fit everything in if I had to worry about stupid things like lipstick and make-up.

CARLA: We have to wait for Fran, anyway... and she's always late. It takes her forever to decide on what jewelry to wear...

PENNY: Which makes no sense since everything she wears looks the same.

CARLA: And that ring she wears! The stone is so large, it looks like she could strain her rotator cuff every time she lifts her left arm.

PENNY: She claims it's a nine carat diamond, but I'll bet anything it's a rhinestone.

CARLA: Sorry to contradict you. It's not a real fake. I saw the same ring at Wal-Mart for thirteen dollars.

MAGGIE: I didn't cancel my private yoga class to talk about Fran. I'm only interested in talking about Bradley.

PENNY: You're right, Mag. It's been twelve years since you suggested we meet once a year to tell stories about that snake we each married... and we've never run out of material.

MAGGIE: It's easy for me... I kept a diary. Sometimes I can't believe how many four-letter words I wrote in there. He had such a beastly temper, and the loudest voice I ever heard.

PENNY: We all remember how easily he would explode. But let's save that for later. I'm glad you're all sitting. I have a surprise. But, I didn't want to say anything till Fran got here.

CARLA: Do we have to wait? I'll have an anxiety attack... and I'll have to eat to calm down.

PENNY: I certainly don't want to be responsible for adding to your body fat. It's about Bradley. He's getting married.

MAGGIE: Again?! Four victims weren't enough?

CARLA: Who is she?

PENNY: Her name is Dee Rogers. I've spent the past two weeks, researching everything about her. I left no stone unturned. I even ordered a report from Ancestry.com.

CARLA: I want to hear everything. Especially if she's awful.

PENNY: Unfortunately, I can't find anything awful about her... here comes our waitress. Thank heavens. She's just in time. I always think more clearly with a martini glass in my hand.

> WAITRESS approaches with a tray, which holds the drinks ordered by PENNY and CARLA. She places them on the table and turns to MAGGIE.

WAITRESS: May I bring you something to drink?

MAGGIE: I never drink alcohol. It's poison for your system. Do you have Masala Chai?

WAITRESS: What's that?

MAGGIE: Spiced tea, made with cloves, cardamom pods and cinnamon. It's a specialty recipe from the Andhra Pradesh region of Southern India.

WAITRESS: I don't think we have that. But, if you'd like, I can ask the bartender.

MAGGIE: If you show me how to get to your kitchen, I can tell the chef how to make it with English Breakfast tea.

WAITRESS: It's this way.

> WAITRESS and MAGGIE walk to the door to the inside of the restaurant. WAITRESS opens the door and they both go inside.

PENNY: Would you believe her?

CARLA: Where does she get the nerve to dress like an aging hippy?

PENNY: And making believe she has a private yoga teacher! It's just a cover for her affairs with Hindu holy men.

CARLA: I never like saying anything good about Bradley, but I can certainly understand why he dumped her. A tea recipe from Southern India! Can you believe? She probably couldn't even find India on a map.

PENNY: And the whole business about not using lipstick or make-up. She has no lips at all and make-up would probably draw attention to all those wrinkles.

CARLA: I'm sure she just wanted to hurt your feelings.

PENNY: I think her comment was directed at you.

CARLA: Let's not argue. But I do think you're going a little heavy on the eye shadow. Doesn't it affect your vision?

PENNY: Quiet! She's coming back.

*MAGGIE returns to the table and sits down.*

PENNY: Carla and I were just saying how lovely you look... are they making your tea?

MAGGIE: Actually, no.

CARLA: No ingredients?

MAGGIE: I forgot to ask. The chef complimented my shirt, and before I knew it, we'd made a date for later this evening. I'm going to teach him some basic yoga positions.

PENNY: How old is he?

MAGGIE: I never asked. I'm sure he's over twenty.

PENNY: You've always been so discriminating, when it comes to men.

CARLA: I want to hear all about Bradley, but could you hold it for a minute? I'd like to use the little girls' room to freshen up.

PENNY: I won't breathe a word till you get back.

*CARLA gets up and leaves the table, walking in the direction of the door to the interior of the restaurant.*

PENNY (*Cont*): You think she'd be embarrassed, the way she's let herself go.

MAGGIE: She does get fatter every year.

PENNY: Obese is a better word.

MAGGIE: I don't like being catty, but I bet she spends as much for chocolate as she spends on rent.

PENNY: Someone should really tell her that light colored clothes just emphasize her weight. She should wear vertical stripes.

MAGGIE: Why don't you suggest that?

PENNY: And hurt her feelings? I'd never do that.

*WAITRESS approaches the table.*

WAITRESS: Excuse me. Is there someone named Penny here?

PENNY: That's me.

WAITRESS: There's a call for you at the bar... a lady.

PENNY: Excuse me, Mag. I'll be right back.

*PENNY and WAITRESS both leave and, a moment later, CARLA returns to the table.*

CARLA: Where's Penny?

MAGGIE: There was a call for her... at the bar.

CARLA: I hate to admit it, but I almost didn't recognize her.

MAGGIE: It's a shame.

CARLA: She should sue her plastic surgeon for malpractice. Her face is drawn so tight, it looks like her cheeks are about to split wide open.

MAGGIE: He's left a permanent smile on her face. What happens when someone gives her bad news and she just keeps smiling?

CARLA: Someone should talk to her about her drinking. I think she uses it as a preservative, but who would want to be preserved, looking like that?

MAGGIE: Thin can be attractive...but she looks like she's trying to get back to her birth weight.

CARLA: Watch it! Here she comes.

*PENNY returns to the table.*

PENNY: It was Fran. She can't make it. When she woke up and thought about Bradley, she developed a migraine and decided to stay in bed.

MAGGIE: Alone?

PENNY: She's between lovers.

CARLA: I've been meaning to call her. I'd be willing to try her leftovers.

*WAITRESS comes over to the table.*

WAITRESS: Will there be anything else?

PENNY: One more lady will be joining us.

*WAITRESS leaves the table.*

MAGGIE: I thought Fran wasn't coming.

PENNY: She's not. It's Dee Rogers... Bradley's fiance.

MAGGIE: You're not serious?!

PENNY: I found her number in the digital white pages, and called her.

CARLA: Why, on earth, would you do that?

PENNY: I told her we'd love to meet her and tell her some wonderful little stories about Brad. What can be more fun than warning her about the worm she's planning to marry.

MAGGIE: That's cruel.

PENNY: You don't like the idea?

MAGGIE: Like it? I love it!

CARLA: I don't know? It doesn't sound right.

PENNY: Did you forget what it was like, being married to that scumbag.

*From the other side of the patio, the WAITRESS is talking to an attractive woman. She points to the table where the three women are sitting.*

PENNY (*Cont.*): That must be her.

CARLA: I hate her already. She looks young... and why did she have to be so pretty?

*DEE walks to the table. The three women stand.*

DEE (*Directing her attention to PENNY.*): You must be Penny. Brad described you perfectly. Slim and very attractive.

PENNY: Was he sober when he said that?

DEE: You're not only very pretty. You have an adorable sense of humor. I never drink, so he's given up alcohol. (*Then, turning to CARLA.*) And you have to be Carla. He described your eyes perfectly. He said they looked exactly like Elizabeth Taylor's eyes.

CARLA: Brad said that?

DEE: Those were his exact words. (*DEE turns to MAGGIE.*) And, of course, you're Maggie. Brad said you never wore make-up and you have the skin of a twenty year old. I can see why he said that.

MAGGIE: He never said anything like that to me.

DEE: He's very shy. But, then, you all must remember how quiet he is around women. Are we waiting for Fran? Do I have her name right?

PENNY: You do. She wasn't feeling well.

DEE: I'm sorry to hear that. Brad asked me to send his love to all of you.

PENNY: He knows you're here?

DEE: Of course. I told him about your call. We tell each other everything.

PENNY: I'd better sit down.

*PENNY sits down. The others, including DEE, also sit down.*

MAGGIE: I think I've changed my mind about my order. When the waitress comes over, I'll have what you're having, Penny. Make it a triple martini.

CARLA: How does he feel about your meeting us?

DEE: He's delighted.

CARLA: He is?

DEE: Oh, yes. He thinks I can learn so much from all of you. He always talks about how lucky he was to have been married to each of you...that those years were sort of a master class to prepare him for our life together.

PENNY: He says that?

DEE: All the time.

MAGGIE: I had no idea he felt that way.

DEE: He's such a dear man.

PENNY: And so unpredictable.

DEE: That's part of his charm.

CARLA: If anyone sees the waitress, I'd like to order dessert.

DEE: None for me. But don't let me stop anyone else. I'm just so pleased you invited me. I can't wait to hear all your wonderful stories about Brad.

*The other women exchange glances. Without a word, en masse, they rise and exit RIGHT. BRADLEY sneaks in LEFT.*

*Lights fade.*

*Blackout.*

### END OF PLAY

# *Student Play Festival Winner 2014*

## Elevate My Life

### by

### Joseph Grosso, Lakewood Ranch High School

Directed by Cinda Goeken

with

Chuck Conlon as Henry

Donna DeFant as Rita

Connie Farris as Emma

Mary Jo Johnson as Savonia

Stephan Pustai II as Sam

Rod Rawlings as Charley

CHARACTERS
HENRY RICHARDS, a man, 40s, dressed in business attire.

SAVONIA LITTLE, a woman, 40s, a former model.

SAM HENKINS, a young man, with Down Syndrome, may be played by either a child, a child with Down Syndrome, or a young adult.

RITA HENKINS, a woman, 30s to 40s, SAM's mother.

ERMA WINDS, a woman, 60s to 70s.

CHARLEY WINDS, a man, 60s to 70s, ERMA's husband.

SETTING
An elevator.

TIME
The present.

*HENRY, carrying a briefcase, enters LEFT and pushes a button on the elevator which he then enters. He waits and while the elevator goes "down," SAVONIA runs on from RIGHT hits the button and briefly awaits the elevator. It opens and HENRY makes a face at the girl, insinuating his attraction to her. SAM runs on from LEFT with his mom in tow.*

SAM: Come on mom! Come on! We'll miss the elevator! (*He drags her by her hand.*)

RITA: Slow down Sam! (*She is yelling, they quickly hop on the elevator.*) Sorry.

*The three wait while the elevator lowers. ERMA and CHARLEY make their way on from RIGHT and CHARLEY pushes the button.*

ERMA: Charley, we aren't ever going to leave this town are we?

CHARLEY: We will dear, we will. Come on.

*The elevator opens and they enter. The elevator continues to go down, then stops, then goes down a little bit and stops. The lights flicker and then shut off, emergency power returns.*

HENRY: What the hell?

SAVONIA: Don't tell me we're stuck.

HENRY: The twenty-first century and they still can't get this shit to work. (*Pause.*)

*CHARLEY goes to the call box within the elevator; it rings.*

CHARLEY: Yeah, we're in the GoGets building on Main, by the waterfront. The elevator's broken (*Beat.*) there's six of us. Thanks. (*He hangs up.*) They said they'll call back in a few minutes with what to do.

*There's a pause as they wait.*

SAM: Mom, I don't wanna be here anymore.

RITA Hush.

SAVONIA: It's okay little man. We'll be outta here in no time.

*The phone rings.*

CHARLEY Hello? Yes. Oh… I see. Alright. Nothing you can do. Yes, we will. (*He hangs up.*) They said we stopped on a floor that was being renovated and its unsafe to evacuate, so we have to wait until they can get the elevator back up and running.

*Everyone groans and responds with distress. SAM sits, SAVONIA follows suit, as does HENRY.*

ERMA: We really will never leave won't we Charley? (*He grasps her hands.*)

SAVONIA: Were you two headed out of town?

ERMA: We were certainly going to try. (*She half-laughs.*) Never taken a honeymoon, thought we finally would.

RITA: Never taken a honeymoon? My goodness.

ERMA: That's what you get when two people must do nothing but work to survive.

SAVONIA: Where were you headed?

*ERMA suddenly becomes very confused.*

CHARLEY: Hawaii dear, we were headed to Hawaii.

SAVONIA: How lovely. I did a shoot out there back a few years.

HENRY: A shoot? Are you a model?

SAVONIA: Yes. (*She hesitates on the tense "are" "were."*) Yes it was by that volcano, for some "Girls with nature" shoot…

HENRY: That's fantastic… the nature I mean, and you I'm sure.

*Pause.*

SAVONIA (*To SAM.*): Didn't you have school today?

SAM (*He looks at his mother for approval to speak; she glances at him.*): Yes ma'am, but I got out early to see the doctor

SAVONIA: The offices on the fourth floor? I did the same! Do you have Dr. Kennedy?

SAM: Yes ma'am. Who's your doctor?

SAVONIA: Samoy, he's a very nice man too.

RITA: The reconstructive surgeon?

SAVONIA (*Hesitantly.*) Yes.

RITA: Figures. (*There is an awkward silence for a moment.*)

SAVONIA (*To SAM.*): Is something a matter with you? Not feeling well.

RITA: Just a check up. Monthly check up. Routine.

SAVONIA: I was going to say, you look perfectly healthy to me.

SAM: I think I am.

RITA: You aren't.

SAM: Sorry, I'm not ma'am. I have Down Syndrome.

RITA: Sam! What did I tell you? You don't need to tell people that. They could care less.

SAM: Sorry.

SAVONIA: There's nothing wrong with that. We all have things that make us unique. See these lines on my eyes, they're the reason I had to quit my job. They make me pretty unique too.

HENRY (*To CHARLEY.*): Did you work upstairs?

CHARLEY: When I was here, son, there was no upstairs. (*He laughs.*)

HENRY: I thought I recognized you.

CHARLEY: Charley Winds. (*They shake hands.*)

HENRY: Henry Richards.

CHARLEY: You married?

HENRY: No... no. (*He half-laughs.*) I'm not a huge fan of the whole marriage deal. Or rather, it's not a fan of me.

CHARLEY: That's a shame. It certainly has treated Erma and I well.

SAVONIA: How did you and your wife meet?

CHARLEY: Well she was on her day off from flying, here in Seattle.

RITA (*To ERMA.*): Were you a flight attendant?

ERMA: Delta!

RITA: Oh what a wonderful life. You must've met some very interesting people.

SAM: How come you weren't a flight person Mommy?

RITA: Because Mommy had you. (*Beat, lights flicker.*) Are they going to get around to fixing this thing or not?

SAVONIA: It's getting a little hot in here.

HENRY: I'll say.

ERMA: Where are we?

CHARLEY: We are headed downstairs dear.

ERMA: Downstairs?

CHARLEY: Downstairs.

ERMA: Did we just visit Little Charles?

CHARLEY: Our boy is in California Erma. We are in Seattle.

ERMA: Oh right. Right. How is he?

CHARLEY: He is quite alright.

HENRY (*To SAVONIA*): So you must've met quite the fella in the modeling world.

SAVONIA: Hardly. (*She smirks.*) Well I mean of course, but you know one Ralph Lauren underwear model you know them all. (*Beat.*) It's Photoshop.

HENRY: What is?

SAVONIA: Their... (*She looks at SAM.*) well, you know.

HENRY: Oh makes sense. But they couldn't have Photoshopped someone as good looking as you.

SAVONIA: Oh please. (*She laughs again.*) Modeling is 90% Photoshop and 10% whatever they throw on you. Too bad there isn't a program good enough to fix this old bag.

RITA: That's why there are people like Samoy.

SAVONIA: Look I don't know what issue you have with me, but what I choose to do to my face is my choice. At least I don't treat my own flesh and blood like some nobody, you are scum.

RITA: Excuse me?

SAVONIA: You heard me. Scum.

SAM: My tummy hurts.

RITA: The doctor says you're fine.

SAM: But my tummy...

RITA: I said hush! (*The conflict slowly becomes calmer, but it is tense.*)

   *HENRY stands to meet RITA.*

HENRY: Kids. You can't live with them, you can't live without them.

RITA: I could certainly live without them. Disgusting little things.

HENRY: Well he seems nice enough.

RITA: He's an abomination. A product of one night of mistakes that lands me with a retard. The doctor's say he'll never get better.

HENRY: Well why did you keep him?

RITA: What would you have done?

   *Phone rings and HENRY answers.*

HENRY: Yes? Okay. When the hell are we going to get out of here?! Well, hurry, God Damnit. (*Hangs up.*) They said there's a bug in the system but it should only be a few more minutes.

ERMA: Charley?

CHARLEY: Yes dear?

ERMA: Where are we Charley?

CHARLEY: We were trying to plan our honeymoon. The elevator stopped on the way down. Remember?

ERMA: I thought we were visiting Little Charles.

CHARLEY: We haven't seen Little Charles in years honey.

ERMA WINDS: I want to see Little Charles, is he married yet? Can we see him?

CHARLEY: He's busy dear.

ERMA: We have got to see Little Charles, he's calling for me. He can't end up like us, (*She goes toward the door and tries to force her way out.*) he can't end up like us. He just can't. Charles! Charles!

CHARLEY: Erma, Erma! Calm down dear before you hurt yourself. (*SAVONIA and HENRY half step in to try and help.*)

ERMA: Charles! Don't do it! Charles! (*She collapses crying.*)

CHARLEY: Erma. Erma! Oh God. Call those people back, her dementia is acting up, tell them we need help now.

*HENRY goes to the phone, while CHARLEY calms ERMA.*

SAVONIA (*To ERMA.*): Are you okay?

ERMA: Who are you?

SAVONIA: Savonia. We met a little while ago. You're in a stopped elevator, Erma.

ERMA: Oh right, right. We were planning a honeymoon you know?

SAVONIA: I heard. To Hawaii? It's beautiful this time of year.

ERMA: We've never been. We've never been to anywhere but our work really.

SAVONIA: I know how that is.

ERMA: Don't let your work stop you. You need to be able to live and explore while you still can. Just getting on a plane is no easy task for me anymore. But promise me this, all of you. You cannot let anything get ahead of your life, or your love. Don't be so busy trying to make a life, that you forget to live. (*She grasps CHARLEY.*)

RITA: But you've had a wonderful life of exploring new places and flying all over the world.

ERMA: I also left my husband and child for months at a time and haven't been able to go on a vacation in forty years. (*She looks at SAM.*) Children are God's gift to us. No matter their disposition, nothing beats growing with your children. Poor Little Charles.

*The elevator starts to kick up again.*

HENRY: Finally! It's about damn time.

*Everyone stands and composes themselves, they have mildly undressed by this point and are in rambles.*

CHARLEY: Well it was lovely to meet you all.

ERMA: Yes wonderful to get to know you.

SAVONIA: Same to you.

HENRY: What a day.

RITA: This has been, interesting to say the least...

SAM: Are we getting off of the elevator now mommy?

RITA: Yes.

SAVONIA: It was nice to meet you little man. Anytime you... and your mom wanna come over and have a play date you sure can. I've got a big puppy who loves to play around.

SAM: I love puppies! (*He looks at his mother who seems to nod.*)

RITA: Did you say Delta? (*To ERMA.*)

ERMA: Yes ma'am. Delta Airways.

> *Doors open and they start to file out with small goodbyes. SAVONIA and HENRY are the last two out.*

HENRY: I was wondering if we could maybe grab a coffee together sometime?

SAVONIA: Just a coffee?

HENRY: Just a coffee.

SAVONIA: Sure.

> *Lights fade.*
>
> *Blackout.*

## END OF PLAY

# Ten-Minute Play Festival

## 2015

**Dates:** April 30th, May 1st, 2nd, and 3rd, 2015

**Location:** Jane B. Cook Theatre, Asolo/FSU Center for the Performing Arts, Sarasota

**Best Play Award**

    High School Reunion by Arthur Keyser

**Runner-Up/Honorable Mention**

    The Coward by Dylan Jones

**Student Playwriting Festival Winner**

    As Long as the Moon Shines by Julien Freij
                      St. Stephens Episcopal School

## *2015 Best Play*

# High School Reunion**

### by

### Arthur Keyser

**High School Reunion is fully protected under the Copyright Laws of the United States of America, Canada and all other countries of the Universal Copyright Convention. Under an agreement between the playwright and ArtAge Senior Theatre Resource Center ("ArtAge"), any use of this play including, without limitation, any performance, requires advance written permission from ArtAge and the payment of any royalties in accordance with the royalty schedule then in effect, ArtAge may be contacted by phone at (800) 858-4998 or through its website at www.seniortheatre.com.

Directed by Louise Stinespring

with

Tom Aposporos as Robert

Dan Higgs as Patrick

John Forsyth as Thomas

## Characters

ROBERT, a man, 62, who is the host in a restaurant.

PATRICK MARTIN, a man, 101.

THOMAS DELANEY, a man, 101.

## Setting

A downtown restaurant in a mid-sized city.

## Time

Twelve-thirty in the afternoon on a mid-week day in late spring.

> *Lights up on ROBERT, standing at a music stand, which is used as a lectern, close to the glass front door of an upscale restaurant. He doesn't notice PATRICK, who is carrying a briefcase and sturdy cane, approaching from the outside. PATRICK taps on the door with his cane. Getting no response, PATRICK hits the door more forcibly. ROBERT quickly walks to the door and opens it. PATRICK walks in and ROBERT closes the door.*

PATRICK: Damned door's too heavy for a man my age to open.

ROBERT: Sorry, Mr. Martin.

PATRICK: Next time, I'll hit it hard enough to break the glass.

ROBERT: I should have noticed you arriving, but I was checking reservations.

PATRICK: It's time you kept up with the rest of the world. The pharmacy's doors open when a customer comes up close.

ROBERT: I'll make sure to mention it to the owner.

PATRICK: I hope you're not trying to humor an old man.

ROBERT: I never think of you as old. In fact, you look quite young.

PATRICK: Don't lie to me. No one at a hundred and one looks young.

ROBERT: I think you're amazing for your age.

PATRICK: The only thing amazing about me is that I'm still alive.

ROBERT: Which one is this?

PATRICK: Our eighty-third.

ROBERT: You don't look a day older than last year.

PATRICK: You'd better have your eyes checked. How old are you now?

ROBERT: Sixty-two.

PATRICK: You probably still have your baby teeth.

ROBERT: You certainly haven't lost your sense of humor.

PATRICK: It's about the only thing I haven't lost.

ROBERT: May I show you to your table?

PATRICK: I don't need any help. If it's my regular table, I can see it from here.

*PATRICK walks to a table, which has only one chair and is set for one person. He sits down. ROBERT has followed PATRICK to the table.*

ROBERT: Your waiter will be Conner. He's in the kitchen right now.

PATRICK: Where's George? He's been waiting on us for almost forty years.

ROBERT: He retired at the end of last year.

PATRICK: It's not like the old days...can't rely on anyone anymore.

ROBERT: He wanted to move to Florida.

PATRICK: He'll be sorry. Nothing there but a bunch of old people.

ROBERT sees an elderly man, waiting at the lectern.

ROBERT: Would you excuse me, Mr. Martin? Someone needs my help.

*ROBERT walks back to the lectern. During a short conversation between ROBERT and the man waiting at the lectern, PATRICK busies himself by opening his briefcase and removing a folder, which he places in front of him on the table.*

ROBERT (*Cont.*): Good afternoon, sir. May I help you?

THOMAS: I'm here for the class reunion. Is Patrick Martin here?

ROBERT: He arrived a few moments ago. I'll show you to his table.

*ROBERT leads THOMAS to the table, where PATRICK is sitting, brings a chair over to the table for THOMAS, and then walks back to the lectern. THOMAS remains standing.*

THOMAS: Good afternoon, Patrick... Tom Delaney. I'm sure you don't remember me.

PATRICK: Don't know where you learned my name. You're at the wrong table. This is the Central High School class of 1931 annual reunion luncheon.

THOMAS: I was in that class.

PATRICK: No you weren't!

THOMAS: I don't want to start an argument, but I was.

PATRICK: If you're looking for a free meal, you're making a big mistake. I may be getting up in years, but I still know a scam artist, when I see one.

THOMAS: I'm not a scam artist. I graduated in the 1931 class at Central... and I'm happy to pay my own way.

PATRICK: There's no way you're a member of our class. I'm the only one still alive.

THOMAS (*Smiling and holding out his left arm.*): Want to check my blood pressure?

PATRICK: Don't try being funny. Just because you're standing here doesn't mean you're not a fraud.

THOMAS: May I sit down?

PATRICK: Not for long. Don't get too comfortable. I have a reunion to run.

*THOMAS sits down on the chair, which had been brought over by ROBERT.*

THOMAS: I remember you from the last one I attended...the twenty-fifth.

PATRICK: I don't remember seeing you there.

THOMAS: I'm not surprised. I never stood out much in school. I should have brought a copy of our yearbook, but forgot it.

PATRICK: I bring mine every year.

THOMAS: If you let me go through yours, I'll show you my picture.

*PATRICK opens his briefcase and takes out a large and obviously worn book. He hands it to THOMAS, who sits down and begins to thumb through the book.*

PATRICK: Careful with that! It's over eighty-three years old.

*THOMAS stops searching and hands the book back to PATRICK, with his finger pointing to a place on a page.*

THOMAS: There I am.

PATRICK: It doesn't look like you.

THOMAS: Check out your picture. Think you still look the same?

PATRICK: Pretty much.

THOMAS: When's the last time you looked in a mirror?

PATRICK: You don't have to be sarcastic.

THOMAS: You don't have to be cranky.

PATRICK: I have a right to be cranky. I'm almost a hundred and two.

THOMAS: So am I... but I don't act like you.

PATRICK: Then there's got to be something wrong with you.

THOMAS (*Smiling.*): If that makes you feel better.

PATRICK (*After hesitating for a moment.*): Where've you been?

THOMAS: Moved out west after college. After I graduated, got married and taught high school chemistry. Retired at seventy-five. Lost my wife when I was eighty and my granddaughter insisted I move back so she could keep an eye on me.

PATRICK: We've had a reunion every year. How come you've never shown up since you moved back?

THOMAS: Never knew this was still going on.

*ROBERT approaches their table.*

ROBERT: Has Conner taken your drink order yet?

PATRICK: Not unless he's a mind reader.

ROBERT: He's probably tied up in the kitchen. I'll take it.

PATRICK: A double Dewer's Scotch on the rocks. Water on the side. Make sure the double is a full double. Pour the whiskey before you add the ice.

THOMAS: You must have a cast iron stomach. Water for me. Tap water is fine. No ice. Just a wedge of lemon.

PATRICK (*To ROBERT.*): Tell Conner to hold up on taking our food order. We never eat until after our business meeting.

*ROBERT leaves the table.*

THOMAS: You're not serious about a meeting?

PATRICK: Couldn't be more serious. We have one every year.

THOMAS: When was the last time anyone else attended?

PATRICK: Seven years ago. After Frank Bellini died, I was the only one still alive... till you showed up.

THOMAS: For the past six years, you've been meeting with yourself?

PATRICK: We've always had a meeting. No reason to change things.

THOMAS: I guess there wasn't a lot of conversation at those last six meetings.

PATRICK: You're being sarcastic, again.

THOMAS: I was trying to be funny.

PATRICK: Didn't sound funny to me. How did you learn about the reunion?

THOMAS: Saw a note about it in the social news section of the weekly Ledger.

PATRICK: Knew I shouldn't have talked to that kid reporter. Robert gave him my name and number and he insisted on asking darn fool questions. It's nobody else's business.

THOMAS: Nobody? If you hadn't spoken to him, I wouldn't be here.

PATRICK: If he hadn't stuck that note in the paper, I'd still be the only class member here.

THOMAS (*Standing up*.): I can leave right now, if it makes you feel better.

PATRICK: Sit down! You don't have to get all worked up about it. I never thought we had anyone else still alive.

THOMAS (*Sitting back down.*): Sorry to disappoint you.

> ROBERT returns with a tray with the drinks and a place setting for THOMAS. He puts the tray on the table and arranges the place setting where THOMAS is seated. ROBERT walks away, but remains close enough to listen to the conversation between the two men.

PATRICK: Before we get any older, let's get on with the meeting.

THOMAS: Is there an agenda?

PATRICK (*Opening the file he had placed on the table.*): There always is. We start by singing our alma mater.

THOMAS: Right here? In front of everyone in the restaurant?

PATRICK: We've never had a reunion without it. Since Frank passed, I've been singing it by myself.

THOMAS: Doesn't it spoil lunch for everyone here?

PATRICK: No one's ever complained, and I wouldn't care if they did. Let's get started.

THOMAS: I don't remember the words and don't sing very well. Why don't you sing without me?

PATRICK: No way. You're not getting out of it that easily. The words are on the inside of the back cover of our yearbook... and nobody sings well at our age. (*Stands up.*) If you don't mind, we always stand, when we sing our school song.

THOMAS (*Standing up.*): I don't want to be the one to break tradition.

*PATRICK opens the yearbook and hands it to THOMAS.*

PATRICK: Are you ready?

THOMAS: Not really, but I'll try.

*PATRICK and THOMAS begin to sing. The music is from an 1857 ballad, <u>Annie Lisle</u>, used by Cornell University and many other schools, for their alma mater.*

BOTH: From the lawns of Central High School
    Where our students strolled...

*THOMAS is clearly off-key and PATRICK stops singing and places a hand on THOMAS shoulder to stop him from continuing the song.*

PATRICK: You weren't lying about your voice. We need a little help. (*Calls to ROBERT.*) Robert! Would you mind joining us? We could use another voice.

ROBERT: It would be my pleasure.

*ROBERT walks over to the standing PATRICK and THOMAS and stands with them.*

THOMAS (*Holding out the yearbook to ROBERT.*): Would you like to share this with me?

ROBERT: After all these years, I know the words by heart.

*The song is then sung by the three men, with no one out of tune and with considerable emotion.*

ALL: From the lawns of Central High School
    Where our students strolled
    We'll not forget that lovely jewel
    Lit by crimson and gold

    Raise our voices, we remember
    Wondrous days of yore
    A new beginning each September
    Of friendships from before

ALL (*Cont.*): In those hallowed halls we'd gather
>As we walked to class
>There's no place that we would rather
>Remember from our past

ROBERT (*Dabbing his eyes with a handkerchief.*): That song always brings tears to my eyes.

THOMAS: Did you go to Central?

ROBERT: No. But, I look forward to hearing that lovely song every year.

*ROBERT walks back to the lectern.*

THOMAS: What's next on our agenda?

PATRICK (*Looking at the agenda from his file.*): We pick the location for next year's reunion.

THOMAS: Has it ever been anywhere but here?

PATRICK: No... but that doesn't mean it always has to be.

THOMAS: Then, I'd like to make a motion that we have next year's reunion here.

PATRICK: I second the motion. All in favor, raise your right hand.

*They both raise their right hands.*

THOMAS: Somehow, I had a feeling my motion would pass.

PATRICK: For an old guy, you have a pretty good sense of humor.

THOMAS: For an old guy, you run a pretty exciting reunion.

PATRICK: Thomas--

THOMAS: What?

PATRICK: Sorry if I was rude. Hope I see you next year.

THOMAS: I'm putting it in my calendar.

PATRICK: Make sure you take good care of yourself.

THOMAS: You, too. I don't want to be alone at the next reunion.

PATRICK: I have an idea! While we're here, let's plan our big one, two years from now. It's our 85th and I don't want this table taken by someone else.

THOMAS: Sounds good to me. Why don't you ask Robert to reserve it?

PATRICK: Remind me when he comes back.

THOMAS: I'm sure you don't need reminders about anything.

PATRICK: Can I count on you showing up?

THOMAS: I wouldn't dream of missing it.

PATRICK: Can we drink to that?

THOMAS: Only if I can drink my water.

PATRICK: I'll let you get away with it this year, but next year, it's going to be scotch.

*They raise their drinks and tap each other's glass.*

THOMAS and PATRICK (*Together.*): To our class reunion!

*Lights fade.*

*Blackout.*

END OF PLAY

## *2015 Runner Up*

## The Coward

**by**

## Dylan H. Jones

Directed by Preston Boyd

with

David Yamin as Sim

Ren Pearson as Jimmy

CHARACTERS
JIMMY, a young man, a frightened American soldier.

SIM, a tan-skinned man, older than Jimmy, droll but determined.

SETTING
A dirty hovel in Iraq.

TIME
2006.

> *Lights up low. It is night, everything washed out by moonlight. In the background we hear automatic weapons sporadically discharging. JIMMY, in desert fatigues and gear is hunkered down by some supply crates, one hand on his rifle: After a few moments SIM, wearing the same outfit but without any gear, and carrying an identical rifle, runs in.*

SIM (*Yelling.*): Where is the armory? The armory, where is it?!

JIMMY (*Raising his gun; in a Southern accent.*): Whoa! Put your gun down. Who are you?

SIM (*Exasperated.*): Oh, no...

JIMMY: Answer me, soldier, name and rank!

SIM (*Setting his gun down.*): Sim. My name is Sim. I am a, uh... (*Checking.*) lieutenant?

JIMMY: The hell you are. You tell me who you really are, or I'm gonna shoot you.

SIM: I told you, I... am... Sim. And I do not care if you kill me, it will save me a lot of time.

JIMMY (*Backing up, going for his radio.*): Captain Burke, this is Private Mills, zone three, I need Fox back here now, we got a possible Haji Flamer.

SIM: A what?

JIMMY: Shut up! Sit down! If you say another word I'll put a bullet in your head.

> *SIM keeps his mouth shut; he looks almost bored. After a second JIMMY tries his radio again.*

JIMMY (*Cont.*): Captain Burke. Captain, do you copy? (*Pause.*) Shit!

SIM: Radio trouble?

JIMMY (*Putting the radio away.*): The hell did I just say?!

SIM: Yes, yes, I heard you: bullet; head.

JIMMY: Then why are you still talking?!

SIM: Because it does not matters if you kill me or not, I will be dead by the end of the day.

JIMMY (*Pause.*): Is that when your timer goes off?

SIM (*He starts to open his shirt.*): I am not wearing a bomb. Here, let me...

JIMMY (*Gesturing violently with his gun.*): Keep your hands where I can see them!

SIM: Fine, then you examine me. Here, I shall put my hands on my head. (*Pause.*) Just look already! Nanna, give me strength!

JIMMY: You do it.

*SIM undoes the shirt and holds it open, revealing nothing underneath.*

JIMMY (*Cont.*): Where'd you come from?

SIM: Sumeria. What is the year?

JIMMY: I can't tell if you're just a smart-ass, or you really want to die.

SIM: It is a simple question, what is the year?

JIMMY (*Pause.*): 2006.

SIM: That is... in the Christian calendar, correct?

JIMMY: Yeah.

SIM: Where are we?

JIMMY: Did you get too close to an IED blast or something? How do you not know the year or where you are, but know your name and where you're from? Why're you wearing the same uniform as me? And where's Sumeria, I don't remember that town, is it near Razzaza?

SIM: It is not a town... it was a kingdom. It no longer exists.

JIMMY: So... what're you, some kind of refugee?

SIM (*Pause.*): Yes, in a way, I suppose, I am.

JIMMY: Are you on our side, or not?

SIM: Of course I am on your side, I always show up on the losing side!

JIMMY: The hell you talking about?!

SIM (*Sighing.*): Please, help me; I need bullets, and to find out where the attack will come from.

JIMMY: Captain said to hunker down, we're waiting for Second Cav to get here.

SIM: Second Cav, whatever that is, will not make it here. No one will. We are all going to die, so we must go fight as hard as we can.

JIMMY: Stop! Look, it's cool you wanna charge out there and get yourself killed, but I don't! You sit tight, we're gonna do what Captain ordered!

SIM: When did you see him last?

JIMMY: Three hours ago. He went on ahead with Stark and Fox, told me to stay.

SIM: So there is no armory; there is nothing except what you have, yes? So... may I have some bullets? Please?

JIMMY (*Pause.*): Why should I trust you?

SIM: By Nanna, I would really rather not die defenseless, if that is permissible?!

> *JIMMY finally lowers his gun, goes over to his gear and finds a clip. He offers it to SIM, who takes it, sits on the floor, picks up his gun, and puts the clip in. JIMMY watches him.*

JIMMY: You close to your grandma?

SIM: What?

JIMMY: You keep talking to your "Nanna." You close with her?

SIM: Oh, no, Nanna is not a person... he is a god. The god of the moon.

JIMMY: God... of the moon? I thought... ain't you Muslim?

SIM: What? ...Oh, because my skin is dark! No, I am Sumerian. We lived betwixt twin rivers, near the mouth of the Great Sea, in the heart of the desert...

JIMMY: You mean this desert? The Iraqi desert?

SIM (*Surprised.*): Iraq? We are in Iraq?

JIMMY: Yeah. Fifty miles south of Ramadi... can't remember this piece-of-shit town's name.

SIM (*Smiling wistfully.*): Oh... I am home. In a manner of speaking.

JIMMY: So you *are* Arab?

SIM: No! I told you… my home has not existed for almost four thousand years. I likely would not even recognize anything here, now.

JIMMY: I don't get it. How is your home four thousand years old?

SIM (*Slight pause.*): Because that is how long ago I died.

JIMMY (*Pause.*): You died… four thousand years ago? But… you're alive. Right now.

SIM: Yes. Each day I awaken in a battle and die, and then wake up somewhere else in another.

JIMMY: Buddy, I gotta take that gun, I think you might hurt yourself.

SIM: Oh, I have been hurt plenty: shot, stabbed, burned up, blown up, torn apart, frozen… I was eaten by lions once; that was strange. I cannot count how many times I have died. The only way I even know how long I have been under this curse is when someone is kind enough to tell me. Like you.

JIMMY: I don't understand? People only die once… well, unless they're cowards.

SIM: Ugh, I despise that saying!

JIMMY: What? "Cowards die a thousand…"

SIM (*Overlapping and finishing it.*): "Die many times before their deaths, the valiant never taste of death but once." Yes, that one. Though it sums up my situation perfectly, Shakespeare never wrote of how to stop it.

JIMMY: Stop what?

SIM: This curse. The more I think on it, I doubt it ever stops… until there are no battles left.

JIMMY: What curse? Who cursed you?

SIM (*Sinking into a mild depression as he recalls the events.*): My commander, in the final battle for our home. The Akkadians came, by the thousands, millions, it seemed… and of our seven hundred men, I alone ran away… and was the only one to survive. I heard him scream, cursing me, from the heart of the fray… but I kept running. That night, in the dark, I slipped on a ledge… and suddenly awoke amongst a small enclave of Jews, about to be slaughtered. That was only the beginning.

JIMMY: I don't believe you.

*SIM hesitates, then carefully takes a very old, very brittle photograph out of his pocket. He offers it to JIMMY, who takes it and stares at it silently.*

JIMMY (*Cont.*): What... is this?

SIM: The Seventh Cavalry, under General Custer. You can see me on the far right. The man who took it, Marcus, died with the rest of us that day. I had it at the end, when an arrow pierced my heart; when I die, things often travel with me. I know not why; makes as much sense as the rest of it all, I suppose.

JIMMY (*Mostly to himself.*): It's gotta be faked...

SIM: You know it is not.

JIMMY: My god... (*Realizing.*) Wait. Are you saying I'm gonna die?

SIM (*Taking back the picture, carefully putting it away.*): Everyone dies.

JIMMY: Yeah, but are you saying I'm gonna die now, today?

SIM (*Pause.*): Yes.

JIMMY: How do you know? How do you know everyone dies, every time?

SIM: I cannot be certain, I know only what befalls me. But I have heard enough to know that even if someone survives, it is an absolute slaughter: I was at Troy, Thermopylae, Philippi, the Alamo, Iwo Jima... countless more that have never even been heard of. Sometimes there are thousands of us fighting; once, there were only five. But always, before the day ends, I die. Matters not whether I fight, or flee... the outcome is the same.

JIMMY: I don't want to die.

SIM (*Sharply.*): Neither did I. Just be sure you fight when the time comes.

JIMMY (*Getting up, close to hysterical.*): There's not gonna be a time!! Second Cav's gonna be here any minute now, Captain's gonna come back, and we're gonna be at base shooting hoops by noon! And I am personally gonna haul your ass into psych! I'm real sorry that you're sick in the head, but stop trying to scare me with this horseshit! We're Americans, we don't lose!

SIM (*Patting the picture in his pocket.*): Yes. You do. I was there, remember?

JIMMY (*Running over and grabbing the gun from SIM.*): Shut up!! Just shut up and sit there!

*SIM sits, closing his eyes, hanging his head. Suddenly the radio bursts with static. JIMMY spins around and hurries back to pick it up.*

JIMMY (*Cont.*): Captain? Captain!

VOICE (*Over the radio, distorted.*): It's Stark; Captain's dead! Second Cav's held up; we got massive incoming! All units to zone one; we're gonna wait 'em out there. Be ca—

> *A gunshot comes over the radio and it goes silent. JIMMY stares at it. SIM looks up at him.*

JIMMY: Stark? Stark? (*Screaming into the radio.*) STARK?!

> *Silence. JIMMY finally shuts the radio off. He sits with his head in his hands. SIM watches.*

SIM: I am sorry... I care for this no more than you do.

JIMMY: There's gotta be a way out. I don't wanna die.

SIM: Death happens eventually. Whether it comes now or later, you have to fight.

JIMMY (*Looking up.*): Why? What's the point?!

SIM (*More firm and loudly than ever before, angry.*): If you need proof that the right thing to do, right now, is to stand and fight, just look at me! I was a <u>coward</u>. And there have always been people, in every battle, just like me, who fled when the end was upon them. And maybe—just maybe—if I can convince enough of them—enough of you—that facing the inevitable is better than living a single more day in shame... maybe... finally... I shall be free. (*Pause; he sighs and stands.*) What is your name?

JIMMY: Jimmy. Jimmy Mills.

SIM: Well, Jimmy... at least give me my gun and show me where "zone one" is. Please.

JIMMY (*Pause; getting up.*): I'm going, too. I'm gonna fight.

SIM (*Smiling, clapping him firmly on the shoulder.*): Good for you!

> *JIMMY gathers his gear, and then gives SIM back his gun. The sound of gunfire increases.*

JIMMY: By the way... where'd you get a gun?

SIM: It is odd... Every time I come to, I have a weapon, some kind of weapon. Lately... it has been guns. (*Beat.*) Once, I awoke with a Zulu spear... that was pretty... cool.

JIMMY (*Grinning awkwardly.*): "Cool," huh? Sound like you've picked up a lot all this time.

SIM: A little. I know hundreds of languages. Or at least how to say "Prepare to die!" in them.

*JIMMY laughs outright, and SIM joins him. The sound of gunfire increases further, accompanied by a mortar blast. They turn to look towards the audience and brace themselves.*

JIMMY: Maybe we'll win. Maybe this'll be your last time.

SIM: Perhaps. There is always... hope.

They both give a war cry and charge towards the audience as deafening gunfire greets them and...

*Blackout.*

END OF PLAY

# Dream On, Merry May

by

Bernard Yanelli

Directed by Preston Boyd

with

Bobbie Burrell as May

David Meyersburg as Tom

Tami Vaughan as Sandie

CHARACTERS
MAY SANDERSON, a woman, 75.

TOM SANDERSON, a man, 76, MAY's husband.

SANDI SANDERSON, a woman, 50, MAY and TOM's daughter.

SETTING
Florida. A living room with a love seat and a table and two chairs. There is also a small Christmas tree on a table and a record player in the background.

TIME
December, 1999.

> Lights up on MAY SANDERSON, an attractive 75 year-old, dressed in a simple house coat, who sits at a table, reading a newspaper.

MAY (*Standing, shouting.*): Tom! Oh, Tom! You have to come see this. It's the article—about me! It's finally here, and it's wonderful! He titled it: "Big Band Singer Merry May Is Alive and Well and Living Right Next Door!"

TOM (*Offstage, shouting back.*): Be there in a minute. Working on something.

MAY (*Mostly talking to herself.*): Oh, all you care about is that damn computer—and your interneting... and whatever else it is you do back there.

TOM (*Offstage, shouting.*): Can't hear you.

MAY (*Muttering to herself.*): Of course you can't, you old coot! I'll come to you.

> MAY rises, but after she hears a doorbell, she changes her direction and proceeds to open a door. SANDIE SANDERSON enters. She's attractive, well-dressed, and carrying a newspaper.

MAY: Sandie, have you seen it? (*She holds up the newspaper.*) Have you seen my article? It's so grand? This is the greatest day of my life!

SANDIE (*Throws her copy of the newspaper down on the table.*): And the most embarrassing day of mine.

MAY: Why? What's the matter?

SANDIE: How could you do this to me? Friends from all over town have been calling, asking why I never told them about my famous mother, Merry May.

MAY: What's so bad about that?

SANDIE: Other than your story being a pack of lies, I suppose nothing.

MAY: But it's not a lie.

SANDIE: Oh, please! You, a Big Band singer? Since when?

MAY: Well, it was a long time ago, when... when I was a young woman living in Indiana. Didn't you read the article? The details are all right there. Well, not all of them, of course. There were so many shows, so many... men. But don't tell your father. I don't want him to know about that part of my "salad days."

SANDIE: Somehow this day just keeps getting better. First, I learn that my mother's a pathological liar; now I find out she used to be "easy."

MAY: Watch your tone there, Missy! Just because you've always been a "Little Miss Goodie Two Shoes" doesn't mean you can talk to me like that.

SANDIE: All right, if this Big Band story is true, why am I just learning about it now?

MAY: You're not. I told you all about my career when you were little, but whenever I did, you started crying, so I stopped.

SANDIE: Why did I cry?

MAY: Who knows? You were always a bit peculiar—I mean when you were younger, always jealous if someone had something you didn't have.

SANDIE: Are you saying I was jealous of your fame?

MAY: Maybe—a lot of women were, you know.

SANDIE: That's absurd. Why would I be jealous of my own mother?

MAY: Beats me. All I know is that one day, when you were six... no, seven, you told me to stop bragging. You said that you were going to be more famous than me, so that's the last time I ever mentioned my singing career to you.

SANDIE: Why don't I remember that conversation?

MAY: Maybe you repressed the memory. Like I said, you used to be a bit peculiar. But look at you now: a back-up singer in your church choir! My, my, what a success story!

SANDIE:(*Glaring.*): Where's daddy? We need to talk.

MAY: In his den, on the computer—emailing, photocrapping... I don't know what the hell he does back there.

SANDIE: It's called photoshopping.

MAY: Crapping, cropping, shopping what's the difference. (*Saddened.*) All I know is that he spends more time on his computer than he does with me.

SANDIE (*Under her breath.*): I wonder why?

MAY: What's that?

SANDIE: Nothing.

MAY: Well, I'll take my newspaper over his computer any day—especially when it has an article about me! (*Holding up the newspaper for SANDIE.*) Tell me the truth. Do you think I look fat in this picture? (*SANDIE rolls her eyes.*) I was eighteen, and the Bob Benderson Band had just rolled into town. I won a talent contest at the county fair, so I got a chance to sing with the band.

SANDIE: You didn't sleep with him, did you?

MAY: Bob Benderson? Heavens, no. He was old and fat and used to fart a lot. But his saxophone player, Slick Willie, now he and I, we had our share of fun. I can still remember a couple of those sultry summer nights when we...

SANDIE: Stop! Stop... before I become ill! (*Suspicious.*) This Slick Willie, what was his last name?

MAY: Oh, I don't remember. It was a long time ago.

SANDIE: Try.

MAY: I... I can't think of it.

SANDIE: Try harder.

MAY: Wait! That's right! It was Clinton. Slick Willie Clinton. And let me tell you, he didn't get his nickname from his musical ability... (*Nudging SANDIE.*) if you know what I mean.

SANDIE: Oh, dear God! I've had enough. (*Shouting.*) Daddy! Daddy! Get in here!

MAY: Shhh! You're not going to tell on me are you?

> *Dressed in a sweater vest, white oxford shirt, and khaki pants, a distinguished-looking TOM SANDERSON, 76, enters, carrying a large poster board with Queen Elizabeth's head photo-shopped with the body of Betty Grable's pin-up photo.*

TOM: What's all the shouting about? (*He sets the poster on a stand that he's also carrying.*)

SANDIE: What on earth is that?

TOM (*Admiring his work.*): My latest creation. I've already got twelve pre-orders from my buddies at the VFW. And I predict my next creation is gonna be even more popular: the face of Eleanor Roosevelt on the bikini-clad body of Raquel Welch.

SANDIE: Daddy, that's downright creepy.

TOM (*Gazing at his creation, not really listening.*): To each his own, Sandie, to each his own.

MAY (*Handing him the newspaper.*): Tom, take a look at my article. Isn't it wonderful?

TOM: Let me see. (*He scans the article.*) It's better than wonderful, May! It's spectacular! Hey, darling! You're famous again!

MAY: I know. I know. It's so exciting!

SANDIE: Daddy, you need to tell me what's going on here.

TOM: We're celebrating your mother's resurgent fame. Isn't that obvious?

MAY: She's jealous, Tom. It's like she's seven years old all over again.

TOM: Oh, no! Not the jealousy phase. That was a tough one, as I recall.

SANDIE: Daddy, we need to speak—in private. (*She pulls her father across the room and speaks under her breath; meanwhile, MAY looks at the newspaper.*) I think mother's finally lost it.

TOM (*Under his breath, as well.*): What are you talking about?

SANDIE: She's losing her grip... on reality.

TOM: Don't be ridiculous!

SANDIE: Come on, Daddy. You must see it.

TOM: Your mother's perfectly fine.

SANDIE: I think it's time for you to consider putting her in some type of home.

TOM (*Sternly.*): She's not going anywhere.

SANDIE: But . . . .

TOM: But nothing! She's getting a little forgetful. So am I. You want to put me into a home, too?

SANDIE: Of course not. But what about this fabricated story?

TOM: Who says it's fabricated?

SANDIE: Oh, come on! Where's the proof that she ever had such a career?

TOM: You want proof?

SANDIE: I do.

>   *TOM walks back toward MAY, puts his hands on her shoulders, and gives her a kiss on the cheek.*

TOM: May, do you remember where I put your scrapbook? I can't keep track of anything anymore.

MAY: It's in your office, I think. Go find it so Little Miss Doubting Thomas over there can stop being so cranky.

>   *TOM leaves the room.*

SANDIE: I'm only doubting you for your own good.

MAY: Sandie, maybe you should go see a therapist about these fits of jealousy. Last week on Oprah I heard a doctor say that they've now got medications for virtually every type of disorder. Of course, I never heard of a jealousy disorder, but I'm sure you're not the first one to...

SANDIE: I'm not continuing this conversation until I see your scrapbook.

TOM (*Reenters with a scrapbook.*): You were right, May. It was in my office all along. Here you go, Sandie.

>   *He gives the scrapbook to SANDIE, who then flips through the pages.*

MAY: It's all right there. Let me know if you have any questions?

TOM (*Looking over SANDIE's shoulder.*): Are you satisfied?

>   *SANDIE hands the scrapbook to her mother, then pulls her father across the room again.*

SANDIE: I don't know what's going on here, but something's not right.

MAY (*Shouting from the other side of the room.*): I was so young. You know, it's strange, but I seem to be wearing the same...

TOM: What's that, May?

MAY: Oh, nothing. Just reminiscing.

TOM: Good.

SANDIE: Are you going to tell me the truth, or do I have to find out for myself?

TOM: Why are you being this way?

SANDIE: Because I've seen this same thing happen with some of my friends' parents and...

*TOM grabs SANDIE by the arm and pulls her further away from MAY.*

TOM (*Glaring.*): Now you listen to me, young lady. You stop this. You stop this right now. Do you hear me? Your mother is my responsibility. You don't get to show up here every two weeks and tell us how to live our lives. Is that clear?

SANDIE (*After an awkward pause.*): All right. I'm... I'm sorry, Daddy. (*Deep sigh.*) I promise to keep my big mouth shut.

*She gives him a kiss on the cheek, causing his glare to turn into a smile. He mouths the words "Thank you." They walk back over to MAY.*

TOM: Which event are you looking at, May?

MAY: I'm not sure. The caption says Chicago, 1947. And that's Bob Benderson up on stage with me. But I don't recall ever singing with his band in Chicago.

SANDIE: Well, that was a long time ago. But you look great. Not fat at all.

MAY: Thank you. I have to admit that I had a pretty amazing figure back in the day.

SANDIE (*Softly touching her mother's hair.*): Sorry that I got so angry with you before.

MAY: That's all right. Nobody's perfect. Besides, maybe your jealous streak was my fault. Maybe I bragged a bit too much when you were little.

SANDIE: Mother, I've got to go, but I'll be back on Sunday for Christmas dinner. Maybe we can look at your scrapbook together.

MAY: That would be nice. And don't worry. (*Under her breath.*) I'll keep my stories clean if your father's at home. He's still a bit old-fashioned about certain things, you know.

*SANDIE smiles, kisses her mother on the cheek, then does the same with her father. She exits.*

TOM: Well, I'm glad our little girl has finally started to appreciate you for who you are.

MAY: Me, too.

*TOM takes the scrapbook and starts thumbing through it.*

TOM: Amazing! What a fox you were—and still are, for that matter! (*He kisses her on the back of the neck.*)

MAY (*She slaps at him.*): Hey, stop that! I may be cheap, but I'm not easy... (*Under her breath.*) anymore.

*TOM gives her another kiss, this time on the forehead. He turns on a record player and the song "I'm Getting Sentimental Over You" by Tommy Dorsey plays in the background. He then opens up the scrapbook and flips through the pages.*

TOM: I'm so glad that I had the bright idea to give your scrapbook to that reporter. He told me that all those pictures really helped make your story come alive.

MAY: So am I. This article is the best gift ever. The only thing is, I don't remember so many of these shows. How can I have forgotten so many wonderful memories?

*With the scrapbook open, TOM stops and stares at his poster, then he looks at the scrapbook again.)*

TOM: Ah, the beauty of photoshop! It makes dreams come true!

*TOM takes MAY by the hand and they start dancing; she has a radiant smile on her face.*

*Lights fade.*

*Blackout.*

END OF PLAY

# It's Time to Move

## by

## Ronnie Pantello

Directed by Don Walker

with

Ren Pearson as Baby 1

Danae DeShazer as Baby 2

CHARACTERS
BABY 1, a man representing a baby boy.

BABY 2, a woman representing a baby girl.

STAGE HANDS, two men or women, wearing physician white coats, responsible for moving the babies in their chairs around the stage.

SETTING
In the womb, and then in the nursery.

TIME
The present.

> *Lullaby music playing. A spot lights BABY 1 and BABY 2, sitting in two chairs CENTER. The rest of stage is dark. BABY 1 is wearing a blue hoodie and blue socks. BABY 2 is wearing a pink hoodie and pink socks.*

BABY 1 (*Squirming around.*): We've been together almost nine months. Aren't you tired of this place?

BABY 2 (*Squirming around.*): No! I like it here. It's warm and there's plenty to eat. I never want to leave.

BABY 1: It's getting a little crowded.

BABY 2: You're the one with the baby weight.

BABY 1: You're not exactly skinny.

BABY 2: I'm just happy, so there fatso!

BABY 1: Well I overheard The Package complaining to Deep Voice about weight gain. You know what that means.

BABY 2: Yea, when The Package is unhappy we don't have to deal with Deep Voice. When The Package is unhappy everybody is unhappy, especially Deep Voice.

BABY 1: Who can stand all that pounding... (*Using his arm BABY 1 mimics in and out to the audience.*) In and out, in and out. Very annoying.

BABY 2: I don't mind it, Deep Voice never stays too long. And The Package is mostly happy when Deep Voice is done.

BABY 1: But who likes being upside down and sideways. Deep Voice only cares about Deep Voice.

BABY 2: Doesn't bother me. I never want to leave. Who knows what's out there.

BABY 1: I think I know a way out.

BABY 2: I'm not interested... all right... tell me more.

BABY 1: You know the pounding noise...

BABY 2: But it stopped.

BABY 1: Yes, but the noise came from down there. (*Points down toward the audience.*) That must be the way out.

   *STAGE HANDS move on stage and stand behind the babies.*

BABY 2 (*Looking DOWNSTAGE toward the audience.*): It's very narrow. We could never squeeze through there. Anyway I am not moving.

BABY 1: That's the way out and I'm going for it.

BABY 2: Not me. Not safe. What would we eat?

BABY 1: There must be food out there. Frankly, The Package's food is terrible. All the fruits, vitamins, vegetables, YUK.

BABY 2: You know, it's not very nice the way you push the food back up!

BABY 1: I'm trying to send a message. Watch this. (*Punches then kicks.*)

BABY 2: Stop with the kicking. That's not nice. Can't you just sit still like me?

BABY 1: The Package loves it when I kick. I'm doing The Package a favor.

BABY 2: I'm not kicking and I am not pushing food back. I'm just going to chill in this nice warm place.

BABY 1: Don't you understand, we have outgrown this place. It's time to move.

BABY 2: No!

   *BABY 1 begins to kick, push and squirm, trying to get out of the chair.*

BABY 1: Uh Oh... I broke something, there's a flood!

BABY 2: Now look what you've done.

   *BABY 1's chair begins to move away from BABY 2. The chairs are spinning.*

BABY 1 (*Scared.*): I falling... follow me... follow the water.

BABY 2: No! I'm afraid.

BABY 1 (*Tension building.*): I'm almost out... almost... almost... I'm out!

   *Stage goes black. We hear a slap. BABY 1 is UPSTAGE..*

BABY 1: Shit! Why did you hit me?

*Lights up on chairs, which are farther apart.*

BABY 1 (*Continuing, to BABY 2*): Go back. Don't come out! Somebody just slapped me… then they put something in my mouth. <u>Don't come out</u>…

BABY 2: Too late! I'm slipping… Oh no!

*BABY 2 puts both hands and feet in the air holding on for dear life. STAGE HAND moves BABY 2 around RIGHT.*

BABY 2 (*Cont.*): Nope… not going.

BABY 1: Where are you?

BABY 2: I'm not coming out… I'm sorry.

BABY 1: You're making everyone nervous… oh no… they're trying to dig you out.

BABY 2: Not going! (*Continues to hold on, feet and hands higher in the air.*)

BABY 1: Oh no, they're going to… on no… open up the package.

BABY 2 (*Curls up in a ball.*) Let go of me.

*Light's dim and come up quickly. The chairs are close together CENTER.*

BABY 1 (*BABY 1's eyes are barely open.*): Open your eyes… it's very bright, but not that bad.

BABY 2: No! I'm not opening my eyes!

BABY 1: Open your eyes, don't be such a baby.

BABY 2: I am a baby stupid. And what's all this noise?

BABY 1: There are others like us. This must be our new home. (*Looking around he waves at the other babies. Flirts, having fun.*)

BABY 2: I hate it! I want to go back… I liked it there.

BABY 1: Too bad. This is our new home and you have to like it.

BABY 2: I don't have to like anything. Why are we so different and yet so close. Will we always be like this?

BABY 1: I don't know. Maybe being different is good. I'll always love you. (*Lovingly touches BABY 2.*)

BABY 2: I'll always love you. But I don't like change. I like the same. I want to go home.

BABY 1: Don't waste time thinking about going back. Go forward.

BABY 2: No. I'm going to spend my time getting back into The Package.

BABY 1: Not me. I'm going to spend my life looking around. Hey, we're moving. Now where?

BABY 2: Stay still... don't move. Maybe they can't see us.

BABY 1: Too late! Deep Voice's got me. We're going somewhere.

BABY 2 (*Startled.*): Now he's got me. What's happening? I hear The Package.

*The chairs move around the stage. The chairs are farther apart.*

BABY 1: Somebody just put me on the Package. Wow... look at those mountains. (*BABY 1's head moves very fast to the right.*)

BABY 2: What mountains?

*Sucking sounds.*

BABY 1: I didn't know I could do this.

BABY 2: Do what?

BABY 1: The mountains have milk... it's good.

BABY 2: I want some.

BABY 1: I'm not done.

*More sucking sounds.*

BABY 1 (*Continues, Angry.*): Wait a minute... I'm not done... put me down.

*BABY 2 begins to cry.*

BABY 1 (*Cont.*): What's with all the noise?

BABY 2: I don't know... I just started to cry... it must mean something.

*BABY 2's chair is moving away from BABY 1. BABY 2 assumes the same head position as BABY 1, head to the side.*

*Sucking sound begins.*

BABY 1: How's it going?

BABY 2: Quiet! I'm busy.

*More sucking sounds.*

BABY 2 (*Cont.*): This is exhausting.

*BABY 2 moves back to original position next to BABY 1. The chairs begin to move.*

BABY 1: Now where are we going?

BABY 2: Back to the lighted room. Maybe we can get some sleep.

The chairs stop moving. They are shoulder to shoulder. They both strain their eyes as they look toward the audience.

BABY 2: What's with that glass wall and all those faces looking at us?

BABY 1: I don't know… they seem happy… smiling… pointing at us. (*Pointing.*) That one looks like the Package.

BABY 2: She does! (*Waves.*) That's weird. They seem happy.

BABY 1: How about some sleep?

BABY 2: Good idea. Maybe this place ain't so bad.

BABY 1: As long as you're here it will be great.

BABY 2: I'll always be here for you.

BABY 1: Let's see what happens tomorrow.

BABY 2: I don't want to think about tomorrow.

BABY 1: Why not? Maybe it will be even better than today.

BABY 2: I doubt that.

BABY 1: Maybe more mountains.

BABY 2: I hope for more mountains.

BABY 1: I think I'm going to like mountains all my life.

*Lights fade.*

*Blackout.*

END OF PLAY

# Nimby

## by

## Robert Kinast

Directed by Louise Stinespring

with

Tammy Halsted as Smokey

Chuck Conlon as Walter

CHARACTERS
SMOKEY, a female, mid-40s to mid-50s, dressed professionally.

WALTER, a male, mid-40s to mid-50s, has a beard and shaggy hair, worn but clean clothes, moves with a limp.

SETTING
A main street in any urban area. At least one sidewalk bench or a table with chairs for outside dining. Possibly a sign encouraging people not to give money to panhandlers.

TIME
The present.

*SMOKEY enters LEFT.*

SMOKEY (*Speaking emphatically, almost angrily, on her cell phone.*): Mr. Commissioner, I've told you before, there is no way the neighborhood association or the business alliance will agree to a shelter for the homeless in this community. (*Beat.*) I realize something must be done about the problem and the idea of a shelter with related services makes perfect sense, just not here. (*Beat.*) That's right: Not In My Back Yard. (*Beat.*) I don't know where. That's your job; that's why you were elected. (*Beat.*) Of course, you can call back any time you want but our position will be the same. There's nothing more to consider. (*Beat.*) All right. Good-bye, and good day to you too.

*WALTER, carrying a backpack or grocery bag with his basic belongings, enters RIGHT during SMOKEY's phone call, approaches her, and holds out a paper cup.*

WALTER: Excuse me, Ma'am, could you spare some loose change, or maybe even some soft money?

SMOKEY: No, I could not. I don't carry any cash, hard or soft.

WALTER: I hear that a lot these days. You know, there's an ATM right around the corner.

SMOKEY: Nice try, but I don't think so. ATMs only give out tens and twenties, and I'm certainly not going to pay a fee if it's not my bank.

*Starts to move past WALTER but he blocks her. This happens several times during the following exchanges.*

WALTER: You just don't want to help people like me, do you? And you could, being president of the Downtown Business Alliance.

SMOKEY: How do you know that?

WALTER: I read the newspapers people throw away; I've seen your picture. You're a person of influence around here; you could make a difference if you wanted to.

SMOKEY: Do you see that sign over there? Can you read it?

WALTER: Of course I can read it; I'm not illiterate. But I don't agree with it.

SMOKEY: Well, I do. Giving money to you panhandlers only makes the problem worse.

WALTER: Worse for who?

SMOKEY: For everybody. Businesses lose customers; neighbors don't want to be pestered on their way home; parents are concerned about their children; people have to clean up your messes.

WALTER: You said "everybody," but I didn't hear you mention the homeless. You probably think we don't have problems, only cause them.

SMOKEY: Well, you do.

WALTER: Just because I ask you for a little loose change, that you don't need anyway?

SMOKEY: Because giving people like you money keeps you hanging around; it makes you dependent, waiting for a handout.

WALTER: You think it's easy asking people for money?

SMOKEY: I wouldn't know; I've never had to.

WALTER: Well, let me tell you, it's embarrassing, and dehumanizing. People pretend they don't see you or hear you, walk past you like you're not really there. Or they suddenly have to check their cell phones. But you know what's the worst? When somebody throws a few coins at you and you have to get down on the ground to pick them up. Now that's humiliating.

SMOKEY: None of that would happen if you worked for a living.

WALTER: I work. I'm working now, and when I'm finished with you, I'm gonna work the other side of the street, and then I'll move over to tenth avenue and work there.

SMOKEY: I don't call that work.

WALTER: That's 'cause you've never done it. Oh excuse me, you've never had to do it. You've never needed help like I do.

SMOKEY: I'm willing to help; I'm even willing to give money if I thought it would be used properly.

WALTER: Ah, and I bet you believe those other signs I've been seeing around here saying all we do with the little bit of money we scrounge up is buy booze and drugs.

SMOKEY: Well, you certainly don't buy new clothes.

WALTER: No, but sometimes I like to wash the clothes I have at a laundromat. And maybe buy a half-decent meal at a restaurant that will serve me, or help out some of the other people I share the streets with.

SMOKEY: I find that hard to believe.

WALTER: That's because you don't really know how I live. You ought to follow me around, see what it's like.

SMOKEY: I don't need to see what it's like.

WALTER: You don't want to see, you mean.

SMOKEY: What I want is for you to get out of my way so I can go home, something else you wouldn't know about.

WALTER: I have a home, several in fact.

SMOKEY: Let me guess: a bench over at Rigby Park, or the school playground, or maybe the public library if you hide in the stacks before they close.

WALTER: All of the above, at one time or another. But you left out the Hillside Memorial Gardens, at least when the weather's nice.

SMOKEY: Those are all public places.

WALTER: So? I'm a member of the public.

SMOKEY: But that's not what they're for.

WALTER: When they're not being used, what's the problem? I'm not hurting anybody; I'm not causing any trouble. In fact, I'm the one likely to be hassled.

SMOKEY: The police are only doing their job.

WALTER: It's not the police. If you're not breaking a law, they don't push it. No, it's a couple of teenage gangs on the prowl around here who like to mess with homeless people. And I admit, sometimes it's the homeless themselves especially the ones who have mental or emotional problems, or maybe just want to rip you off if you have something they want.

SMOKEY: If it's that risky, why don't you go the City Mission Shelter?

WALTER: Too many rules: when you can check in; when you eat; where you sleep; when you have to leave. It's too confining. Don't get me wrong. Those folks do the best they can. I just like my freedom, and my space.

SMOKEY: I do too. So if you'll go "work" the other side of the street or settle in to whatever "home" you're staying at tonight, I'll be on my way.

*WALTER steps aside this time and gestures SMOKEY on.*

SMOKEY (*Cont.*): Thank you.

WALTER: You're welcome. It was nice seeing you again... Smokey.

SMOKEY (*Stops, slowly turns around to face WALTER*): What did you call me?

WALTER: Smokey.

SMOKEY: No one has called me that since college. How do you know my nickname?

WALTER: "The Seacoast Sound." The band that put the smooth in smooth jazz.

SMOKEY (*Steps closer, looks intently at WALTER*): Are you...

WALTER (*With a gesture miming playing the keyboard.*): Walter Stevens, on keyboard, accompanying our lead singer, Smokey Duval.

SMOKEY: I don't believe this. Walter Stevens. I haven't heard from you since the band broke up.

WALTER: And I would remind you, the band broke up because you left.

SMOKEY: I wanted to pursue other goals, Walter. You knew that. Besides, you could have gotten another singer.

WALTER: Not like you, Smokey. You were the Suncoast Sound. And the other guys were ready to move on to different things too.

SMOKEY: What about you?

WALTER: Music was my life. I couldn't imagine doing anything else. So I formed another band. We played backup for singers who didn't have their own band or fronted for headliners who came through town. We caught on, started getting invitations to tour, traveled all over.

SMOKEY: Sounds like you were successful. What happened?

WALTER: What happens to a lot of people who go homeless: a crisis, a tragedy, some situation that feels overwhelming and doesn't leave many options. At least, none you can see, or want to pursue.

SMOKEY: What was it in your case?

WALTER: You really want to know, or are you just curious?

SMOKEY: I really want to know. After all, we spent a lot of time together before the band broke up. (*Gestures toward a bench.*) Here, sit down.

WALTER: Can't sit for long.

SMOKEY: Why not?

WALTER: It's part of my story.

SMOKEY: Tell me.

WALTER: One night about a year ago, we were playing right here in town. I was driving to our hotel a couple miles from here with Sammy the Stick Man, our drummer. There was construction on the road, lane changes, and it wasn't lit very well. All of a sudden, around a bend, out of nowhere comes this SUV—the wrong way. I swerved to the left but the SUV swerved to the right and we hit almost head-on.

SMOKEY: How awful.

WALTER: No, fatal. Sammy didn't survive, and I stopped playing.

SMOKEY: You can't hold yourself responsible for what happened, Walter.

WALTER: I don't, but that's not the reason I don't play anymore. I can't. I had a lot of injuries from that accident and without insurance, I didn't get the best surgery or rehab. Fact is, I can't play or even sit very long without being in pain.

SMOKEY: There must be pain medicine you can take.

WALTER: There is, when I can afford it, which depends on what I make panhandling.

SMOKEY: But there are other things you can do with music to make a living—teach, compose, manage a group, be an agent.

WALTER: Oh, there are all kinds of things I could do, if I wanted to—but I don't. Since that night, I've had no desire, no motivation, just like a lot of the homeless people I know. To paraphrase a song we both know, it was the night the music died, my music anyway.

SMOKEY: But living on the street is certainly not the answer.

WALTER: It's not that much different from the life I was living before the accident. You know, moving around a lot, staying in different places, no fixed address or steady income, no permanent friends—it works for me.

SMOKEY: For you maybe, but not for every homeless person.

WALTER: You'd have to ask them about that—why they're homeless, whether or not they want to be. In fact, I think you should ask them if you're really serious about solving the "problem" of the homeless. Get their stories and you might get the solution.

SMOKEY: How would I do that? I don't know any homeless people.

WALTER: You do now. And I could introduce you to a lot more.

SMOKEY: How would I contact you, if I wanted to meet... the people you know?

WALTER: I'm around here most of the time. And I know how to find you. Just think about it. (*Struggles to his feet.*) And now, I better get going before "one of the people I know" takes my spot for tonight. It was good seeing you again, Smokey.

SMOKEY: It was good seeing you too, Walter. I think.

*WALTER offers a goodbye gesture and exits. SMOKEY watches him leave, ponders for a moment, then takes out her cell phone, punches in a number and waits a moment.*

SMOKEY (*Cont.*): Mr. Commissioner, regarding our earlier conversation? I think we need to talk.

*Lights fade.*

*Blackout.*

### END OF PLAY

# The Dancing Lessons

**by**

## Connie Schindewolf

Directed by Pam Wiley

with

Sarita Roche as Miriam

Lynne Doyle as Catherine

Cammy Harris as Young Miriam

Logan Junkins as George

CHARACTERS

MIRIAM, a woman, 80, suffering from Alzheimer's and unable to talk or make eye contact.

CATHERINE, a woman, 50 to 55, MIRIAM's daughter.

YOUNG MIRIAM, a woman, 22, dressed in an evening gown.

GEORGE, a man, 23, dressed in a suit or tuxedo.

SETTING

A nursing home with two chairs (or one chair and a wheelchair for MIRIAM).

TIME

The present.

*When MIRIAM is thinking of herself and GEORGE as young, Young MIRIAM and GEORGE are on stage and dance then stop and have dialogue. When they dance, there is music that fades when they speak. When they finish speaking, the music comes up and they dance again for a few seconds before CATHERINE resumes her dialogue. They hold each other and move very slowly when CATHERINE is speaking and no music can be heard.*

*Lights up as MIRIAM sits in chair as CATHERINE enters.*

CATHERINE: Hi Mom. (*She bends down and kisses her.*) How are you today? (*Pauses.*) Is this your sweater? (*Looks at tag.*) No. It's Nancy Johnson's. Looks nice on you though. She certainly shopped at the right places. I'm still going to complain though because there's no reason they should be mixing up your laundry when your name and room number are on it. I have a surprise for you. I found this box of... old mementos I guess, from your past. The old music I played didn't work, and I know you're thinking in there. Remember when I was still in high school and we went to see Aunt Liz in that nursing home in Dixon? We thought she'd know us, but all she could talk about was the nuns. We found out when she was little she went to a small Catholic school... well that's where her mind was... stuck with the nuns. She looked us in the eyes though... just thought we were nuns. So where are you, Mom? Where are you stuck right now? Is it a happy place? (*She takes out a certificate and puts it in MIRIAM's hands.*) It says George and Miriam, "Most Improved." What were you most improved at? It doesn't say.

*Music starts and YOUNG MIRIAM and GEORGE enter, dancing. CATHERINE does not see or hear them as they are in MIRIAM's mind. They slow down and stop during dialogue and music fades.*

YOUNG MIRIAM: We are getting better, aren't we? I mean, "Most Improved" that's something isn't it?

GEORGE: It certainly is. You know, as much as I hate to admit it, I'm glad you talked me into these dancing lessons. We'll never be Fred and Ginger, but it's fun and I get to hold my favorite lady.

YOUNG MIRIAM: Do we have to keep it a secret?

GEORGE: Absolutely! You don't think I want the guys to know I ballroom dance, do you? They'd laugh all the way through our next poker game.

YOUNG MIRIAM: All right, all right. You know this is such good exercise, and it's something we can do all of our lives.

GEORGE: We'll see M'Lady!

*Music fades up and they dance for a few seconds then stop. The music fades out.*

CATHERINE: Mom, what are you thinking? (*She takes the certificate from her.*) I just want one little sign that you understand I'm here every day, and that you know what I'm talking about. (*She takes a shell out of the box and puts it in her hands.*) Look, it's a little shell. What does this represent? Is it from the Gulf?

*Music plays and YOUNG MIRIAM and GEORGE dance then music fades and they stop dancing and speak.*

YOUNG MIRIAM (*She has felt something in his pants pocket.*): What's this?

GEORGE: Nothing.

YOUNG MIRIAM: Come on. It's not your keys. Take it out.

GEORGE: Okay, okay. (*He pulls out a shell.*)

YOUNG MIRIAM (*Taking it.*): A shell? Is this one we got from that beach?

GEORGE: Yes.

YOUNG MIRIAM: The sandbar where you took me on our first date?

GEORGE: Okay, so I'm a sentimental sucker. It reminds me of you so I keep it in my pocket, and when I'm frustrated at work or somewhere, I feel it and it's like I have you with me.

YOUNG MIRIAM: That's so romantic! I have the other half of that clam-shell you know, I'm going to start doing the same thing. That was such a beautiful da… when we were lying on the sand and the sun was so warm and you said…

GEORGE: Miriam, you are so beautiful. I knew then I was going to marry you. What I didn't know is you'd sign me up for dancing lessons!

YOUNG MIRIAM: You love it and you know it!

GEORGE: I know I love any reason to hold you in my arms!

YOUNG MIRIAM: Isn't this better than watching TV on a Wednesday night?

*Music up and they dance and then it fades out.*

CATHERINE (*She takes shell from her and picks up a little bank from the box.*): Look Mom, I don't know why you kept this little bank. (*Shakes it.*) No money in it. Why would you keep an empty bank? You did teach me a lot about saving. I never saw you and Dad use credit cards… you saved for everything. And you know I think I've taught Bob that too. When we first got married, he was clueless about budgeting and saving. So, thanks, Mom. You and Dad didn't have luxurious things but they were really yours… you owned them free and clear. And another thing, I didn't know what I put you guys through when I was in college and having to move back and forth with all my junk. Well, I know now since we had to move Shelby back up to North Carolina again. And would you believe she lives on the third floor of her dorm with no elevator! She really didn't act very appreciative of all the work Bob and I did moving her at our age. I doubt I acted very appreciative to you and Dad either, and I'm sorry, Mom. What goes around comes around, I guess. (*Pause.*) What could this bank mean to you?

*Music up, dancing, then music fades.*

YOUNG MIRIAM: I counted the money today in the bank… $350.

GEORGE: Only $150 more!

YOUNG MIRIAM: I'm so excited just thinking about it! I mean I know we've only been married six months but… a baby! We're so smart in waiting. I mean the hospital bill's going to cost us at least $400, and we know there will be other expenses.

GEORGE: I really haven't missed the pocket change we've put away every day. I just can't wait to start trying… over and over and over. (*Laughs.*)

YOUNG MIRIAM: Oh it will be rough, won't it?

GEORGE: Will you still love me as much when there's the pitter-patter of little feet in the house?

YOUNG MIRIAM: Always! We may have to stop our dancing lessons for a while though.

GEORGE: I think I can handle that. I'm sure we'll get enough exercise.

YOUNG MIRIAM: Let's always remember how happy we are right now, okay?

GEORGE: Sure thing.

YOUNG MIRIAM: No, I'm serious. You know we'll have some rough spots. When that happens, will you remember me this way? In this dress at this age and the way we are dancing?

GEORGE: Yes. And when I'm old and gray, will you remember me like this… just like tonight?

YOUNG MIRIAM: Absolutely!

*Music up, they dance and then it fades out.*

CATHERINE: Did I tell you Bob and I are saving for an Alaskan cruise? We've never been and I've heard everyone rave about how beautiful it is, and how they got to see whales. It won't be for a while so don't worry… I'll still be here every day. And I'll be home for Christmas too. We're not going to Bob's parents this year. Speaking of whales. There's one caught in the canal by Old Pass. I don't remember what kind it is. It's not a killer whale but it's about that size, and they're trying to get it back to the Gulf. They're not common around here, but sure enough it swam into the bay and got stuck in the canal. They don't understand why the poor thing's just stuck there. There's not enough food for it to eat. The news showed people standing on their docks throwing it raw meat… but it doesn't touch it. It's sad. (*Takes another item out of box.*) Mom, look what else is in the box. (*She holds up a tiny baby outfit.*) It still has the tag on it so I'm confused. If it were mine, I would have worn it. Why did you save this? Here, feel it. (*She puts it in MIRIAM's hands.*)

*Music up but instead of dancing, GEORGE is leading YOUNG MIRIAM by the hand and they're walking. The music is slower. It fades and they speak.*

GEORGE: Come on, let me see a smile. You look so beautiful tonight.

YOUNG MIRIAM: No, I don't. The dress is still pretty, but I'm not… not tonight. We shouldn't have come.

GEORGE: We've missed two lessons, and the Dr. said it'd be all right. You know Miriam, we shouldn't have bought all the baby stuff… being only two months. I mean I started it. I brought home that tiny little outfit. I just knew it was going to be a girl. I'm so sorry.

YOUNG MIRIAM: I'm the one who is sorry. I'm just so thankful we didn't tell anyone. Promise me you won't.

GEORGE: I won't. We're lucky we're so young… we'll get pregnant again.

YOUNG MIRIAM (*She is visibly upset.*): Lucky? How on earth can you say I'm lucky? I can barely get out of bed in the morning, and I can't even get the dishes done!

GEORGE: Miriam, I'm sorry. I won't use that word again. (*He holds her.*)

CATHERINE (*She takes the baby outfit from MIRIAM.*): It is awful cute even if I don't understand why you kept it. Mom, is that a tear? (*Wipes it for her.*) Does this make you sad? You know they're coming up with all kinds of new medication that might help you... maybe to even speak. But, we don't really have to talk to understand each other. Mom, will you just look at me?

*Music starts but fades quickly.*

GEORGE: Come on, let's dance, please?

YOUNG MIRIAM (*She looks confused.*): No, I have to do something... wait.

*The music has completely stopped. YOUNG MIRIAM leaves GEORGE and walks to MIRIAM. CATHERINE is seated and bent down with head in hands. Standing by MIRIAM, YOUNG MIRIAM moves MIRIAM's head so she's looking at CATHERINE and then picks up her hand and puts it on CATHERINE's head and pats it. YOUNG MIRIAM smiles. CATHERINE looks up to her mother and realizes she has communicated with her. She takes her hand and kisses it, then she hugs her. YOUNG MIRIAM moves back to GEORGE as the music starts up and they dance around.*

*Lights fade.*

*Blackout.*

### END OF PLAY

# The Locket

by

**Mark E. Leib**

Directed by Pam Wiley

with

Tony Boothby as Nathan

Gabrielle Lennon as Deborah

Jan Wallace as Shana

Ben Kalish as Kit

CHARACTERS
NATHAN, a man, 45.

DEBORAH, a woman, 41, NATHAN's wife.

SHANA, a woman, 51, NATHAN's sister.

KIT, a man, 27, SHANA's son.

SETTING
An old-fashioned bedroom. A bed, a night table, a tall chest of drawers, a dressing table with a mirror, various drab artworks on the walls, and the door to a bathroom.

TIME
2015

*Lights up as NATHAN, DEBORAH, SHANA, and KIT enter.*

KIT: So now we violate her bedroom. Terrific.

NATHAN: It's harmless. We're just going to look around and go.

SHANA: It's so musty in here. I can't imagine how anyone could stand it.

NATHAN: Shay, you look in the tallboy. I'll check the night table. Deborah, you look in the bathroom over there.

DEBORAH: How do I know if I've found it?

NATHAN: It's a roundish gold locket on a thin golden chain. Easy to spot.

KIT: We're like a bunch of thieves. I feel like a criminal.

NATHAN: We're not thieves. We're not going to take anything. You look in the dressing table drawers.

KIT: How's it going, Aunt Lainie? Now that you're dead we've decided to ransack your bedroom. It's how we pay our respects.

SHANA (*Holding up a pendant on a chain.*): Here's something. Is this it?

NATHAN (*Going over to her.*): Let's see. (*He takes the pendant.*) No, this is like a cameo. The one I'm looking for opened. That's the main thing: it had a hinge. (*He gives it back.*)

KIT: You know there's something to be said for leaving mysteries mysteries.

NATHAN: I have to know this. Otherwise I'll be wondering the rest of my life.

SHANA: If she didn't want you to know when she was alive, why do you think it's okay now?

DEBORAH (*Sticking her head out of the bathroom.*): She had a lover. Big deal.

NATHAN: It is a big deal. We're talking about a woman who hardly ever left her house. Who never left the state of Florida. Who never married, never dated, was never even seen on the street talking to an eligible male. But there was someone in that locket. And she <u>cried</u> over him. I swear I saw her crying.

SHANA: It was probably a relative, then. Grandpa Neil. She was crying over her father.

NATHAN: If it was Grandpa, why wouldn't she say so when I asked?

KIT: She liked privacy. Ever heard of it?

NATHAN: Plus I'm sure that she wore it when Grandpa was still alive. In fact, I can't think of a time when she wasn't wearing it around her neck.

DEBORAH (*Returning.*): It's not in the bathroom

NATHAN: You sure?

DEBORAH: There's Q-Tips, nail-clippers, a toothbrush and toothpaste. Nothing slightly necklasoid.

KIT: Tell me about the crying episode.

NATHAN: I was maybe ten years old in 1970 or something, and she came over to babysit for me and Shana. So at one point we're watching television and I say, Aunt Lainie, do you mind if I go play in my room? And she says, no, of course not, go on. So I'm in my room for twenty minutes and I can't find one of my Soldiers of World War II figures. I go into the TV room to look for it, and there she is, all alone staring into this opened locket in her hands, and crying, really sobbing. And I say, "Aunt Lainie, what's the matter?" And she immediately closes the locket, puts it back inside her blouse, and says, "I'll tell you some other time. Now go back to your games." And she wouldn't say anything else.

SHANA: Where was I?

NATHAN: In your bedroom, I think. Being characteristically anti-social.

DEBORAH: So did you ask her again later?

NATHAN: Yeah, like three times, including an instance just a few years ago, when I caught her looking at it all teary-eyed. But she refused to explain it.

KIT: Nothing in the dressing table.

SHANA: Actually, it's kind of neat that she had a secret. She was so old-fashioned in every other way. Having a lost love makes her more interesting.

DEBORAH: Even if we find it, the photo could be unidentifiable. What if it's someone from her childhood, or her high school? We could be looking at the guy and still have no idea.

NATHAN: I'm prepared to pursue it.

KIT: Meaning what?

NATHAN: We're a big family. Someone will recognize him.

SHANA: If it's a him.

DEBORAH: You think it's a woman?

SHANA: If she was so reluctant to show it. And like I said, she was old-fashioned.

DEBORAH: Talk about rocking your world. Dreary, conventional Aunt Lainie.

SHANA: Here's something.

NATHAN: Let me see. (*He goes over to SHANA and looks at the jewelry in her hand.*) Well, at least it's on a necklace, that much is right. But it doesn't open.

KIT: We're not going to find anything. If it was that important, she probably had it on when she died, and she's probably wearing it in her coffin.

NATHAN: I asked the funeral director.

DEBORAH: You did what?

NATHAN: Since there wasn't a showing, I figured he was my only good source. And he said he didn't remember anything.

KIT: How long have you been thinking about this?

NATHAN: Since my childhood. Since the first time I found her crying.

DEBORAH: Maybe it's better that we not know. Maybe we respect her memory more by allowing her her secret sadness and accepting that she was a lot more than the drab picture everyone seems to have of her. I'm not going to look any further.

NATHAN: Forty years, sweetie, I've been wondering. I've got to have it in my hands finally.

SHANA: You said you wouldn't take anything.

NATHAN: I don't have to: I'll just take a picture with my phone. And then I do my Sherlock Holmes bit.

KIT: Is it just me, or does anyone else feel *mortified* about being in the home of a woman who just died and who was fanatically private to the point of never having a companion? Does anyone else feel like getting out of here before they desecrate another inch of this deceased woman's memory?

NATHAN: She promised she would tell me. I'm just holding her to her promise.

DEBORAH (*Surveying the room.*): What a sad life. I'm looking around here and all I see is stasis and isolation.

SHANA: She wasn't sad. She was vibrant and funny and just very frightened of everything. She didn't like to leave her house.

KIT: Aunt Lainie, you keep your secret. You keep it and forgive us for trying to unmask after your death what you kept sacrosanct during your life.

SHANA: This is the last possible drawer. If it's not in here, it's not anywhere.

DEBORAH: I kind of hope it's not there.

NATHAN: There are other places to look. Other rooms. This is just the start.

DEBORAH: I know who it was. It was the one boy that touched her. Fifty years ago, under a tree outside class, some boy smiled at her like no-one else ever did, and she took his picture from the school yearbook and she put it in her locket and forever after she remembered the one time when she nearly made a contact with a world of love -

KIT: Maybe there never was anyone. Maybe that's what she was crying over – that there was no-one to cry over.

DEBORAH: I don't want to be here anymore...

SHANA: I found it.

NATHAN (*Rushing over to her.*): Let me look.

SHANA: This has got to be it. The real thing. Hinge and all.

NATHAN: This is the one. Yes, I'm sure of it.

KIT: We're sorry, Aunt Lainie. We're sorry we persisted.

NATHAN: I can hardly believe it. All those years. Do you want to open it?

SHANA: No, you. It means so much to you. You should be the one. Here. Good luck.

*She hands him the locket.*

NATHAN: I'm shaking.

DEBORAH: You ought to be.

NATHAN: I've been searching for this so long... (*He opens the locket and stares, shocked. Pause.*)

KIT: Well?

NATHAN: It's Kennedy.

SHANA: Say that again?

NATHAN (*Staring.*): It's John F. Kennedy.

SHANA: Let me see. (*She takes the locket from him and looks.*) Cut from a magazine. Yeah, it's Kennedy. Anybody else want to see?

KIT: Sure. (*SHANA hands him the locket. He looks.*) How about that? John Kennedy.

*He looks up. No-one speaks.*

*Blackout.*

END OF PLAY

# Why

## by

## Marvin Albert

Directed by Jenny Aldrich
with
Lilian Moore as Madeline
Danae DeShazer as Loretta

CHARACTERS
MADELINE FALLON, a woman, 50.

LORETTA WILLIAMS, a woman, 35.

SETTING
MADELINE's front porch.

TIME
The present.

*Lights up on MADELINE, who is alone on her front porch when she hears a car door slam. She looks up and is startled to see LORETTA approach.*

LORETTA: I would like to speak to you if I may.

MADELINE (*Startled.*): Why?

LORETTA: It's rather personal.

*MADELINE doesn't respond.*

LORETTA (*Cont.*): It's important.

MADELINE: Is it?

LORETTA: Yes.

*MADELINE doesn't respond.*

LORETTA (*Cont.*): I'm...

MADELINE: I know who you are, Loretta.

LORETTA: You... You know...

MADELINE: Why are you here?

LORETTA: If you know who I am then you'll know why I'm here.

*MADELINE doesn't respond.*

LORETTA (*Cont.*): I need to know why. I need to know about me.

MADELINE: You know about you. You are a very lucky lady who has it all. You had a good education, parents who love you And judging by that car, a pretty good job. Yeah, I'd say you are a very lucky young lady.

LORETTA: How could you have...

MADELINE: How could I? What were my choices? Oh yes, I did have choices. I could have gone to some back alley (*Makes quote sign.*) doctor and had you flushed down some toilet. Would that have been a good choice?

LORETTA: Maybe.

MADELINE: Not for me. I could never have done that to you.

LORETTA: At least then I wouldn't have felt...

MADELINE: What, abandoned? You have no idea what abandoned is.

LORETTA: I need to know.

MADELINE: Why?

LORETTA: You gave me away!

*There is a pause. The two women stare at each other.*

MADELINE (*Long pause.*): Okay, story time. Once upon a time there was a fifteen year old girl with an eighteen year old boyfriend. She got pregnant. End of story.

LORETTA (*Excited.*): That's not the end of the story. The choices. What about the choices?

MADELINE: Right, the choices. I already told you that I would never would have had an abortion. I then chose to go to my parents for help. I just came out and told them.

LORETTA: And?

MADELINE: My father beat the hell out of me. Did anyone ever beat the hell out of you?

*LORETTA just stares.*

MADELINE (*Cont.*): No? I didn't think so. Then my father had my boyfriend arrested for statutory rape. He was sent to prison and was killed by his cellmate... Nice story so far?

*LORETTA doesn't respond.*

MADELINE (*Cont.*): Okay, I'll go on. Next, they sent me to a home for (*Makes quote sign.*) <u>wayward</u> girls. That's where you were born and that's when my choices ended. They handled everything. All they told me was that you would be adopted by a wonderful family who would provide for you all of the things that I couldn't.

LORETTA: So you just gave me away.

MADELINE: With love. Unselfish love. What kind of life would you have had with me?

*The two women stare at each other in silence.*

LORETTA: How did you know my name?

MADELINE: I had a cousin who worked for the State. She helped me find you and I never lost track. I watched you grow up. I came very close to totally ruining your life right before the adoption would have been final. I was tempted but I knew that would be the worst thing for you. But I did watch you grow up.

LORETTA: What do you mean, watch me?

MADELINE: I knew where you lived, where you went to school, I even was at your college graduation.

LORETTA: You were there?

MADELINE: I even shook your hand and wished you well. That was the closest I ever came to telling you about me. I wanted to so much.

LORETTA: Why didn't you say something then.

MADELINE: Why? I knew how well off you were. Nothing like my childhood. Nothing like the life you would have had with me. (*Beat.*) Loretta, I'm sorry the way I acted when I first saw you. I panicked. I thought my heart would burst I... I'm so sorry.

LORETTA (*Nods and pauses.*) : What happened to you?

MADELINE: I grew up. I never went back to school but I got a job as a waitress and...

LORETTA: What about your parents?

MADELINE: They threw me out and I was totally on my own.

LORETTA: And then?

MADELINE: A few years later I met a man. He was a lot older than me. He was very kind and he loved me. We got married and I had a baby, a girl.

LORETTA: I have a sister?

MADELINE: And a brother.

LORETTA: Do they know about me?

MADELINE: No.

LORETTA: And now, will you tell them? I want to meet them.

MADELINE: I don't know. I will think about it.

LORETTA: How old are they?

MADELINE: Douglas is twenty-eight and (*Beat.*) Loretta is thirty.

LORETTA (*Angrily.*): You gave her my name?!

MADELINE: It was a choice I thought about it for a long time, but yes.

LORETTA: I... I don't know what to say.

MADELINE: What's to say, It was my way of keeping a piece of you.

LORETTA: I... I...

MADELINE: It was something I had to do.

LORETTA: Your husband, does he know?

MADELINE: He died four years ago. But yes, he did know.

*LORETTA looks faint.*

MADELINE (*Cont.*): Are you okay?

LORETTA: I... I don't know. I guess all my life it was all about me. I didn't have good thoughts about you. How can a person give a part of them away just like that?

MADELINE: It was never, "just like that."

LORETTA: Please tell them about me...

MADELINE: If I tell them about you, I'll be telling them about me. (*Beat.*) I always thought that someday something like this would happen. And now you're here. (*MADELINE takes LORETTA's hand.*) I'm sorry. So sorry.

LORETTA: I had to find you.

MADELINE: Why now?

LORETTA: So many reasons, so many questions. But now there is another reason. I'm getting married and someday, I hope I'll have children of my own. Funny, I never thought I would ever want children but now...

MADELINE: I can see you're bitter.

LORETTA: Yes I am or at least I was when I first got here.

MADELINE: And now?

LORETTA: More confused than bitter.

MADELINE: Can you understand my side of the situation?

LORETTA: A little, I guess. Maybe more than a little, but I can't turn off all of those feelings.

MADELINE: When did you know you were adopted.

LORETTA: I always knew. My folks read me stories every night when I went to sleep. I don't remember them in the beginning but they became my identity, who I was, who I am, They all started the same way. There once was a mommy and a daddy who loved each other and wanted to share that love with a baby girl. One day they adopted this beautiful little girl and their love was then complete. So, there was never a time that I didn't know I was adopted. It was when I found out that there were other children who were not adopted that I started to wonder. I felt...

MADELINE: What?

LORETTA: Different. Not worse but different.

MADELINE: And it always bothered you?

LORETTA: Not always but sometimes. I started to have questions. Especially when I went to a doctor and had to fill out a sheet asking about my illnesses. Then at the end of the sheet they ask about my family. It took me a long time to realize that those things had nothing to do with my health.

MADELINE: So now that you are getting married?

LORETTA: I would like to know what my child could look forward to.

MADELINE: I understand that but that was not your only reason for finding me.

LORETTA: No. I was so angry at you and all that anger was, well, hurting me.

MADELINE: I can only ask you to understand and forgive me and believe that what I did was for you. Can you see that?

LORETTA: I can see your choices were limited.

MADELINE: I guess that's a start.

*LORETTA stares at MADELINE.*

MADELINE (*Cont.*): What?

LORETTA: I would really like to meet my, eh, sister and brother.

*MADELINE doesn't respond.*

LORETTA: Even if you don't tell them who I am.

MADELINE: Maybe. I will think about that. It wouldn't be easy for me because it will not be easy for them.

LORETTA: I just want to see them.

MADELINE: Do your parents know you're here?

LORETTA: They know.

MADELINE: And?

LORETTA: They know that I love them and they...

*Just then, the phone rings loudly. Both women are startled. MADELINE answers.*

MADELINE: Hello... I was just talking about you... Yes, it was good. Are you on your way home. Please, can you stop here first... Yes, It is important... (*She looks at LORETTA and takes her hand.*) There's someone here I want you to meet.

*MADELINE hangs up the phone. They stare at each other then they hug and both cry. MADELINE cries out softly.*

MADELINE (*Cont.*): Oh my God, oh my God.

*The hugging continues.*

*Lights fade.*

*Blackout.*

## END OF PLAY

*Student Play Festival Winner 2015*

# As Long as the Moon Shines

by

**Julien Freij**

Directed by Daniel Greene

with

Ben Kalish as Danny

Tori Greenlaw as Susie

Tami Vaughan as Joan

CHARACTERS
DANNY, a young man, 17.

SUSIE, a girl, 9, his sister.

JOAN STEVENS, a woman, 30s

SETTING
A rural road in western Massachusetts.

TIME
October 1965.

> *The lights go up on DANNY and SUSIE walking together. They stop in front of a store and SUSIE sits on a bench. They are both carrying beat-up backpacks.*

SUSIE: Danny, I'm hungry.

DANNY: Don't worry, Susie, I'll bring you something later after I cash in my paycheck.

SUSIE: But you said the same thing yesterday!

DANNY: I know, I know, but... Hang on for a minute. Let me see if this store will cash my check.

> *DANNY exits, then reenters with a candy bar and a worried look on his face. He hands the candy bar to his sister.*

DANNY (*Cont.*): Here, I got you this.

SUSIE: Gee, thanks! (*She starts to take off the candy bar wrapper.*)

DANNY: Don't eat that now. (*He looks around nervously toward store.*) We have to get going right away.

SUSIE: Is something wrong?

DANNY: No, but we have to go... to a friend's house. And we're late.

> *He takes SUSIE by the hand and they run offstage. The lights go down for a few seconds. When the lights come back up, DANNY and SUSIE run back onstage, panting.*

DANNY: Let's rest here for a minute.

SUSIE: Why do you look so scared?

DANNY: I sort of lost my paycheck.

SUSIE: Then how did you get the candy bar?

DANNY: Well, you see... I had to... Uh...

SUSIE: You stole! You stole!

DANNY: Ssssh!

SUSIE: But you always said that stealing is bad.

DANNY: Susie, it was either that or watching you go hungry another night.

SUSIE: What about you?

DANNY: Me? I'm fine. My friend will probably have some food for us to eat when we get there.

SUSIE: Which friend is it? (*Pause.*) Cause your last friend wasn't very nice to me.

DANNY: This one's a nice lady. We met when I was looking for work. She has a daughter about your age. She wants you to meet her.

SUSIE: What's her name?

DANNY: I'm not sure, but I think it's Molly.

SUSIE (*Smiling.*): That's a nice name. I think she'll be my new best friend.

DANNY: That's exactly what I've been hoping.

SUSIE: Danny, how far away is your friend? I'm getting tired and I don't want to sleep in a park again.

DANNY: It's not that far.

SUSIE: I still don't understand why we had to leave that home.

DANNY: It's kind of hard to explain, but the people were... um... doing some bad things.

SUSIE: What kind of things?

DANNY (*Stares at her as he thinks of a response.*): I'm not sure exactly, but I had to get you out of there. I promised our dad that I would watch over you and find you a...

SUSIE: Find me a what?

DANNY: Never mind. It's not important.

SUSIE: Can you tell me what happened to mommy and daddy again?

DANNY: Susie, I already told you that story a bunch of times.

SUSIE: I know, but I like hearing it. It makes me feel good. Please?

DANNY: Ok. Fine. About ten years ago, right before you were born, mommy and daddy loved each other very much, so they decided to have you, so you could keep me company.

SUSIE: What did she look like?

DANNY: She was beautiful... the most beautiful mom I've ever seen. You look a lot like her, but younger.

SUSIE: Like her? (*Giggles.*) Really?

DANNY: Yes, you have the same smile and eyes.

SUSIE: Why did she have to die? I don't understand.

DANNY: She got really sick a few months before you were born. It was some kind of virus. I remember dad got really angry because the doctors didn't know what to do. A few weeks after you were born, she got worse and worse, and then... then she left us to be with God.

SUSIE: Is she up there now?

DANNY: Yeah. I'm sure she's watching us right now and happy that we're talking about her.

SUSIE: Is daddy up there too?

DANNY: I don't know.

SUSIE: What do you mean?

DANNY: After mom died, he got really sad and he began to act differently. Pretty soon, he wasn't the dad I knew anymore. People kept calling the house about bills he owed, and then he lost his job at the factory.

SUSIE: Did he cry?

DANNY: I never saw him do that, but I never saw him smile either.

SUSIE: So what happened?

DANNY: One night, he took you out of your crib while you were still sleeping and put you in my arms. He said, "Watch after your little sister. Daddy has to go away for a while. I am taking you to see some nice people."

SUSIE: Where did he take us?

DANNY: He dropped us off at a foster home, but we only stayed there for a couple years. He promised that he would come back to get us after he found a new job, but that was six years ago.

SUSIE: I wish I remembered him.

DANNY: Before he got sad, when mom was still alive, he loved to hold you and sing you lullabies.

SUSIE: Which ones?

DANNY: Your favorite was "Twinkle, Twinkle, Little Star." You used to giggle whenever he sang it to you.

SUSIE: Will you sing it to me now?

DANNY: But you're almost ten.

SUSIE: I don't care. I want to hear it.

DANNY: Ok, but I only remember the first verse.

SUSIE: That's all right.

DANNY: Here goes:

> Twinkle, twinkle, little star,
> How I wonder what you are.
> Up above the world so high,
> Like a diamond in the sky.

SUSIE: Hey, maybe our mom is a star, and that's how she sees us at night.

DANNY: *(Smiling.)* That's a good thought! Susie, thanks for not complaining about how things are going. I know that it hasn't been too easy lately.

SUSIE: It's all right. I know you're doing your best.

DANNY: Thanks. We should get going, but I have to use that payphone to make a call first. (*He steps to the side.*) Hi. It's Dan Hayes. We're on our way. We should be there in 10-15 minutes. Yes, I have it with me. (*He reaches in his pocket and pulls out a piece of paper.*) Thanks again for what you're doing. (*Walks back to SUSIE.*)

SUSIE: Who was that, Danny?

DANNY: My friend. She said her daughter can't wait to meet you. Before we get there, I want to show you this special place.

SUSIE: What kind of place?

DANNY: It's a park. Mom, dad, and I used to go there when I was little before you were born.

SUSIE: What did you do there?

DANNY (*Thinks and smiles.*): We had lots of fun. We would listen to the radio and sit around and eat peanut butter and jelly sandwiches. After that, dad and I would play catch. He and I would throw the ball back and forth and talk about the Red Sox.

SUSIE: I never heard you tell this story before.

DANNY: Some of the happiest memories of my life were going to that park.

SUSIE: If your friend doesn't live too far away, we can come back here and play, right?

DANNY: I hadn't thought of that, but... yeah, that's a good idea. The last time I was here with mom, she told me: "Danny, even though I'm sick, don't ever forget that I'll always love you... as long as the moon shines. Please remember that whenever you come back to this place."

SUSIE: That's a nice story, but it also makes me kinda sad.

DANNY: I know, but I want you to remember this place when you come back here with...

SUSIE: With you, right?

DANNY: Yeah, when we come back here together.

SUSIE: Good.

*They walk a bit, then DANNY points into the distance.*

DANNY: Susie, look! I can see my friend's place up ahead.

SUSIE: Where? I can't see it?

DANNY: It's right there... (*Points again.*) the big house on the hill.

SUSIE (*Excited.*): Now I see it!

*They keep walking.*

DANNY: Well, here we are.

SUSIE: You didn't tell me it was a farm. Look at all the horses.

*DANNY grabs SUSIE's hand. The lights go down, then up on a door. DANNY knocks and a woman, JOAN STEVENS, opens the door.*

DANNY: Hi, Joan.

JOAN: Hey, Dan! You finally made it.

DANNY: This is my little sister Susie.

SUSIE: Hi!

JOAN: I have a daughter named Molly who's really excited to meet you. Why don't you go inside and say hi to her?

*SUSIE looks at her brother for a moment, then he gives her a long hug before she exits.*

JOAN: I'd like to look at her birth certificate and the notarized letter from you that says you'd like us to take care of Susie until you can find a permanent place to live.

DANNY: Sure. Let me get them.

*DANNY reaches into his bag and produces a folder and a birth certificate. He hands it to JOAN who looks through the folder. She puts the folder under her arm and nods approvingly to DANNY.*

JOAN: Thanks, Dan. Don't worry, my husband and I will take good care of her. Do you want to say goodbye?

DANNY: No, just... Do you mind leaving a message for me?

JOAN: Sure.

DANNY: Tell her that I'll be back for her as soon as I can. Tell her that no matter what, I'll love her for as long as the moon shines.

JOAN (*Thinks for a second.*): I sure will.

DANNY: I should probably get going.

JOAN: Do you have any money on you?

DANNY: No, but I'll be all right.

*JOAN reaches into his pocket and gives DANNY $50.*

JOAN: Here, take this. I only have fifty dollars on me, but this should help a little.

DANNY: Thank you. Thank you, Joan, for everything.

JOAN: You're welcome. Now go and make something of your life, and don't worry about Susie.

*JOAN closes the door and DANNY walks away. He holds out his thumb to hitch a ride. We hear a car engine, and DANNY gets an excited look on his face. We hear the car stop.*

Voice (*Offstage.*): Where ya headed, kid?

DANNY: Nowhere in particular... just wherever there is a moon.

*Lights fade.*

*Blackout.*

## END OF PLAY

# Ten-Minute Play Festival

# 2016

**Dates:** May 5th, 6th, 7th, and 8th, 2016

**Location:** Jane B. Cook Theatre, Asolo/FSU Center for the Performing Arts, Sarasota

**Best Play Award**

    Hands by Sylvia Reed

**Runner-Up/Honorable Mention**

    Clarinet Licks by Fredric Sirasky

**Student Playwriting Festival Winner**

    Brothers in Arms by Julien Freij
                                    St. Stephens Episcopal School

## *2016 Best Play*

# Hands

### by

### Sylvia Reed

Directed by Seva Anthony

with

Nicole Cunningham as Sophie

Joshua Brin as Jack

CHARACTERS
SOPHIE, a young woman, 20s.

JACK, a young man, 20s.

SETTING
A desk in an office in a building on a street in a city.

TIME
About 6 p.m., Friday, December 14, 2012.

> *As the lights come up, SOPHIE is sitting on the floor under a desk. Her chair is to the side. Her head is in her hands. After a fairly long moment, JACK enters. He carries SOPHIE'S denim jacket. He approaches the desk slowly.*

JACK: Sophie?

SOPHIE (*After a bit, in very small voice.*): Yeah?

JACK: What's going on?

SOPHIE: Nothing.

JACK: It doesn't feel like nothing.

> *Long pause.*

JACK (*Cont.*): Everyone else has gone home. Your boss said he tried to get you to come out but you wouldn't. And he couldn't wait around because he had to be somewhere. Something about a wedding, a rehearsal dinner?

SOPHIE: His niece is getting married.

JACK: Oh... Well he called me and asked me to come check on you. And lock up.

SOPHIE: Does he think I'm crazy?

JACK: He's just worried about you. He was... concerned.

SOPHIE: How did he get your number?

JACK: I don't know. Maybe he looked on your phone? (*Sees her phone.*) It's here on your desk.

SOPHIE: Oh.

JACK: He left the key on his desk so I could lock up. Sophie?

SOPHIE: Yes.

JACK: Do you think you could at least pick your head up and look at me?

*SOPHIE slowly picks her head up. Her hands shake.*

JACK (*Cont.*): What's going on?

SOPHIE: Look at my hands.

JACK: They're shaking.

SOPHIE: I know.

JACK: Wow. They're really shaking. What's the matter?

SOPHIE: They won't stop.

JACK: Do you need to eat?

SOPHIE: I'm not hungry.

JACK: 'Cause I know sometimes you get hypoglycemic. Did you drink a lot of coffee this afternoon?

SOPHIE: No.

JACK: Tea? You really like iced tea.

SOPHIE: No.

*After a moment.*

JACK: Chocolate?

SOPHIE: It's not about food!

JACK: What's wrong with you then?

SOPHIE: What if they never stop shaking?

JACK: They can't shake forever.

SOPHIE: Really?

JACK: Nothing is forever.

*Long pause.*

SOPHIE: Did you ever make a handprint in pre-school?

JACK: Umm... I think so.

SOPHIE: I remember when I was 4, my teacher – Miss Amy – painted my hand green and I pressed it onto the paper and it made a tiny print.

JACK: I remember doing something like that.

SOPHIE: My mom put it on the fridge. With a magnet with my picture.

JACK: That's nice.

SOPHIE: My picture was in the magnet. And the magnet held up my handprint.

JACK: Ok.

SOPHIE: It's funny the things you remember. She also has a picture of me on Patches. The pony. I think everyone has a picture like that. (*Pause.*) I can still see my handprint. I was really proud of it.

JACK: Umm. I brought your jacket. You left it at my apartment the other night.

SOPHIE: Thanks.

JACK: The temperature's dropping really fast. I was going to give it back to you tonight when you came over. But then you didn't come over. (*Pause.*) Is this about you not wanting to come over?

SOPHIE: No.

JACK: Oh, good. (*Pause.*) You're not just saying that to spare my feelings, right?

SOPHIE: No. It's not about that.

JACK: You think you could come out then?

SOPHIE: I've been making a list in my head about hands.

JACK: A list?

SOPHIE: Yeah. Sometimes when I worry I make lists in my head about things.

JACK: Oh. That's... good.

SOPHIE: Hands are... important.

JACK: Yes they are.

SOPHIE: They... conduct music.

JACK: Uh huh.

SOPHIE: They write poetry... And they fold... In prayer. (*Pause.*) And they have four fingers and a thumb, which are important too.

JACK: Yep. Thumbs are important. As are fingers.

SOPHIE: Fingers do things. (*Pause.*) They twirl hair, button shirts, tie shoes, flip switches. (*Pause.*) They grow nails, wear polish, play pianos, scratch itches. (*Pause.*) And they pull triggers...

JACK (*After a moment.*): Pull triggers?

SOPHIE: I bet those kids made handprints too. (*Pause.*) When they were younger.

JACK: So that's what this is about.

SOPHIE: Sounds absurd, doesn't it? To say "when they were younger"? About a classroom of six-year-olds? (*Pause.*) You think their mothers are searching for their tiny handprints tonight? The ones they made when they were still alive and in pre-school? (*Pause.*) So they can press their own hand against it like they can still touch them?

  *Long pause.*

JACK: You know I love this about you. Your empathy. But you can't do this to yourself.

SOPHIE: They probably have wrapped presents under their Christmas trees. Presents they'll never get to open or play with. How will their parents survive this?

JACK: I don't know. I don't know how they will. It's terrible.

  *Long pause.*

I think... things are gonna change because of it. I really do. I really believe this is gonna make the politicians wake up and... do something about this.

SOPHIE: You really do?

JACK: I do. (*Pause.*) So... I was in the middle of making us a really nice dinner.

SOPHIE: You were?

JACK: Yes I was. I got us a couple of lobster tails. And I was gonna make us a really nice salad. I was chopping everything up and getting it ready so I could just throw it all together and we could hang out.

SOPHIE: Like a celebration?

JACK: Yeah

SOPHIE: It doesn't feel right to celebrate.

JACK: I know. I made the plan to celebrate earlier this week. Of course I didn't know it was gonna turn out to be a terrible day.

  *JACK paces, out of SOPHIE'S view.*

SOPHIE: What were we gonna be celebrating?

*JACK pulls a small box from his pocket and looks at the engagement ring he was planning on giving her. He looks at the ring as he speaks.*

JACK: Nothing... really. Because it's Friday? (*JACK puts the ring box back in his pocket.*) I got champagne too...

SOPHIE: Wow. You really <u>are</u> happy it's Friday.

JACK: And then your boss called and he was really worried.

SOPHIE: Do you think he's gonna fire me?

JACK: He wouldn't do that. You always say he's a jerk but he really sounded like he cares about you.

SOPHIE: He did?

JACK: Yeah. He seems like a really good guy.

SOPHIE: I know. It's me. I'm disappointed in myself.

JACK: Why?

SOPHIE: Because I went to college for four years and have all these student loans and now I'm working as an assistant in a law office because I can't get a job at a newspaper and I wouldn't have had to go to journalism school for four years to work here and I wouldn't have all these loans if I didn't go to college and you see what I mean, right?

JACK: Everything's going to be fine.

SOPHIE: The twenties suck.

*JACK paces for a moment. He looks out a window.*

JACK: It gets dark so early these days. (*Pause.*) The moon is barely visible tonight. Just a tiny sliver.

SOPHIE: Even the moon wants to hide.

*JACK sits on the desk. His feet dangle in front of SOPHIE. After a moment.*

SOPHIE (*Cont.*): What are you doing?

JACK: I'm thinking.

SOPHIE: What about?

*Silence. SOPHIE finally pokes her head out from under the desk and looks up at JACK.*

SOPHIE (*Cont.*): Jack?

*Silence. SOPHIE inches up a little more.*

SOPHIE (*Cont.*): Why aren't you talking?

*SOPHIE is practically out from under the desk.*

SOPHIE (*Cont.*): You're always talking. You never shut up, actually. I love that about you…

*As she's coming out from under the desk.*

JACK: I'm making a list.

SOPHIE: About

JACK: Hands.

*SOPHIE looks at her hands. The trembling has subsided somewhat.*

JACK (*Cont.*): Hands sign petitions. Hands wave protest signs. Hands have fingers that write blogs and posts to Twitter. (*Looks at SOPHIE.*) You could be part of the change.

SOPHIE: I could?

JACK: You could. You're a great writer. And you're not so bad looking either.

*JACK gets off the desk. Reaches for SOPHIE'S hand. She takes his hand. She gets up off the floor. They hug each other. And then—*

SOPHIE: You really believe this time things are gonna change?

JACK: I don't see how it couldn't.

SOPHIE: Me either.

*Lights fade.*

*Blackout.*

END OF PLAY

## *2016 Runner Up*

## Clarinet Licks

### by

### Fredric Sirasky

Directed by Helen Holliday

with

Fredric Sirasky as Bill

Ann Gundersheimer as Jane

CHARACTERS
JANE, a woman, 75.

BILL, a man of the same age, her husband.

SETTING
The comfortable den of a suburban home.

TIME
The present.

> *Lights up on BILL, who sits in a hard chair holding a clarinet. He's dressed casually in a pair of well-worn chino pants and a faded golf shirt, except that he wears his boxer shorts <u>outside</u> of his chinos. He plays a blues lick on the clarinet. He sits back with a contented smile. JANE enters.*

JANE: That sounded great, Honey.

BILL: Yes. I think I'm ready to get back with the boys. They sure need me. I mean, whoever heard of a Dixieland Band without a clarinet? (*He plays a quick lick, holds up the clarinet and speaks to it.*) You and me Pops! (*He speaks to JANE.*) They said to come over this afternoon about... what did I say?

JANE: About one thirty.

BILL: That's it, one thirty, over at, uh...

JANE: Jim's house.

BILL: Yeah. Jim's house. Is that okay? You can drive, right?

JANE: Of course... and I'll pick you up after I leave Brenda's. It's our last day to brush up before the bridge tournament. Now, I know you're just having a rehearsal...

BILL: An old fashioned jam session!

JANE (*Pause.*): Yes. But don't you think you should wear the new slacks and shirt we bought for you at Macy's the other day?

BILL: Oh, no. This is a big day for me. I've been working up to this for six months. But I've got to admit, I'm a little scared. To nail the charts, I need to feel really comfortable. And these are my lucky chinos and lucky shirt.

JANE: Bill... it's...

BILL: What?

JANE: We had an agreement. Remember?

BILL: Agreement?

JANE: You promised you... wouldn't get dressed without my help.

BILL: I don't need your help. I'm a big boy. (*He plays a few lively bars of "Stars and Stripes Forever."*) And don't you forget it.

JANE: Look, I love the fact that you're back to playing. But what's with this new Harpo Marx thing?

BILL: Harpo Marx?

JANE: Punctuating your conversation, like Harpo with his ooga horn. It's not right.

*He jokingly blows a blast on his horn, trying to imitate the "f" word.*

BILL: —k'you! Hah!

JANE: You put your underwear on over your pants!

*He looks down at his boxer shorts.*

BILL: So what? Who cares?

JANE (*More calmly.*): I care. Now stop playing that thing for a minute, and please go change. For me.

BILL: Okay. You know I love you. (*He kisses her on the forehead, and starts off.*)

JANE: And, Bill, leave the clarinet here. You can't carry it around all day.

BILL: Look. Since the... the incident, I admit I forget things once in a while. But Doc Johnson said the music would help. Just bear with me a little longer. Okay? (*He plays one long, sour high note.*) I got that note from Artie Shaw... and, boy, was he glad to get rid of it!

*He carefully puts the clarinet on its upright stand and exits. She stares at the clarinet, then picks it up and speaks to it.*

JANE (*Quietly, but with great intensity.*): All right, Pops, now listen to me. This is not what I signed up for. So I'm counting on you to do your thing... do your thing, Pops, so we can all get back to normal. And, by Jupiter, if you let me down I swear I'll...

*She takes the clarinet by the neck as if to strangle it. BILL enters, still wearing his boxer shorts on the outside.*

BILL: Hey, careful with that! That's my number one reed. (*He takes the clarinet from her and puts it back on its stand.*) Listen, I thought I'd better eat something, and while I was in the kitchen, I thought, why not make you something, too? You hungry?

JANE: I thought you were headed for the bedroom.

BILL: The bedroom? It's noon. Why would I go to the bedroom?

JANE: To change your clothes.

BILL (*He looks down at his clothes.*): But these are my lucky...

JANE: Fine! Keep the lucky clothes. But go into the bedroom and put your underwear on <u>under</u> your pants. That's why they call it <u>under</u>-wear. And do it before you go to the kitchen. Got it?

BILL: Underwear, underwear. Got it.

*He exits. She points at the clarinet.*

JANE: Remember what I said, Pops. Mother of God. (*Her cell phone rings.*) What now. (*She takes out her phone and answers it.*) Yes... Oh, hi, Jim... Yes, one thirty. We'll be there... Well, he remembers the music all right. In fact he's obsessive about it, almost like a... an idiot-savant. But the rest of it. Well, be patient. His doctor says we've got to keep "expanding his horizons." so I'm doing everything I can to keep, well, kicking him in the ass... (*She laughs.*) Yeah, that'll expand his horizons. And Jim, do me a favor. In couple of minutes, call Bill on <u>his</u> phone to make sure he's coming ... Well, he depends on me for everything. We're trying to get him to recover his sense of independence... Good.

*BILL enters, wearing the new shirt and slacks from Macy's, with his underwear properly underneath the slacks.*

BILL: Ta-da!

JANE: Now that looks great.

BILL: Hey, I don't need no lucky chinos. (*Picks up the clarinet.*) I've got it all covered. (*Plays a couple of beautiful soft notes. Then, on purpose blows a loud sour one.*) I can't do it. (*Plops into the chair, puts the clarinet on its stand, and shakes his head.*)

JANE: What?

BILL: I can't do it. Not in public... or even with the boys. I'm not scared. I'm terrified.

JANE: Now wait a minute, Buster. It's not that easy.

BILL: I know it's not easy. That's what I'm saying.

JANE: That's not what I mean! I'm not talking about playing, I'm talking about quitting.

BILL: Quitting?

JANE: Come hell or high water, you are going to Jim's, you are going to play with the boys, and you are going to get back into the goddamned swing of things.

BILL: I can't. I never heard you swear before.

JANE: Don't say you can't! You think I'm going to let you crawl into a hole and die? I've seen what happens when some of our friends give up the fight. I am <u>not</u> going to spend the rest of my days taking care of you while you gradually waste away. I'll help you as much as I can. But you have to show me every day that you're still in the battle. And playing at home won't hack it.

BILL (*Taps his head with a finger.*): Look, we both know where this could be headed. I can't even put my pants on straight. Why add to the strain by getting involved in a situation where I'll just embarrass myself?

JANE: This is not just about <u>you</u>! What about <u>me</u>? Bill, you had a stroke. Bad luck. But look how well you're playing. My God, you're a phenom! You could be a test case for all the others in your condition. Doc Johnson says so. But you've got to take the next step. Now pack up the horn and I'll drive you over to Jim's.

BILL: No, no, no! I'm telling you I can't do it!

JANE: That's your decision?

BILL: It's not a decision. It's a reality.

*She snatches the clarinet from its stand and blows an ugly, awful note.*

JANE: —k'you!

*She thrusts the clarinet into his hands.*

BILL: That's no way to talk.

JANE: I'm angry!

BILL: <u>You're</u> angry?

JANE: Of course! You were going to Jim's. I was going to Brenda's. Now I'm stuck, sitting around here all day listening to you talk to your horn! Well, I'm sick of it!... And <u>you</u> call him.

BILL: Call who?

JANE: Jim! To let him know you're not coming.

*He takes out his old flip-top cell phone.*

BILL: I...

JANE (*Instructing him on how to use his phone for the hundredth time.*): Hit CONTACTS, scroll down to JIM, and hit OK three times. (*She hands him back his cell phone.*) I need a drink. (*She starts to exit. Stops.*) And tomorrow we can visit Sunnyside.

BILL: What?

JANE: Arlene Davis lives there. She says it's a lovely facility.

BILL: Are you serious?

JANE: You're damned right I'm serious.

BILL: It's a hell of a time to bring that up.

JANE: So when is a good time? We got the brochure, we've talked about it. This is the time. I'll help a fighter. I won't help a wimp. If you quit, I quit.

BILL: A wimp? I'm not a wimp! I can handle myself alright. I just need a little assistance.

JANE: Exactly! It's called Assisted Living! And Sunnyside's the perfect place for it.

BILL: I don't believe this. If you needed help, I'd help you. Sunnyside? That sounds to me like a legal separation. So, after we visit Sunnyside, we'll visit a lawyer! In the meantime, run off to your goddamned bridge club. I don't need you or anybody else. I've got everything I need right here.

JANE: Yeah. You've got Pops. And you make a lovely couple. Enjoy yourselves. Me? I'm having a scotch.

BILL: Aren't you going to Brenda's?

JANE: Don't be silly.

BILL: What?

JANE: You know I can't leave you alone.

> *She exits. He sits, staring into space. As his mind wanders, his jaw drops, and his face assumes dull look we've never seen. Then he suddenly comes to and looks around confused.*

BILL: Wasn't Jane here? Where the hell... (*Picks up the clarinet.*) Just you and me, Pops. (*He plays a couple of soft blues licks, closes his eyes and gives Pops a great big kiss.*) I love you, Pops. Hey! Remember this one?

> *He plays 16 bars of the old Ray Henderson standard "Sunny Side Up" then snaps his fingers in rhythm trying to remember the lyrics. JANE enters with two glasses of scotch.*

BILL: What are those words?

JANE: You're losing it, kid.

BILL (*Keeps snapping his fingers.*): I'm better than I ever was. I just ...

JANE (*Sings in rhythm with his finger tapping.*):
"Keep your Sunny Side Up, up,
Hide the side that gets blue."

BILL: That's it!

BOTH: "If you have nine sons in a row,
Baseball teams make money, you know.
Keep your funny side up, up,
Let your laughter come through, do."

BILL: Big finish! (*He rises.*)

BOTH: "Stand up on your legs,
Be like two fried eggs,
Keeeeep youuuur Sunny Siiiiiiiide Uuuuuuuup!"

*He finishes on a loud, high note on the clarinet, and they laugh together.*

BILL: Where the hell did that come from? I haven't played that one in years.

*JANE hands him a glass of scotch, raises her glass and proposes a toast.*

JANE: To Sunnyside.

BILL: Sunnyside? On, yeah. Isn't that where Arlene Davis moved after Ben died? We ought to pay her a visit. Of course, the place is probably filled with incontinent old geezers who can't find their shoes, but so what. Keep your Sunny Side Up.

*They drink.*

BILL (*Cont.*): The boys'll love that one. They sure need me. I mean, whoever heard of a Dixieland Band without a clarinet? They said to come over this afternoon about... what did I say?

JANE: About one thirty.

BILL: That's it, one thirty, over at, uh...

JANE: Jim's house.

BILL: Yeah. Jim's house. Is that okay? You can drive, right?

*JANE is overcome with emotion, and takes a moment to answer.*

JANE: Yes. I can drop you off on my way to Brenda's.

BILL: Great. Now put down that scotch. You think I want my chauffeur arrested for D.U.I?

*Lights fade.*

*Blackout.*

### END OF PLAY

# A Tender Moment

## by

## Frank Motz

Directed by Bob Trisolini

with

Nancy Denton as Woman

Ryan Fitts as Man#1

Dylan Jones as Man#2

CHARACTERS
HAROLD (MAN#1), a man of any age.

MS. LATEER/MARTHA (WOMAN), a woman, 20s to 30s, dressed as an elderly woman.

LOUIS (MAN#2), a man of any age.

SETTING
A living room cluttered with boxes. There is a couch.

TIME
The present.

> *Lights up on an old, frail looking MS. LATEER looking through one of the boxes. A knock is heard. She goes to the door and opens it. HAROLD is standing there.*

HAROLD: Forgive me for intruding, but is this where Peter Lateer lived?

MS. LATEER: Yes?

HAROLD: Are you related to him?

MS. LATEER: I'm his sister.

HAROLD: I'm so sorry.

MS. LATEER: Thank you.

HAROLD: May I come in?

MS. LATEER: Well, I really have a lot I need to do....

HAROLD (*He politely brushes past her into the room.*): I will only be a minute. I promise. I believe you are his closest living relative?

MS. LATEER: That's right.

HAROLD: And his only heir?

MS. LATEER: Yes. But who are you?

HAROLD: I am one of the millions of people who loved your brother. I never missed his radio show. He was one of those people who touches the lives of others in a way that they never forget.

MS. LATEER: It's very kind of you to say that.

HAROLD: It's true.

MS. LATEER: Thank you, Mr.?

MS. LATEER: Would you? Thank you.

HAROLD (*He speaks as he leaves the room.*): Of course. (*His voice is heard from the other room.*) There's nobody here. What's in all the boxes?

MS. LATEER (*Raising her voice to be heard.*): They were sent over from the studio where he did his radio broadcasts. I think he had more things at the radio studio than here in his apartment. I have been too upset to go through them. (*She opens one of them and looks through it.*) Wait! I think I found it!

HAROLD (*Rushing back into the room as she pulls the microphone out of the box.*) Yes! That's it! (*He goes to her and takes it and admires it as he holds it up.*) You cannot imagine the inspiration this microphone can be for those who loved your brother so much. Thank god it is safe. (*He goes to her in a tender way.*) Ms. Lateer, I know I am asking a lot. I'm sure this has meaning for you as well and it certainly would be worth a lot of money to collectors who would display it in their home. My request is to use it to carry on the great work your brother did. To keep helping the people to whom he meant so much.

MS. LATEER (*Starts to cry.*): You are such a wonderful man and what you want to do with this would have meant so much to Peter.

*A knock at the door.*

MS. LATEER: Excuse me.

*She goes to the door and speaks to LOUIS. HAROLD sees him and turns his back to the door.*

MS. LATEER (*Cont.*): May I help you?

LOUIS: I am so sorry to bother you at a time like this. I am here to see Peter Lateer's sister.

MS. LATEER: I am his sister.

LOUIS: May I come in? (*Like HAROLD, he politely walks past her into the room looking around.*) I feel bad coming to you at a time like this. It's about your brother's microphone. I'm a scout leader and the kids just loved listening to your brother on the radio. (*He looks out at an imaginary microphone.*) It would mean so much to them if I we could have his microphone sitting there when we have our meetings.

MS. LATEER (*Gestures to other man.*): Oh my. This kind man is also interested in it.

*LOUIS turns around and HAROLD recognizes him.*

HAROLD: Walters. Ben Walters.

MS. LATEER: (*Leading him to the door.*): Thank you Mr. Walters. Now, if you don't mind, I have a lot of work to do here sorting through his things and preparing for the funeral.

HAROLD: I understand and I am terribly sorry to bother you at a time like this. I would not do it if it were not such an important thing that I have come here to talk to you about.

MS. LATEER: Alright, Mr. Walters. I'm listening.

HAROLD (*Leads her to the couch*): Come over here. Sit down. (*They sit.*) Ms... ?

MS. LATEER: Lateer.

HAROLD: I see. Ms. Lateer, I should tell you that I have come to see if I could acquire Peter's microphone for the benefit of all of us who loved him so much. For us, it is a symbol of the great things he did.

MS. LATEER: His microphone?

HAROLD: That's right. The one he used on his radio show. The legendary microphone. Everyone knows that microphone.

MS. LATEER: I see...

HAROLD (*Gets up and becomes very dramatic.*): Ms. Lateer, I want to make certain that your brother's work carries on. That the things he did, the things he stood for, the very life that he led, live on for future generations to benefit from.

MS. LATEER (*Moved.*): What a wonderful thing. My brother would have loved that.

HAROLD: However, I am afraid someone may have broken in here and stolen it.

MS. LATEER (*Afraid, looking around.*): Why do you say that?

HAROLD (*Goes to the door.*) Come here. I want to show you something.

*She goes to the door and he shows her.*

HAROLD (*Cont.*): Do you see the marks where someone has used a screw driver to open the door without a key?

MS. LATEER: Oh dear. Do you think someone could still be in the apartment?

HAROLD (*He goes over and puts his hand on her shoulder.*): No, but why don't I look around to be sure.

HAROLD: Absolutely.

*MS. LATEER comes over and takes the microphone from him and heads toward LOUIS.*

HAROLD (*Cont.*): I'm sure the patients at the hospital will understand.

MS. LATEER (*Stops and turns.*): At the hospital?

HAROLD: Yes, there are also some things you don't know about me, Louis. I volunteer at the hospital to help lift the spirits of the most seriously ill people there. They've all been hoping I could get the microphone for them, but I'm sure they would prefer that the kids have it.

MS. LATEER: Oh dear, I don't know what I should do.

HAROLD (*Gets emotional.*): In fact, there is one patient in particular. Emily is her name. She has a terminal illness. She never missed listening to your brother.

LOUIS (*Melodramatic.*): I can't help but think the microphone would mean the world to her.

HAROLD: You are so right. It would.

LOUIS (*Even more melodramatic.*): Might even help her hang on and keep living.

HAROLD (*Emotional.*) Wouldn't that be something?

LOUIS: Yes. It reminds me of little Larry.

HAROLD: Little Larry?

*LOUIS gets so emotional, he can't speak.*

HAROLD (*Cont.*): What about little Larry?

*LOUIS waves his hand as if to say he is too emotional to speak.*

MS. LATEER: Oh dear. I think he is too emotional to speak.

HAROLD (*Amused.*) Is that right, Louis? Are you too emotional too speak?

*LOUIS shakes his head affirmatively.*

HAROLD (*Cont.*): Let me guess. Little Larry is also terminally ill?

*LOUIS shakes his head affirmatively.*

HAROLD (*Cont.*): And you think the microphone might save his life?

*LOUIS shakes his head affirmatively.*

LOUIS (*Annoyed.*): Hello, Harold.

HAROLD (*Also annoyed.*): Hello, Louis.

MS. LATEER: You know each other?

HAROLD: Yes, we do. I didn't know you were a scout leader.

LOUIS: There are a lot of things you don't know about me, Harold. I see you have the microphone.

MS. LATEER (*To HAROLD.*): I thought your name was Ben Watson.

HAROLD (*To MS. LATEER.*): It is. Harold is my nickname. (*To LOUIS.*) The scouts instill such wonderful values. Isn't there a motto the kids repeat before each meeting?

LOUIS: Yes. (*To MS. LATEER.*): I always read it to the kids from a card. I get choked up every time.

HAROLD: Could you say it for us?

LOUIS: I don't have the card.

HAROLD: Paraphrase.

LOUIS: That wouldn't be right.

HAROLD: Surely you can tell us something from it?

LOUIS (*Exasperated. Raises his right hand.*): I promise to always do the right thing. (*He pauses. They both wait, looking at him.*) In sickness and in health. (*He pauses again. They both look at him quizzically.*) And I will always uphold the scout motto.

   *Silence.*

HAROLD: Which is?

LOUIS: Wherever I go. Whatever I do. I will do it with honor, dignity, love, devotion, goodness, and decency. (*Silence.*) And finally, I will always be prepared. (*Silence.*) For anything. (*Silence.*) That may come along. (*Silence.*) So help me God. (*Silence.*) Amen.

HAROLD and MS. LATEER: Amen.

   *LOUIS breathes a sigh of relief.*

HAROLD: That's touching.

MS. LATEER: Oh, yes. (*To HAROLD.*) I really think it should go to the kids, don't you?

MS. LATEER: Oh dear.

HAROLD: Louis, this kind lady wants to do the right thing. Maybe we can work something out that could benefit the kids and the seriously ill.

*LOUIS shakes his head affirmatively.*

MS. LATEER: Oh, that would be wonderful. What a tender moment. Could you two go into the next room and see if you could work something out?

HAROLD (*To MS. LATEER.*) We certainly can. (*To LOUIS.*) Louis?

*LOUIS shakes his head affirmatively.*

MS. LATEER: If you two only knew how much this moment means to me. It gives such meaning to my brother's life. I can never thank you enough.

HAROLD: It means so much to us too, doesn't it, Louis?

*LOUIS nods his head affirmatively. They exit RIGHT.*

*MS. LATEER removes the wig and the clothes she is wearing, revealing a young woman made up to look old. She admires the microphone and smiles. She exits leaving the door open. The two men enter and LOUIS goes over and picks up the clothing and wig and looks at HAROLD.*

LOUIS: Martha?

HAROLD: Martha.

*Lights fade.*

*Blackout.*

END OF PLAY

# Call These Delicate Creatures Ours, and Not Their Appetites

by

Peter A. Balaskas

Directed by Helen Holliday

with

Dylan Jones as Kieran

Paul Mullen as Willem

CHARACTERS
KIERAN, a man, mid-20s, American.

WILLEM, a man, late 40s/early 50s, Irish (with accent).

SETTING
A small pub in Dublin, Ireland.

TIME
The present, evening.

*Lights up on a bar DOWNSTAGE, with a row of stools behind it. On the bar are a variety of snacks and drink condiments. Hanging LEFT, facing the bar, is a television where the customers can watch the programs. Crowd noises of a busy pub provide background noise.*

*At the bar in the center is KIERAN, watching a golf game on the TV and drinking a pint. WILLEM enters from RIGHT, carrying a pint. WILLEM, who appears to be a regular sees the TV and sits next to KIERAN. KIERAN turns and sees WILLEM.*

KIERAN: How are you doing?

WILLEM: Fair to midland. Yourself?

KIERAN: Likewise.

*KIERAN looks back at the TV. WILLEM does the same.*

WILLEM: Ah, one of the PGA County Tournaments. Know where?

KIERAN (*Looking closer.*): Can't tell.

WILLEM (*Squints.*): Bloody hell, this is embarrassing. My family has been here for four generations and I can't recognize my own country. It's a sin, really. (*Pause.*) How do you like our golf?

KIERAN: Honestly, I haven't been paying attention. It's just seems... peaceful watching them play.

WILLEM: I know what you mean. If this were a boxing or football match, this whole pub would be like a mini stadium: lots of cheers, catcalls and fisticuffs. Golf? Well... like watching a pleasant sunset: quiet and tranquil. (*Pause.*) Or it's like watching paint dry, depending on your present frame of mind. (*KIERAN chuckles and nods. WILLEM holds out his hand.*) I'm Willem.

KIERAN (*Shakes hands.*): Kieran.

WILLEM: Now, judging by your accent, where in the states are you from? Or, is it Canada?

KIERAN: It's the US. And I'm from California.

WILLEM: What brings you out here?

KIERAN: One-month long vacation. Ireland for three weeks and London for one.

WILLEM: Ah. (*Pauses, then frowns.*) Why the hell would you want to spend a week in London?

KIERAN: It's a birthday vacation. I'm Irish, so I wanted to absorb my heritage here. And as far as the London connection is concerned, I'm seeing some Shakespearean plays over there, which coincides with my birthday: April twenty-third.

WILLEM: Like the Bard himself! Well, I forgive you, then. And since both of your birthdays are in a couple of weeks. (*Raises glass.*) Happy birthday, Kieran.

KIERAN (*They both clink their glasses and drink.*): Cheers, Willem.

WILLEM: I happen to know a thing or two about old Bill, as I usually call him. Besides teaching Irish literature, I'm also professor of Elizabethan and Jacobean theatre at Trinity College.

KIERAN: So am I! I mean... I'm a professor of literature at University of California Irvine.

WILLEM (*Looks him over.*): You're awfully young to be a university professor.

KIERAN: A little. I'll be 25. I jumped ahead a couple of grades in high school and during my undergrad. I earned my PhD when I was 22.

WILLEM: God, do I feel old!

KIERAN: Don't be. Ever since I saw Dead Poets Society as a child, I always wanted to teach, especially when it came to the Bard. Shakespeare is my favorite class to teach.

WILLEM: Well then, my young friend, I must ask you the necessary questions: favorite comedy, tragedy, historical and romance.

KIERAN: Willem, I'm on vacation. I'm not supposed to think.

WILLEM: Now, now. If the Bard is in your blood, it should come second nature. Don't disappoint a fellow Shake-o-phile... Shakespearian-phile... whatever the hell we're called these days.

KIERAN (*Thinking.*): Historical: Henry V. Comedy: Midsummer Night's Dream. Romance: The Tempest. And Tragedy: Romeo and Juliet.

WILLEM: Ah, very good choices. Historical: <u>Richard III</u>. Comedy: <u>The Merry Wives of Windsor</u>. Romance: <u>The Winter's Tale</u>. And Tragedy: <u>Macbeth</u>. But I also love the sonnets.

KIERAN: Me too. I'm afraid my favorite is less than original: Number 18. "Shall I compare thee to a summer's day..."

WILLEM: "Thou art more lovely and more temperate." (*Pause.*) I'm more partial to Number 152, especially when it ends with "For I have sworn thee fair; more perjured eye/To swear against the truth so foul a lie!" (*KIERAN looks at him.*) Very dark, I know. But the tone and the tempo have a lyrical nature to it. Old Bill is tied with Joyce as my favorite. It's the Irish connection, you know.

KIERAN: I love Joyce, as well. <u>The Dubliners</u> and <u>Portrait of an Artist as a Young Man</u> had a huge influence on me growing up. They changed my life, both as an Irishman and as a lover of literature.

WILLEM: Well, you couldn't be in a better place than spending three weeks here. And how do you like it so far?

KIERAN (*Pause.*): It's quite a magical, mercurial place.

WILLEM (*Noticing KIERAN's dark mood.*): Well, don't sound so enthusiastic.

KIERAN: I'm sorry, Willem. Ireland is truly divine. It possesses... a spirit which moves me deeply. It's just...

WILLEM: What's wrong? (*Pause.*) Look, Kieran, I know we just met. But rumor has it that I am an unbelievably wise, yet humble, listener. Maybe talking about it will help. It *is* your birthday, after all. You should be savoring your native culture during the days and... burning the candle at both ends during the nights. My God, a literature professor quoting metaphorical clichés. I should be flogged.

KIERAN: This trip was supposed to be for two: me and my girlfriend. She loves and teaches Shakespeare, as well.

WILLEM: Same university?

KIERAN: No, she works at Chapman. Unfortunately, I found out she was cheating on me with her ex for the past year. And when I confronted her, she didn't deny it.

WILLEM: I'm surprised she didn't lie so she could get a free trip out of you.

KIERAN: The proof was too evident; a mutual friend of ours grew a conscience and told me. The accommodations were easy to change, but I had to eat the extra plane ticket because they don't do refunds.

WILLEM: Ouch. I'm so sorry, lad.

KIERAN: We were together for three years and I actually expressed my love, which was an unbelievable mistake.

WILLEM: No, it wasn't. Just because one bad apple tore up your emotional innards, doesn't mean the entire tree is spoiled.

KIERAN: It was going to be the first trip where I wouldn't go alone…a trip that I would be sharing with someone that I cared about. (*Pause.*) You know, when I got here, I made a promise to myself to get blind drunk, pick up a beautiful Irish lass and… uh…

WILLEM: Shag the memory of your ex away? (*KIERAN nods.*) I completely understand. (*Pause.*) So, it's been a week. Have you found a conquest?

KIERAN: More like she conquered me. I was walking around Dublin lost and I saw a cathedral in the distance. I couldn't find out which one it was. So, this stunning blonde walks up, and I asked her its name, which happened to be St. Patrick's. I was so embarrassed that I didn't recognize it. She used to be a travel agent, and she was extremely knowledgeable about the landmarks and locales. After a few minutes talking about me and my passion for literature, she suggested being my unofficial tour guide.

WILLEM: Well, there you go. A luscious blonde to hold you by the hand and to offer a bountiful bosom to cry on.

KIERAN: Silken, golden hair. Sparkling green eyes. And a smile that penetrates your core. She reminded me of a young Miranda Richardson from <u>The Crying Game</u>.

WILLEM (*Whistles.*): Stunning, indeed!

KIERAN: April was her name. And I have to tell you, Willem, at the time, I thought it was a beneficial omen. I mean, meeting a lovely woman named April on the month of April, <u>my birth month</u>? I don't consider that a coincidence.

WILLEM: It's more than that. It's the magic of Cupid… or Dionysus, depending on how much drink you've had at the time.

KIERAN: Well, there was one major obstacle: her wedding ring.

WILLEM (*Pause.*): Oh dear.

KIERAN: But I figured it was…just her being hospitable and friendly. (*WILLEM looks at KIERAN.*) <u>I know, I know!</u> But she was so giving and generous, driving me around in her car, showing me the eastern coasts and downtown Dublin, crossing the Liffey Bridge, checking out the museums, and the local pubs and theatres.

KIERAN (*Cont.*): We went cross-country to Cork, the cemeteries and the grassy plains… it was peaceful and sublime, like something from a Yeats poem. We drove and toured the country, and then we had dinner and drinks during the evenings. We even saw <u>Pride and Prejudice</u> at the Gate Theatre. We had a phenomenal time. But she never spoke about her husband; she strictly focused about me. I was tempted to ask if he was going to miss her. But…

WILLEM: You didn't want to spoil the mood.

KIERAN: I just didn't want to be alone. (*Pause.*) Later in the week, I did share with April what happened with my girlfriend, maybe too much, I suppose. And her emerald eyes just peered into me. She could tell the wounds never healed; she even held my hand and gave me a huge hug when the evening was done, as though part of her soul was being infused into mine. The next day, she picked me up at my B & B and we went to Phoenix Park during the late afternoon. She packed a picnic basket with sandwiches and wine. While we were sitting on the blanket, talking and laughing, I noticed she wasn't wearing her ring.

I finally asked her about that. She said she understood what it meant to be in an unloving relationship. Although the man she was married to was a decent provider, he was reserved, uptight, stern, cold and distant, both emotionally <u>and</u> physically. She was still working as a travel agent at the time, which was some consolation. But they basically had nothing in common. She tried to make it work by having a child. Unfortunately, she had to quit her job in order to raise him, while the husband was still business as usual with his work—whatever that was—and his fishing. In fact, he took their son for a father-and-son fishing trip the week she met me. She felt more alone in the marriage than being single.

It was my turn to hold her hand. We looked at each other and the next thing I knew we were kissing passionately for who knows how long underneath this gigantic, billowing ash tree. It was like a scene from a Jane Austin novel. It was enchanting, Willem… in more ways than one.

WILLEM (*Pause.*): What happened after the picnic?

KIERAN: We silently drove back to my B & B. It was evening and… (*Pause.*). We were together throughout the entire night. The way she moved… I'm mainly talking about, you know, the times in between where…

WILLEM (*Interrupting.*): Wait… wait a moment. (*Pause.*) <u>Times</u>? How many times were you…

KIERAN: Two, maybe three.

WILLEM: <u>Maybe</u> three? God's wounds, I'd be lucky if I could get through the one.

KIERAN: It was more than just pent-up, carnal energy being released. When we were resting in each other's arms, I felt her become more... at peace. I think she was happier during those moments than the sex.

WILLEM: After what you shared with me about that cold fish husband of hers, I'm not surprised. The poor woman.

KIERAN: The next morning, we ordered breakfast in bed, she kissed me goodbye and hinted about getting together again. I mainly hung out at Bewley's Tea Café, bathing in the afterglow. Then, I received a call from her. She said her husband was coming home early and was on his way back with their son. She couldn't be with me anymore. So, we wished each other goodbye, good luck and that was it.

*Silence*

WILLEM: How do you feel now?

KIERAN: After being cheated on myself, I thought I would be the last person to be "the other man." But, Willem, I was tired of being the victim. After what April shared with me about how her husband had treated her all those years, I figured I wasn't hurting anyone. At the time, it felt good not being the cuckold anymore.

WILLEM: Understandable. But now?

KIERAN: Now... I feel both cuckolded and opportunistic. Instead of afterglow, I feel hung over. All those literary classics I've read and taught that romanticized adultery are just inane fantasies.

WILLEM: That's because if the authors wrote about the hard cold <u>realities</u> that stems from adultery, people wouldn't be buying their books. They would fade into absolute obscurity.

KIERAN: Needless to say, April's husband may be a jerk, but he didn't deserve what I just did. And I feel like crap because of it.

*They drink in silence. Then, WILLEM gently pats KIERAN on the shoulder.*

WILLEM: Believe it or not, what you are feeling, right now, is actually good. (*KIERAN looks at him.*) It means you have a conscience, Kieran. You're human, you made an error in judgment and you feel regret. That is called temporary loss of ethics. You're young, you'll learn, and you'll make sure not to do it again. Simple as that. No judgment here, my young friend.

KIERAN (*Smiles with relief.*): Willem, thank you... for listening and especially for the words of wisdom.

WILLEM (*Nods, clinks glasses with KIERAN.*): Comes with age. And I totally understand the complexity that is called marriage. It takes work... and a lot of stamina.

KIERAN: You're married, too? (*WILLEM nods.*) I feel like a total ass talking about myself all this time. Well, it's your turn. The way I feel right now, I really do need to hear a happy story about marriage. Let's start with her name.

> *WILLEM just looks at KIERAN and smiles. KIERAN smiles back, but not getting what is going on. After a few more seconds, he finally gets the point and is stunned. He is about to get up and leave, fearing the worst. But WILLEM just gently holds his arm and guides him back to his chair, showing no anger at all.*

WILLEM: There's an old saying that you never really know what goes on with a marriage unless you're inside the couple's bedroom. Well, Kieran, I'll do the next best thing.

April was correct when she shared with you that I was reserved and uptight. I am a serious man who cherishes literature as a way of preserving our heritage and our humanity as a whole. But I also understand that I need to, for lack of a better term, lighten up. Twenty years ago, I was looking for a special woman who possessed that... unique brand of energy, that sense of adventure. I thought April was that person. She was... is vibrant, witty, jubilant. I oftentimes pinched myself thinking, "How could this wild, passionate woman think of me as her husband?" Well, during those early years, we complimented each other perfectly: April with her energetic, adventurous drive, and me with my logic and stability.

But as the years went by, April wanted more. More traveling, more partying, more nights on the town with her girlfriends, more, more, and more. I kept stressing the importance of pacing yourself, that the true sense of adventure was growing older and evolving with a spouse, savoring the subtle, quiet intimacy between two souls. However, according to April, that's just quote/unquote "literary tripe created by authors who hadn't been shagged or even snogged in ages." We were beginning to lead separate lives. It was I, not April, who wanted a child. I called it the most wonderful adventure that a man and woman could ever explore together. I used those exact words to her.

When Stephen was born 10 years ago, that made things worse for April. She couldn't work as a travel agent anymore. And she had to stop going out to those wild, nightly parties with her girlfriends. She finally decided to join me in attending the academic soirées and galas at Trinity, something she previously declined until our son was born. And surprisingly enough, she seemed to click very well with my colleagues and their spouses.

WILLEM (*Cont.*): But as you well know, the underbelly of academia is a nasty world of itself. The professional pettiness, competitive jealousies... and cold-hearted infidelities. Three months ago, I heard a rumor that April and a colleague of mine—in the same department, I might add—were having an affair. Apparently, she found this particularly younger professor more exciting, energetic and adventurous than I.

For the past two months, I've had a private investigator chronicle her daily activities, including her indiscretions. However, the investigator shared with me something fascinating: my colleague wanted April to divorce me and marry him, which she vehemently refused. After all, I was tenure and there was no way in hell she would give up her style of living. So, they broke up. And I thought that life was back to normal.

But then this past week, when I returned from the fishing trip with my son, the investigator showed me pictures of her latest symbol of adventure: you. And then he showed me pictures of April and my colleague together once again. Apparently, she only dallied with you in order to cuckold <u>him</u>, to make him jealous. After spending the night with you, he caved in to April's demands to keep the relationship as is, while the clueless husband—me—continues being unexciting, yet provide for her financial needs.

*WILLEM gets up and pays for both of them.*

I'm not angry at you, Kieran. I should thank you, actually. If it weren't for you being here, I would have continued thinking that there would have been hope. But with all the evidence I gained, I can finally prove April's unsuitability as a mother and get custody of Stephen. Who knows, if the furies of vengeance smile upon me, this scandal might even get my treacherous colleague terminated from Trinity. (*Silence.*) I do have to wonder, though... among the three of us—you, me, and my colleague—who is the <u>true</u> cuckold here?

*He pats and squeezes KIERAN'S shoulder, not in malice, but sympathy.*

WILLEM: Give my best to Old Bill in London.

*WILLEM strolls out of the bar, leaving a forlorn KIERAN in his thoughts. The sounds of the crowd and the golf game on TV grow louder as the lights fade.*

*Blackout.*

END OF PLAY

# Chopping Celery

### by

### Connie Schindewolf

Directed by James Thaggard

with

Nicole Cunningham as Emma

Andrea Dovner as Marsha

Louise Stinespring as Grandma

CHARACTERS
EMMA, a woman, 19, a college student.

MARSHA, a woman, 50ish, EMMA's mother.

GRANDMA, a woman, 68 to 75.

SETTING
The three women are each sitting at a small desk or table, writing. MARSHA is CENTER with her laptop, EMMA is RIGHT with a tablet or texting on her phone, and GRANDMA is LEFT writing letters by hand. Throughout the entire play they are writing to each other and talking out loud as they write, but not directly communicating. At times EMMA is writing to a friend. There is a spot light on each but they all remain lit until the end when GRANDMA's light goes out.

TIME
The present.

> *Lights up with EMMA typing on her tablet to her friend, talking out loud as she types.*

EMMA: Oh my God, the party's Wednesday before Thanksgiving? Are you kidding? I don't think I can go. That's when we all have to go to Grandma's and chop celery. It's for the turkey or something. I'm not even going to eat the turkey this year since I've gone vegetarian, almost vegan. I could tell Mom I can't get a ride home until Thursday morning and then I'll drive over myself.

GRANDMA: Dear Marsha, I can't believe how early it's getting dark now. I'm so happy you're all coming Wednesday night to help me get the meal ready. Did Emma ever say if she got the little drip coffee pot I sent her? She said she did a lot of late night studying, and that's what helped you, coffee, when you were a freshman, remember? I'm sorry I haven't learned to email or spacebook or any of that computer stuff, but I just like to write letters. It's ok that you type yours, print them out, and mail them to me. I just don't want to forget how to write in cursive. That's a dying art you know. Last time I subbed grade school the teachers had just about given up.

MARSHA: Emma, what can be so important Wednesday night that you have to go to a meeting? Isn't everyone going home Wednesday? I guess you could drive yourself over to Grandma's Thursday, but she'll so miss having you there to chop the celery and break up the bread. Did you send a thank you to her for the coffee pot?

EMMA: Mom, I just haven't had time to write Grandma a thank you note. The coffee pot is so old fashion. I mean, Starbucks is within walking distance. (*Pause.*) Does she know I don't eat turkey any more?

MARSHA: Humor her, Emma. It was a gift and she expects a written thank you! I taught you that. I'll have a nice little card; you sign it and give it to her, ok? No, I haven't told her about your new eating habits yet.

EMMA: Hey, Whitney. What's up? My Mom's still pressuring me to go to my Grandma's with them Wednesday, so, I'm not sure about the party. This is just kind of a ritual with them the night before Thanksgiving, and we go through the same thing after church on Christmas Eve. It used to be fun when my cousins were there, and I was in third or fourth grade.

MARSHA: Yes, Mom, Emma got the little coffee pot and she loves it. I'm sure she has a thank you ready to get in the mail. Mom, about Thanksgiving. I just want you to know ahead of time that Emma doesn't eat Turkey any more.

GRANDMA: Did she develop an allergy or something?

MARSHA: No, she just doesn't eat turkey any more... or any meat.

GRANDMA: Oh, no Marsha. She's not become a vegetarian has she? You know she'll never get enough protein. She can eat turkey on Thanksgiving and Christmas at least. You don't go your whole life eating meat and then one day stop cold turkey... no pun intended.

MARSHA: Mom, I know it may be hard for you to understand but I've learned to pick my battles, so let's just humor her and not get on her case, ok?

GRANDMA: So, what's she going to eat, Marsha? There's meat in the gravy and the dressing. You mean I can't even put bacon in the green beans?

MARSHA: You fix the meal as you always do. She's not going to starve for God's sake!

EMMA: So, on Wednesday night before Thanksgiving my cousins and I would all sit around Grandma's dining room table, and she'd bring in the celery, cutting boards, and the paring knives. That made us feel grown up.

MARSHA: She eats lots of beans and tofu. She says there's protein in just about everything. I've just quit worrying about it.

GRANDMA: What is tofu, Marsha?

MARSHA: I'm not exactly sure.

GRANDMA: Well, don't you think you better find out?

MARSHA: Mom, she's 19. Was your mother telling you what to eat when you were that age?

EMMA: After we chopped like a gazillion stalks of celery, Grandma would set, like, five stale loaves of bread in front of us and tell us to have fun. We'd start breaking it up for the dressing. Then we'd ask Grandma if we could have some grape juice in her good crystal water glasses. She'd get them down from the china cabinet and ask us to just be careful. I don't think she ever got it… just what we were doing.

GRANDMA: The world is different now, Marsha. I just worry about her, and you and everyone in the family. That's what Grandmas do you know.

MARSHA: Don't worry. Thanksgiving is not just about food you know. One of the best days of my life was at your house on Thanksgiving. It was Emma's first. Daddy was still alive. It was like the whole family just revolved around Emma and how blessed we all were. Do you remember Aunt Sally giving her her first taste of your pumpkin pie?

GRANDMA: Of course I remember that day. But listen to yourself. Your description came right back to food again. Food is a major part of the holidays, part of our tradition. You're trying to change our traditions on me and it's like pulling a rug out from under my feet.

EMMA: So, we broke up the bread and with our fake wine we pretended we were taking communion. Grandma was in the kitchen by then simmering the celery so she didn't see us. My cousin Jack would say, "This is my body, broken for you. Take and eat." With much giggling, we would. Then he'd say, "This is my blood, take and drink. Do this in remembrance of me." Then Grandma would finally yell, "What's going on in there?"

MARSHA: Dear Emma, How are you? I told Grandma about you not eating turkey and she didn't take it very well. Do you think you could make an exception just on the holidays, honey, for her? Do you know if you're coming home Wednesday night yet?

EMMA: Mom, I knew the two of you would make a big deal out of this! What difference does it make what crosses my lips on Thanksgiving? Can't we just be thankful for the important things in life, and not what I eat?

MARSHA: Ok, so what are you thankful for, Emma? I really want to know, because you don't seem to be thankful for family or anything we do for you.

EMMA: Well, I know one thing I'm thankful for, and that is that Thanksgiving is only once a year! See ya Thursday morning cuz the meeting is still on. Have fun chopping celery.

MARSHA: Mom, Just a heads up, Emma may not come with us Wednesday night. She has a meeting or something on campus. But we'll be there.

GRANDMA: Dear Marsha, Sorry Emma doesn't think she can miss her meeting. You know I've always insisted that we have the holidays here at my house but maybe Christmas you could make the turkey. I've been feeling a little tired lately, and I may be getting ready to concede and let you fix the dinner.

EMMA: Whitney, Guess what my cousin Jack said one year. He saw Grandma pulling body parts out of the butt of that turkey, and one of them looked like a penis, and a big one too!

MARSHA: Mom, are you really feeling tired or are you just trying to punish me for my daughter being a vegetarian?

GRANDMA: Dear Marsha, I can't believe you even have to ask me about that. I would never joke about my health. I'm just tired, not comatose, so forget I said anything. Looking forward to seeing you Wednesday.

EMMA: Then Grandma would start baking the pumpkin pies. Thank God there's no meat products in pumpkin. The smell of her house the night before Thanksgiving and Christmas is almost as good as opening presents... almost!

GRANDMA: Traditions seem to be going by the wayside.

EMMA: Mom, I don't want you and Grandma to worry about me not getting enough protein so I'm going to pick up a Tofurkey and some hummus for me.

MARSHA: Dear Mom, Emma is bringing her own Tofurkey and hummus so don't worry. Everything will be fine and we'll have a wonderful holiday. I love you.

GRANDMA: Dear Marsha, What in the hell is "Tofurkey" and isn't humus, manure? I won't have it on my table, and you shouldn't be letting her eat that!

MARSHA: Mom, Tofurkey is a brand of soy stuff they squish together, and you bake it like a turkey. And you're thinking of humus that Daddy used to put in the garden. It's something entirely different.

EMMA: Did you tell Grandma about the Tofurkey?

MARSHA: Is there any reason you can't talk to Grandma?

EMMA: Like I have time to write letters or talk on the phone! I have lots of studying to do, Mom. You need to talk her into getting on line and emailing, and Facebook. And while you're at it, why don't you talk her into using her dishwasher so we don't have to do the Thanksgiving dishes by hand?

MARSHA: I told her you were blogging now and you know what she said? She said, "I didn't know Emma danced!" Isn't that a hoot?

EMMA: Mom, I've told you to please not use the word "hoot". It makes you sound so old.

MARSHA: I just wish you could live by her traditions for one more Thanksgiving.

*GRANDMA's light goes out. Pause.*

EMMA: Whitney, if I didn't tell you, thanks for coming to the funeral home the other night, I meant to. It meant a lot to me, and I know you had to miss a couple of classes. We're doing ok.

MARSHA: Emma, you were such a big help before, during, and after the service. Thanks. I love you.

EMMA: Mom, you know what I just thought of? We forgot to give Grandma that thank you note from me for the coffee pot. And, I want to tell you that I'm sorry for missing the Wednesday night celery chopping. Hope you are ok. Sorry I had to get back to classes so soon, but it's not that long until Christmas.

MARSHA: Grandma knew you loved her, honey.

EMMA (*Starts typing on her laptop then closes it, takes out pen and paper and writes to GRANDMA in cursive.*): Dear Grandma, It's so strange I'm writing you since I never did before and now you're not even here. I mean I know you can't really get this. I don't even know what I'll do with it... put it in my drawer by my bed I guess. Maybe there's some way you'll know I'm writing, and I think it will help me too. I'm sorry I never wrote you a thank you for the coffee pot. I'm using it now and saving some money on fewer trips to Starbucks, so thank you for your thoughtfulness. I have to be honest; if it hadn't been for Mom, I probably would never have ever written a thank you to you. You see she'd buy a card and I'd just sign it like I had taken the time to get it. I'm sorry I didn't take more time for you, and I'm sorry I wasn't there to help you on the Wednesday before Thanksgiving this year. The party I went to instead wasn't that much fun. I'm sorry my Tofurky made you sad, but your pumpkin pie was still the greatest! I love you, Grandma, and I want you to know that Christmas Eve after church, I'm going to ask Mom if I can be in charge of celery chopping. Love, Emma.

*She puts the letter in an envelope and seals it.*

*Blackout.*

## END OF PLAY

# Miss O'Hara, I Have a Confession to Make

by

Bernard Yanelli

Directed by Bob Trisolini

with

Melliss Kenworthy as Maureen O'Hara

Ryan Fitts as Martin O'Rourke

CHARACTERS
Maureen O'HARA, a woman, 70, aging star of the Silver Screen.

Martin O'ROURKE, a man, 46, a journalist/failed screenwriter.

SETTING
The living room of Maureen O'Hara's suite at the Beverly Hills Wilshire Hotel, which contains a couch, chair, coffee table, and a desk with a phone.

TIME
1990.

*Lights up on Maureen O'HARA, 70. Dressed in an expensive suit jacket and skirt, she sits in a chair, flipping through a bound script. She rises, plops the script on a coffee table that holds a few others, then stares at the phone. After hesitating, she picks it up and dials.*

O'HARA: Hi. It's Maureen. Any word yet on casting? (*Listening.*) I see. Don't apologize. I was probably too old for the part, anyway. (*Listening.*) No, the other scripts were dreadful. Call me old-fashioned, but I doubt my fans of The Quiet Man would accept me as the wife of a space alien who becomes the next U.S. president... I've got to go. I'll talk to you later. Bye.

*After hanging up the phone, she lets out an audible sigh, then gets startled when the doorbell rings. She takes out a compact, fixes her hair, then answers the door.*

*O'ROURKE enters. Dressed in a rumpled jacket, shirt, and slacks, he looks like he may have slept in his clothes.*

O'HARA (*Cont.*): Please, Martin, come in and make yourself comfortable. Would you like a drink?

O'ROURKE: No thanks. And, Miss O'Hara, I'd prefer it if you called me Marty.

O'HARA: Only if you call me Maureen.

O'ROURKE: Oh, I could never do that.

O'HARA: Then, Martin it is. (*He smiles, then gazes into her eyes, creating an awkward moment.*) (*She tries to break the awkwardness.*) How long have you been with the L.A. Times?

O'ROURKE: Pardon?

O'HARA: The Times, how long have you...? (*Sitting in a chair, she motions for him to sit on the couch.*)

O'ROURKE: Less than a year. I'm one of those journalists who bounces around a lot—that and I used to have hopes of making it as a... Ah... screenwriter. (*He sits.*)

O'HARA: So how did you get stuck interviewing _me_?

O'ROURKE: You're joking, right? Everyone was jealous when I got this interview.

O'HARA: Nice to know that my name hasn't been completely forgotten.

O'ROURKE: Absolutely not! In fact, I've seen all 42 of your films, including _Comanche Territory_.

O'HARA: Ah, yes. Not one of my best choices.

O'ROURKE: I wish I could disagree.

O'HARA: You mean, you weren't mesmerized by all those close-ups, as I gazed off into the horizon? (*She sits upright and gazes at nothing in particular.*) Well, I'm glad the _Times_ sent out a dedicated fan. Besides, I think I detect a slight trace of an Irish brogue?

O'ROURKE: We moved to California from Ireland when I was ten. (*In an Irish brogue.*) County Clare.

O'HARA (*In a heavier Irish brogue.*): As a Dubliner, I won't hold that against ya, me-boy-o.

> He looks down and sees several scripts lying on the coffee table, then picks up the top one and looks at the cover.

O'ROURKE: You're not trying to make a comeback, are you?

O'HARA: Heavens no! (*She grabs the script back, then sets it and the others on the floor.*) For some reason, my old agent keeps sending me these scripts—even though I tell him not to.

O'ROURKE (*Taking out a notebook from his briefcase.*): Shall we get started?

O'HARA: Yes, but before we do, please tell me your age, Martin. Knowing that will help me determine how much detail I should go into as I answer your questions.

O'ROURKE: I'm in my late 30s... Actually, I don't know why I just said that. I'm 46.

O'HARA: Oh, so you're the same age as my daughter.

O'ROURKE: You mean Bronwyn.

O'HARA: Yes. I keep telling Bron that she needs to find a good man. Are you single?

O'ROURKE: I am, but I doubt she'd be interested in a struggling journalist.

O'HARA: Your career's hit a rough patch, has it?

O'ROURKE: To be honest, my entire career *has been* a rough patch. Thankfully, though, we're not here to talk about me, but rather you and your... enormous body of work.

O'HARA (*Deadpan.*): I'm glad you added the words "of work." Otherwise, you would have made me cry.

O'ROURKE (*Equally deadpan.*): And to think a critic once said you lacked a sense of humor.

O'HARA (*Smiling.*): The nerve of that man.

O'ROURKE: Any subjects off limits?

O'HARA: Such as?

O'ROURKE: The failure of your first two marriages; the tragic death of your third husband Charles?

O'HARA: Oh, so it's going to be *that* kind of interview? I thought you might go for the movie star who walked away from the Silver Screen at 50, only to regret it after she turned 70.

O'ROURKE (*Aggressively.*): Miss O'Hara, you could pass for 50 any day of the week. Your beauty is... well, it's as timeless as a setting sun.

O'HARA: Wow! Now, there's an image. Maybe you should chuck journalism, Martin, and go back to writing screenplays.

O'ROURKE: Actually, I borrowed that line from a review of <u>Comanche Territory</u>. One of the critics wrote, "Framed in Technicolor, Miss O'Hara seems more significant than a setting sun."

O'HARA: Well, that's all very lovely to hear, but let's not forget he wrote that review 40 years ago.

O'ROURKE (*Overly intense.*): That's irrelevant! What he said still holds true.

O'HARA: You know, Martin, I like you. You're good for my ego. And with me, flattery will get you everywhere—except, of course, my bedroom. That's off limits.

O'ROURKE: Miss O'Hara, this is <u>great</u>! You've already given me a glimpse of your legendary feistiness, which leads me to my next question. Did you really punch director John Farrow in the face?

O'HARA: I'd prefer to leave that story alone.

O'ROURKE: How about off the record?

O'HARA: Off the record, I slugged that bastard good and hard. I meant that punch for him and every other Hollywood mogul who tried to get his hands on this... this well-endowed Irish Catholic body. (*She smiles and strikes a pose while sitting.*)

O'ROURKE (*After he bursts out laughing.*): Do you think that punch may have hurt your career?

O'HARA: Probably, but my iron-willed Irish mother told me to live life on my own terms, and no one in Hollywood was ever going to change that.

*O'ROURKE abruptly stands, then paces in a frenetic manner.*

O'ROURKE: Good for you, Miss O'Hara! Good for you! Like I said, this is <u>great</u>!

O'HARA: Martin, are... are you all right? (*He looks confused, then stops pacing.*)

O'ROURKE: Yes. I... I mean, no. (*Sighs.*) Miss O'Hara, I'm sorry, but I have a confession to make.

O'HARA (*Suddenly concerned.*): What kind of confession?

O'ROURKE (*Forlornly.*). I don't write for the <u>L.A. Times</u> anymore. I did when I set up this interview with your secretary, but I got laid off a few hours ago.

O'HARA: Then I'm confused. Why are you here?

O'ROURKE (*Sighs.*). Because I've idolized you ever since I was twelve. That's when I saw you in <u>The Hunchback of Notre Dame</u>. I've watched that movie so many times I've lost count.

O'HARA (*Slowly rising.*): Martin, I appreciate all of your compliments, I really do, but you're starting to scare me a little. I think you should . . . yes, you should go now.

O'ROURKE: I understand. (*He stuffs his notebook in his briefcase.*) I'm sorry if I upset you. I just thought you should know there's someone out there who thinks you're the greatest actress—no, the greatest movie star—the world has ever seen. Thank you for your time. I promise to never bother you again. (*He smiles grimly, then heads for the door.*)

O'HARA (*Hesitates.*): Martin, wait. (*He turns back.*) Maybe I shouldn't have been so harsh. Would you like to stay and finish your interview? Perhaps you can... who know, perhaps you can get it published somewhere else.

O'ROURKE: Oh, Miss O'Hara, I'd really appreciate that. And I promise to be on my best behavior. I'll even stand on the other side of the room, if that'll make you feel more comfortable. (*As he speaks, he awkwardly walks across the room.*)

O'HARA (*Chuckling.*): That won't be necessary. So go ahead; ask me anything you'd like. And please sit.

O'ROURKE (*Smiling.*): Thanks, but I think better when I'm standing.

O'HARA: Suit yourself. (*She sits back in the chair.*) Ready when you are.

O'ROURKE: How difficult was it to walk away from Hollywood while you were still in your prime?

O'HARA (*Reflecting.*): It was one of the most difficult decisions of my life.

O'ROURKE: I thought so, but do you mind explaining?

O'HARA: Well, it was difficult because I had worked so hard to convince myself that I didn't care about the limelight, but, the truth is, I did—and I still do. Pathetic, huh? I'm 70 years old and still crave fame. (*Her voice quivering.*) And I hate myself for it. (*After she composes herself.*) I wouldn't wish fame on my worst enemy. It's like a drug that never leaves your system. (*Sighs.*) I discovered that ugly truth right after the studios stopped calling.

O'ROURKE: But... but <u>you're</u> the one who shunned Hollywood, not the other way around.

O'HARA: That's what I kept telling myself. But the fact is by the time I hit my late 40s, the phones had already started growing quiet.

*O'ROURKE retrieves his briefcase and stuffs his notebook in it.*

O'HARA (*Cont.*): What are you doing?

O'ROURKE: I can't write this.

O'HARA: Why not?

O'ROURKE: It's too personal.

O'HARA: But I want you to write it. I'm finally ready for people to know the truth.

O'ROURKE: Then find another journalist.

O'HARA: I'm confused. I thought this was the article you wanted to write.

O'ROURKE: Not anymore. Miss O'Hara, I'm won't let you destroy the image I have of you in my head.

O'HARA: Martin, you need to shed whatever illusions you have about me. You have no idea how many mistakes I've made in my life. No idea.

O'ROURKE: Name one.

O'HARA: That I should've been a better mother to Bron. My own mother was a spectacular role model—always there, always ready with some homespun piece of advice—but I failed my daughter in so many ways. I was too busy chasing fame. (*She rises, picks up a script from the floor and throws it on the coffee table.*) And now look at me—an actress well past her prime, still hoping her fans will find her... relevant.

O'ROURKE: Please don't talk that way.

O'HARA: Why? So you can carry on with your little fantasy, pretending I'm someone I'm not.

O'ROURKE: No, because my life is already sad enough, and now I've made yours sad as well.

> *O'HARA takes the script on the table and throws it into a trash can. She continues to toss out the other scripts as she speaks.*

O'HARA: You haven't made me sad, Martin. You've actually done just the opposite; you've jolted me back to reality.

O'ROURKE: How so?

O'HARA: By making me realize what a *fool* I've been.

O'ROURKE: I'm not sure what to say.

O'HARA: Good, then it's my turn: Why did you fail as a screenwriter?

O'ROURKE: A little thing called lack of talent, I suppose.

O'HARA: I don't believe you. You actually seem quite insightful; a little odd, perhaps... (*She chuckles at her own joke.*) but definitely insightful.

O'ROURKE: The truth is I do have some talent, at least according to my former agent. Last year, he swore to me that my most recent script was producible, but I told him not to distribute it. By that point, I had already experienced too many rejections,

O'HARA: How many screenplays have you written?

O'ROURKE: Five. The first three were okay; the fourth was good; the last one was damn good.

O'HARA: What was it about?

O'ROURKE (*After first looking away.*): I'd rather not say.

O'HARA (*Forcefully.*): What is it about, Martin?

O'ROURKE (*Hesitating.*): A fifty-year-old actress who leaves a remarkable career behind and never looks back.

O'HARA: You wrote a screenplay about... me?

O'ROURKE: Not about you directly, but it was inspired by how I saw your life unfolding.

O'HARA (*After an awkward silence.*): Send me a copy.

O'ROURKE: Why? Are you going to sue me?

O'HARA: No. If it's as good as you say, then I'll try to help you get it produced.

O'ROURKE: But you just told me that my ending doesn't ring true.

O'HARA: When's the last time someone in Hollywood actually cared about the truth?

O'ROURKE: You mean, you'd... you'd really help me, even though we just met? Even though I just lied to you?

O'HARA: Of course I'll help you. I already told you, I like you, Martin. And you're definitely seem like someone who deserves a break.

*Fighting back his emotions, O'ROURKE starts to speak, but stops. O'HARA then reaches out and takes his hand in hers.*

O'HARA (*Cont.*): Please—let me help you, if I can.

O'ROURKE: I'm touched, Miss O'Hara. I truly am.

O'HARA: By what?

O'ROURKE: The, ah... the timeless beauty of a setting sun.

*As the lights fade, O'HARA holds his hand to her face, then gives him a hug and pats his back, much as a mother might do to her child.*

*Blackout.*

### END OF PLAY

# Silences

## by

## Mark E. Leib

Directed by James Thaggard
with
Joshua Brin as Ralph
Nancy Denton as Susan

CHARACTERS
RALPH, a man, any age.

SUSAN, a woman of like age to RALPH.

SETTING
An outdoor café.

TIME
The present.

*RALPH and SUSAN sit at a table in the café, sipping their coffee quietly.*

RALPH (*After a brief period of silence.*): Then there's the silence when you've been stopped by a cop. You know you were speeding, you're sure you're gonna get a ticket, he's turned off his siren and you're just watching him get out of his car in the rearview mirror. And the headlights: you're seeing his headlights. And all you can do is sorta...

*He tries to show what the silence is like.*

SUSAN: I've done that one.

RALPH: Yeah, but you had your looks and your feminine wiles. You were thinking how to get out of it.

SUSAN: My feminine wiles didn't spare me a $200 ticket.

RALPH: When you're a guy you're aware that there's no wiggle room whatever. That's why the silence is so intense. It's like... doom. In black boots. All that's left is the details.

SUSAN: I still don't think it's that different. Anyway, how about: the silence of the ocean. From your hotel window, at midnight. You look out into the distance, but it's such a calm night that though you can see the moon reflecting on the water's surface, you can't hear a thing. No waves crashing. No radios blaring. Just the moon on the water and...

*She models the silence.*

RALPH: Lovely.

SUSAN: Really lovely.

RALPH: Are there people on the beach?

SUSAN: You don't see any. If there are, they're as silent as the ocean.

RALPH: Nice. That's one of your best ones.

SUSAN: Yeah. Just listen again...

*She models the silence again.*

RALPH: All right, I've got one. The silence of grief.

SUSAN: Too depressing.

RALPH: Life is depressing sometimes. When my mother was buried. The standing by the coffin. The knowledge that this person who affected your life so much even from before you were born, this person will never speak to you again, will never hassle you again, will never offer you a glass of wine or a cheese Danish or a napkin. All that's left now is the coffin. And you stand there looking at it like...

*He tries to show what the silence is like.*

SUSAN: That's too hard.

RALPH: Life is hard sometimes.

SUSAN: How about the silence of sunrise in Pigeon Forge, Tennessee. Where the mountains are so high, you can't see the sun till eleven a.m. And when it appears, over the mountain, it's because it's climbed higher than the Smokies, and you just look at it grateful that it's surpassed that last mountain and presented itself for you. The silence of...

*She models the silence.*

RALPH: Nice.

SUSAN: So... miraculous. And though you knew it would happen, still unpredictable.

*Pause.*

RALPH: Listen...

SUSAN: You been to Pigeon Forge?

RALPH: I missed it.

SUSAN: That's where Dollywood is. The Dolly Parton theme park. Right near Gatlinburg. I was there with Ed a couple of years ago.

RALPH: Amazing Ed.

SUSAN: We had a pretty good time when we weren't arguing.

RALPH: Angry old Ed. (*Pause.*) Listen, I was walking downtown yesterday...

SUSAN: This is too much fun.

RALPH: I was downtown right by a Starbucks...

SUSAN: When you've wanted something, could be a really pricey dress, or shoes or a car, let's say it's a car. You've always wanted a Jaguar, you've always thought you'd never own one, and then you have a good week at the brokerage and the first thing you do is go to the auto showroom and buy an amazingly sleek, gray Jaguar MK54 and you fill out all the papers, and they hand you the keys, and then you get in your Jaguar, all yours now, you close the door, look around. And it's like...

*She tries to show what the silence is like.*

RALPH: I've got something to say here.

SUSAN: We really shouldn't stop: The silence of exhaustion. You've played three good sets of tennis, you can hardly move you're so sore, you lie down on the bench and wipe the sweat off your face, let your deep breathing turn into shallow and finally the silence. Just like...

*She tries to show the silence.*

RALPH: Accomplishment.

SUSAN: Yeah. You've had a real workout.

RALPH: You're tired but you're proud.

SUSAN: Yeah: it's a proud silence.

*Pause.*

RALPH: The silence of... of being in love. And walking downtown near Starbucks, a few tables and chairs right out there on the terrace. And thinking you see the woman you're crazy about. At a table. And she doesn't see you.

SUSAN: Now, that's a nice silence. The beloved from afar.

RALPH: Unfortunately, you notice... that she's not alone. That there's a man sitting across from her, someone you don't recognize. And you see her reaching across the table – and he's reaching across the table – and they've got their hands clasped together. Seeing that. Which is just like...

*He models the silence.*

SUSAN: That's rough.

RALPH: Yeah, it's rough.

SUSAN: It must feel pretty bad.

RALPH: Doesn't have to. There could be an explanation.

*Pause.*

SUSAN: Look, you're a real nice guy...

RALPH: Don't say this. Don't say this.

SUSAN: I so much enjoy spending time with you.

RALPH: Not <u>this</u> conversation, anything else...

SUSAN: Being that woman. Enjoying a cup of coffee and a cinnamon roll and a madeleine with a wonderful new friend. And realizing, with some regret perhaps, that those few minutes with that new person mean worlds to you more than you've been feeling with someone else maybe you've been seeing a few months. But feeling so grateful to that familiar someone, liking him so much, not wanting to hurt him, that all you've been able to do all this time is keep silent when the subject should have been broached.

RALPH: How long?

SUSAN: Three weeks?

RALPH: And you couldn't say so?

SUSAN: You know, sitting in that café, drinking coffee and talking, maybe she sees you out of the corner of her eye, and suddenly precisely at that moment she knows just what to do. So she reaches out for the hand of her new friend for the first time, and she knows you're watching, and she knows what you're thinking so she just sits there, grasping her new friend's hand. Kind of like this...

*She takes his hand and models the silence.*

RALPH: I'm falling from a height. And there's no bottom. I'm in freefall.

SUSAN: I'll help you. I'll cushion your landing.

RALPH: I can't... imagine... that I'll ever land. So much falling.

SUSAN: We'll just sit here for awhile. And I'll fall with you.

RALPH: For how long?

SUSAN: A while. Till you've... got your balance back.

*Pause.*

RALPH: If I'm not... in your mind... I'm nowhere.

SUSAN: You're in my mind. Always will be. I promise.

RALPH: I'm falling. I can't stop.

SUSAN: It's all right. Fall awhile.

*They sit quietly holding hands. She looks into his eyes, smiling. He looks at her, trying to hold back tears.*

*Silence.*

*Lights fade.*

*Blackout.*

**END OF PLAY**

# The Clown

## by

## Larry Hamm

Directed by Seva Anthony

with

Andrea Dovner as Natalie

Chris Hines as Billy

Chuck Conlon as The Clown

CHARACTERS
NATALIE, a woman, 28 to 38.

BILLY, a man of like age.

THE CLOWN, a man or woman, in white face with a red nose and a costume that should make the character appear gender neutral.

SETTING
A kitchen. A table sits UPSTAGE CENTER with a chair on either side. A birthday cake sits in the middle of the table. If possible, a full-sized swinging door can be positioned LEFT, but this may be indicated by pantomime.

TIME
Present day.

*NATALIE and THE CLOWN, wearing a noise maker (e.g. a bicycle horn, kazoo, triangle) on a string around his/her neck, enter RIGHT. Throughout the play, THE CLOWN should react to the dialogue, walking that fine line that exists between interacting with and upstaging the other characters.*

NATALIE: Thank you for coming to the backdoor. We want to make sure Janey's surprised.

*CLOWN honks twice.*

NATALIE: Did you have any problems finding the house?

*CLOWN honks once.*

NATALIE: Oh, I get it...you don't talk.

*CLOWN honks twice.*

NATALIE (*Unconvincingly.*): That's cute.

*CLOWN shrugs shoulders, feigns a blush.*

NATALIE: I thought it would be great if you could entertain the children until its time for me to bring out Janey's cake. I don't want to start until everyone's here, so I hope you don't mind waiting.

*CLOWN gestures thumbs up.*

NATALIE: Well, if you could stand over here (*Leads CLOWN UPSTAGE below table.*) out of the way, I'll be running in and out of the kitchen. Oh, and watch the cake. (*Walks LEFT.*) And, please don't come near the door. These swing open and Janey might see you. (*As NATALIE pantomimes cracking the door and looking out LEFT.*) Oh, that's wonderful... Margaret Porter is here. She's big in the Arts, you know. It's quite a coup getting her and her daughter at Janey's party.

NATALIE (*Cont.*): And, look, Juliana Rodriquez and Naomi Winters are here with their daughters. We'll have such a good ethnic mix. (*As she talks BILLY enters RIGHT and CROSSES to NATALIE, where BILLY embraces/grabs her from behind.*). Oh! (*Jumps.*)

BILLY: Hey, sweetheart.

NATALIE: Jeezus, Billy Yeardley, you scared the crap out of me.

BILLY: Don't worry, I'll make it up to you.

NATALIE (*Breaking away.*): I told you I don't want to see you anymore. not like that. Justin is getting suspicious.

BILLY (*Following.*): Oh, Natalie baby, you know you don't mean that.

NATALIE: I just can't take the chance of him finding out.

BILLY: C'mon, you know it's worth… (*Sees CLOWN.*). Who's that?

NATALIE: Just some clown. He's here for Janey's birthday party.

BILLY: But he heard us. Will he say anything?

NATALIE: Apparently not.

BILLY: Gawd, he looks kinda creepy.

   CLOWN *waves*

NATALIE: He's harmless.

   CLOWN *honks twice.*

BILLY: Are you sure?

NATALIE: Of course. You aren't one of those people afraid of clowns are you?

BILLY: Me?

NATALIE: You know, Coulrophobic?

BILLY (*Nervously.*): Killer what?

NATALIE: No, Coulrophobia is the fear of clowns.

BILLY (*Weakly.*): Ha. No.

NATALIE: Well, I promise this one won't hurt you. He's only here to do a few tricks for Janey's party. Make some balloon animals. Anyway, he's bonded.

BILLY: He's glued there?

NATALIE: No, the company he works for, *Par-tays by Pagliacci*, ensures him for theft, property damage, liability…

BILLY (*Looks suspiciously at CLOWN.*): That makes him sound dangerous.

*CLOWN waves.*

NATALIE: Hardly. Billy, you are so foolish, sometimes.

BILLY: Well, I'm sorry. It's just that I had this fantasy of throwing you down and having my way with you , but the other dude in the room has thrown me off my game.

NATALIE: I told you, <u>no more</u>. You've got to behave. And… do you really think that's a man?

BILLY: I dunno. I guess we could ask. Hey, are you a dude?

*CLOWN makes a body builder pose.*

NATALIE: There's your answer.

BILLY: Whatever the hell that means.

NATALIE: It doesn't matter what he or she is. I just need a clown to entertain a group of eight-year-olds for an hour. Which reminds me, I am the hostess and need to go make certain my guests are settling in. You might want to take this opportunity to leave. (*Exits LEFT.*)

BILLY (*After NATALIE's gone.*): That's not happening until I get what I came for. (*Walks to door LEFT, peeks out. Turns and looks at CLOWN.*) So, what are you all about?

*CLOWN shrugs.*

You are a dude, aren't you?

*CLOWN shrugs.*

It's kinda freaky, wearing makeup and shit.

*CLOWN shrugs.*

Are you some kind of peed-o-file?

*CLOWN shakes head "no" vigorously.*

I mean it's really odd to hang out with little kids, playing with balloons and such. Do you ride in one of those little cars?

*CLOWN honks once.*

What does that mean? Is that a "yes"?

*CLOWN honks once.*

BILLY (*Cont.*): Fuck. What does that mean?

*CLOWN shrugs.*

You're a pain in the ass. (*Returns LEFT to door.*)

*CLOWN honks twice.*

Um-um. (*Looking LEFT out door.*) I'll tell ya, clown boy, there are some nice-looking MILFs out there. Does that interest you? You know what I'm talking about, don't ya? Mothers I'd Love to...

*CLOWN quickly honks twice.*

Yeah, I figured you'd know. (*To CLOWN.*) You've got a nice gig for meetin' 'em. But I don't know that getup is going to move you from meetin' to mountin'. (*Looking out door again.*) Me, I'm exactly what they want. Exactly what they need. Natalie, she's been all over me for weeks. And, oh yeah, there's Sin-your-eata Rodriquez. Those Latinas all have such nice hips and live for a toss. Comes from years of Catholic breeding.

*CLOWN throws up hands in disgust.*

What's the matter? (*To CLOWN.*) You a little sense-tive? You one of those illegals hiding behind some paint to take our jobs? Popping out bastards on this side of the border to make 'em sit-zens?

*CLOWN shrugs shoulders, honks once.*

I didn't think so, but they're everywhere you know. Even Rodriquez in there probably doesn't have a green card. None of 'em do. They brought down our econ-mee with their cheap labor and getting all that free hospital care. Who do you think pays for that? We do. That's who.

NATALIE (*Entering through door LEFT.*): What are you still doing here?

BILLY: Oh, baby. (*Changing demeanor instantly.*) You know you don't want me to leave.

NATALIE: Yes, I do. We can't do this anymore.

BILLY (*Approaches her.*): You don't mean that.

NATALIE: Please, Billy. (*BILLY embraces her and begins to kiss her neck.*) Please.

BILLY: I want you, baby.

NATALIE: No.

BILLY: C'mon, the clown won't mind. He's some kind of pervert anyway.

NATALIE (*Pushing away.*): It's my daughter's birthday party!

BILLY: I just thought we'd celebrate, too. (*Thinking.*) Hey! You need something pretty to make you feel better. I've got a present for you in the car.

NATALIE: I don't need anything...

BILLY: I'll be right back. (*Exits RIGHT.*)

NATALIE: My god, what have I gotten myself into?

*CLOWN honks twice, wags finger at her.*

Are you judging me?

*CLOWN shakes head, "no."*

That's good... because you have no idea what it's like being married to a man who works 60 hours a week and is always too tired when he is home to do anything other than plop his ass in front of a TV. Add a child who demands most of your time and energy to that picture and you're looking at a world where everything is flowing out of you and nothing's flowing in.

*CLOWN just looks at her.*

You don't get it, do you?

*CLOWN honks twice.*

No, I don't think you do. Billy's an asshole, but he doesn't take a lot of work and he feels good at the time. He's fun. Sometimes that's all you need.

*CLOWN does "happy hands" (palms out, fingers spread, shaking back and forth).*

Right. You should know what fun means to a person. (*Sits and CLOWN sits.*) My whole life is remembering or planning. I don't like looking back or looking forward all the time. Sometimes I want to just be right here right now. See, you understand. I didn't want to be unfaithful. I didn't really even want Billy Yeardley. I just wanted something else. Something for me.

*CLOWN points right to where BILLY exited, and gestures, "why?"*

You're right. Billy was a big mistake. And now I don't know how to get out of it. I wish I could undo it, but I wish I could go back ten years and undo all of this.

*CLOWN gestures "poof" with hands and then wipes hands.*

NATALIE (*Cont.*): But how?

*CLOWN points to his/her heart.*

Following my heart?

*CLOWN makes palms down wavering motion to indicate "not quite."*

Being true to myself?

*CLOWN honks twice, rises and goes to her.*

But who am I? I don't have a clue where to start?

*CLOWN places hand on her shoulder, points to her heart again.*

I know. I just have to keep being truthful to myself and everyone. You know that's going to disrupt everything?

*CLOWN nods head, "yes."*

But it's the only way to get things right, isn't it? The only person in that room out there I care about is Janey, and she has never even truly met me. I'm hiding in here because I don't want to talk with any of them. Margie Porter and the Arts? Hell, real art would scare the shit out of everyone in this town. And, I don't know an ethnic mix from trail mix. I don't really know anyone, but I want to. I do.

BILLY (*Enters RIGHT.*): Baby, come here. I've got something pretty for you.

NATALIE (*Crossing down to him.*): Billy, that isn't going to change anything.

BILLY: Here, I want you to have this.

NATALIE: Aw, Billy, a gold heart. That's sweet, but... with an inscription. This is really... E Y?

BILLY: Ever Yours, baby.

NATALIE: Or Estelle Yeardley. This is your wife's!

BILLY: Not anymore.

NATALIE (*Handing the heart back.*): You are a total idiot. (*To CLOWN.*) I feel good. I'm ready to talk to Justin now, too. I'm starting over, but I'm doing it for the first time.

*CLOWN honks twice.*

BILLY: Oh, you're getting advice from a clown now?

NATALIE: Yes, I've found that he's a sympathetic listener.

BILLY: Oh yeah, he's *simplethetic*. Walking around with a smile on his face, sticking his red nose in other people's business. Acting like the world is supposed to be some happy place like one of those bleeding heart liberals. (*To CLOWN.*) That's it, isn't it? You think the rest of us ought to take lessons from you?

*CLOWN shrugs.*

Well, we don't want to. We've got it all under control here. If people like you would just follow the rules, instead of making a joke of everything.

NATALIE: Please don't attack the clown.

BILLY: What the hell. Are you on his side? That's the way they work, you know. They start off with their liberal media and their liberal schools teaching everyone liberal ideas, and then they send in the clowns. Oh sure, he's got a white face, but inside he's got colored ideas. And those spread like wildfire. Pretty soon it will be all out war. Like it says in Revulations, it will be them against us.

*CLOWN goes to BILLY, shaking his head sadly.*

BILLY: (*Continues, backing away.*) Don't touch me. I do own a gun.

*CLOWN gestures for BILLY to lean toward him/her.*

What do you want from me? (*BILLY leans down.*)

*CLOWN kisses BILLY on the forehead.*

CLOWN: Don't be so afraid. (*Looks at* NATALIE, *points toward door LEFT.*)

NATALIE: Oh, yes. Please join the children. Make them laugh. I'll be right out with the cake.

*CLOWN gives NATALIE thumbs up, exits LEFT.*

BILLY: That was one weird fucking clown.

NATALIE: Aren't we all?

*Lights fade.*

*Blackout.*

END OF PLAY

## *Student Play Festival Winner 2016*

# Brothers in Arms

### by

### Julien Freij

Directed by Preston Boyd
with
Tom Aposporos as Old Hans
Alex Beach as Hans
Jacob Schweighofer as Peter
Tami Vaughan as Frau Schmidt

## Characters

OLD HANS, a man, 60s.

HANS, a man, 18.

PETER, a man, 18.

MR. SCHMIDT, a man, 60s.

BRITISH SOLDIER, a man, early 20s.

## Setting
Germany

## Time
World War I

*Lights up on OLD HANS. He stands CENTER, peering out into the audience.*

OLD HANS (*Adjusting his glasses.*): Good morning, lads. Today I want to discuss some of the horrible tragedies of WWI. But before I do, let me tell you about how my friend Peter and I decided to fight for the Kaiser. We were both 8, sitting in a classroom, much like you.

*OLD HANS steps off stage. Cue flashback, while the song "O' Tannenbaum" plays offstage. Lights up on MR. SCHMIDT, who stands behind a table, talking to his class. PETER is asleep with his head resting on his desk, while HANS doodles in a notebook.*

MR. SCHMIDT (*Pounding his fist on the table.*): It is your <u>sacred</u> duty as able bodied young Germans to fight for the fatherland! The Kaiser himself demands your allegiance and patriotism! And so do I.

*PETER wakes up and looks confused.*

PETER: Mom, five more minutes. Please!

*HANS thunks his friend on the head.*

PETER (*Continuing, lifts his head up and puts on his glasses.*): What'd I miss?

HANS: He's at it again.

PETER: The war? Who cares? It's all the guy talks about.

MR. SCHMIDT: Gentlemen, you'll not only fight the British and French, but you'll also embark on adventures that I cannot even begin to describe.

*Sitting upright, HANS and PETER pay closer attention.*

PETER (*Nudges HANS.*) Did you hear that, Hans? Maybe the old codger has something important to say for a change.

HANS: Yeah, adventure. Sounds, um, heroic. I'll show those Limies and Frogs a thing or two. (*He strikes a pose, flexing his muscles.*) What do you think?

PETER: I think the only thing you can show them are those flimsy arms of yours. (*Laughs to himself.*)

HANS: At least I can pass all my classes, Mr. D+.

MR. SCHMIDT: Hans! Peter! Pay attention! Don't make me warn you again!

HANS: Sorry, sir, we were just, ah, just wondering where the nearest enlistment center was.

PETER: That's right!

MR. SCHMIDT (*He adjusts his bow tie.*): Glad to hear of your eagerness, lads! Come see me after class. I have all the paperwork right here.

*The bell rings.*

MR. SCHMIDT (*Cont.*): Okay, class dismissed. I expect every one of you lads to follow in the footsteps of Hans and Peter!

*HANS and PETER walk forward.*

PETER: So, Hans, how long do you think it'll take before we start fighting?

HANS: How about we enlist first, then go grab a snack. I'm starving.

*They arrive at MR. SCHMIDT's desk.*

MR. SCHMIDT: First ones!

HANS: Yes, Sir. You know, Peter and me. Always eager to show our patriotism.

MR. SCHMIDT (*He's skeptical, so he adjusts his glasses and glares at the boys before smiling.*) Yes, well, right. Good for you! (*He opens a folder and takes out a few forms.*) Please sign your names here. (*He points to separate sheets of paper, where each one signs.*) All right. Take these forms home and get your parents to sign. They'll be proud of your commitment.

HANS: Yes, Sir. You know, Peter and me, always eager to show our... our patriotism.

MR. SCHMIDT: You'll be notified within a few weeks where to report for duty. And don't worry, the Kaiser is sure the war will be over by Christmas.

*HANS, PETER, and MR. SCHMIDT exit, as the song "Over There!" plays in the background.*

*OLD HANS reenters.*

OLD HANS: My friend Peter and I had no idea what we were getting into. Neither did the rest of our friends. The <u>horrors</u> we witnessed on the western front were beyond description. We were trapped in the trenches for weeks on end. There was no chance to escape. None at all.

*OLD HANS exits, as the song "Over There!" plays again in the background. Lights up on PETER and HANS, who are crouched behind a small wooden barrier. The sounds of gunfire and explosions can be heard at regular intervals offstage. Each time this happens, both boys get jumpy, especially PETER.*

HANS: Peter, are you all right?

PETER: No, Hans. I'm not. (*Scared, shaking.*) This isn't what they promised us. It's gonna be Christmas tomorrow, and this war is nowhere near being over.

HANS: I know, Peter. Our teachers...our parents...the Kaiser, they all lied to us. Everyone of them.

PETER: This isn't an adventure. It's a massacre.

HANS: How many of our classmates are left, do you know?

PETER (*With sadness.*): Just us, I think.

*After a solemn pause, we hear more sounds of gunfire and bombs.*

HANS: "Dulce et Decorum Est Pro patria Mori."

PETER: What's that?

HANS: It's from Horace, the Roman poet. We learned it last year in Latin. "It is sweet and fitting to die for one's country."

PETER (*Fighting back tears.*): That's complete bullshit and... and you know it!

HANS: I know, Peter. (*Pause.*) I don't know why it came to me just now.

PETER (*Still shaking*): I don't care. I'm scared, Hans. I just wanna go home.

HANS: I do too, but our only way out is to keep fighting. Don't you quit on me.

PETER: I'm finished, Hans. I... I can't go on. (*Starts to break down.*)

HANS: What are you talking about? Peter, pull yourself together! If you don't, you're going to end up out there with those unlucky bastards in No Man's Land. (*He points to the battlefield.*)

*PETER doesn't respond. He just stares off into space. More sounds of gunfire and bombs.*

HANS (*Cont.*): Here, I grabbed a a bottle of brandy from the commandant's table when he wasn't looking.

*He opens a small bottle and hands it to PETER, who takes large frantic gulps.*

HANS (*Cont.*): Easy, Easy! Don't drink the whole thing. (*He grabs the bottle back from PETER.*) If you get drunk, you'll never get make it of this hellhole.

PETER: What if this is our last battle, Hans? Have you ever thought about that? What if we never make it back home?

HANS: Don't talk like that, Peter.

PETER: Why not? (*He looks up.*) Grenade!

*HANS and PETER duck down at the same time as we hear a loud explosion offstage.*

HANS: That was a close one.

PETER: They're all close ones.

HANS: You're right.

PETER: Let's run for it. What do you say? Get out while there's still a chance.

HANS: No! That doesn't make any sense.

PETER: Then I'm leaving without you.

HANS: If you desert now, they'll shoot you in the back.

PETER: I don't care. I can't stay in this trench anymore. I'm going to lose my mind if I do.

HANS: Wait! Do you hear that?

*The sound of a battle cry rings out offstage.*

PETER: Those damn Brits. They're charging us again.

HANS: They must be mad. They'll be sitting ducks.

*PETER and HANS grab their rifles, stand up and shoot, then duck back down.*

HANS (*Cont.*): I'm getting sick of all this back and forth shit.

PETER: If they're charging us, that means it'll be our turn soon.

HANS: Don't worry. When we go, just stay by my side. I'll protect you.

PETER: Didn't you say the same thing to Franz and Schneider last week? Now look where they are. (*He points out into No Man's Land.*)

HANS (*Barking.*): Hey! At least I tried.

PETER: I'm sorry, Hans, I know you did your best, which is more than anyone else did.

HANS: I'm sorry I yelled at you. Let's not argue, okay?

PETER: Sure.

> *Offstage, someone barks an order in German, which is followed by lots of men yelling offstage.*

PETER (*Cont.*): There is it is—the order for our counter-charge. (*Gulps.*) Let's get this over with.

> *HANS and PETER climb over the barrier and run offstage, screaming a battle cry as they do so. Sounds of gunfire and men screaming are heard offstage. A few moments later HANS reenters, but he's by himself.*

HANS: (*He sighs as he climbs back into the trench.*): Wow! We survived again! Thank mercy. (*He looks around and seems confused. Frantically.*) Peter? Peter!

> *The shooting stops. HANS runs back and forth in the trench yelling PETER's name.*

HANS (*Cont.*): Peter! Peter! Where are you?

> *After an awkward sound of silence, the sounds of the British soldiers singing "Oh, Christmas Tree" can be heard offstage. HANS seems confused. He climbs over the barrier, carrying his rifle. When he sees an unarmed BRITISH SOLDIER, HANS points his rifle at him.*

BRITISH SOLDIER (*With his arms raised.*): Hey! Hey! Relax. Please put your gun down. Have you not heard the news?

HANS: What news?

BRITISH SOLDIER: There's been a truce called.

HANS: I don't believe you. (*His rifle is still raised.*)

BRITISH SOLDIER: They're calling it the "Christmas Truce."

HANS: What are you talking about?

BRITISH SOLDIER: It's true. Some men are singing, and over there, some are playing football. Do you want to join in?

HANS: No. I... I have to find my friend Peter. He didn't make it back into the trench after the last charge. (*HANS lowers his rifle.*)

BRITISH SOLDIER: What does he look like?

HANS: He's my size. Dark hair. And he wears glasses.

BRITISH SOLDIER: Sorry, I haven't seen any German who looks like that.

*The BRITISH SOLDIER pulls out a cigarette and he offers it to HANS.*

BRITISH SOLDIER: Want one?

HANS: Yeah, sure.

*HANS takes the cigarette, but he drops it because his hands are shaking. The BRITISH SOLDIER picks it up and gives it back to him.*

BRITISH SOLDIER: Do you want me to help you find your friend?

HANS: Please.

BRITISH SOLDIER: What's his name, again?

HANS: Peter.

*As they walk off together, they both call out PETER's name, but then they head off in separate directions. As they do so, we hear German soldiers singing "O' Tannenbaum" offstage. HANS comes across a body that is slumped behind some wooden debris. He turns it over and sees that it's PETER.*

HANS (*Shocked*): Peter! Peter, are you all right?

*Lying in HANS's lap, PETER opens his eyes slowly and gasps for breath.*

HANS (*Cont.*): Peter! It's me, Hans. Please... please talk to me.

*After PETER doesn't respond, HANS opens up PETER's jacket, then HANS looks up and realizes he has blood all over his hands.*

PETER (*Gasps, then shaking.*): Hans? Is it over? Did we win?

HANS: Sure, Peter, the war is... it's... it's all over. We won! We did it!

PETER: The Kaiser should be... he should be happy.

HANS: Stay here, Peter, while I go get some help.

PETER (PETER *grabs HANS's arm.*): No. Don't go. It's too late.

HANS (*His voice cracks with emotion.*): No! No, Peter, it's not. I promise.

PETER: Why, Hans? Why did we decide to fight?

HANS: I don't know, Peter. Maybe it's because we were young and naive. But it doesn't matter. I'm gonna get you home. I... I promise.

*We again hear the German soldiers singing "O' Tannenbaum" offstage.*

PETER: What's that?

HANS: You wouldn't believe it. The Germans and British are singing Christmas carols together. Please rest up, while I go find the medic.

*PETER suddenly sits up and grabs HANS by the arm.*

PETER: When you get back home, you tell that bastard teacher of ours that he was wrong—wrong about everything.

*PETER's body suddenly slumps back down into HANS's lap. HANS shakes PETER's body, but it does not move.*

HANS: Peter! Oh, Peter!

*As HANS fights back tears, the BRITISH SOLDIER returns.*

BRITISH SOLDIER (*Solemnly.*): Is that your friend?

*HANS nods. As HANS stands to composes himself, the BRITISH SOLDIER reaches down and takes PETER's dog tags, then gives them to HANS. HANS and the BRITISH SOLDIER pick up PETER's body and slowly exit.*

*Offstage we hear both "Oh, Christmas Tree" and "O' Tannenbaum" sung at the same time. The lights dim.*

*OLD HANS walks back onstage and addresses the audience.*

OLD HANS: War is a bitter and savage institution. It always was. It always will be. Man killing his fellow man for what? A flag? Personal glory for the leaders? My greatest regret in life is that I tried to protect my friend Peter, but failed. Still, I'll... I'll never forget our friendship or his laughter. The poet Horace once wrote, "Dulce et Decorum Est Pro patria Mori." "It's sweet and fitting to die for one's country." There was nothing "sweet or fitting" about Peter's death. Nothing at all.

*Lights fade.*

*Blackout.*

END OF PLAY

# Ten-Minute Play Festival

# 2017

**Dates:** May 4th, 5th, 6th, and 7th, 2017

**Location:** Jane B. Cook Theatre, Asolo/FSU Center for the Performing Arts, Sarasota

**Best Play Award**

    The Best Ten Minutes Ever by Dylan Jones

**Runner-Up/Honorable Mention**

    Always by Stephen Cooper

**Audience Favorite**

    I'm Dead When I Say I'm Dead by Ron Pantello

**Student Playwriting Festival Winner**

    Amazing Grace by Luke Valadie
                        St. Stephens Episcopal School

## *2017 Best Play*

# The Best Ten Minutes Ever

by

## Dylan H. Jones

Directed by Sara Logan

with

Phillip Troyer as Eli/Don

Johana Davila as Barbara/Anne

Sandra Musicante as Kay

CHARACTERS
BARBARA/ANNE, a woman, in her mid-20s.

ELI/DON, a man, in his mid-20s.

KAY, a woman, 60s to 70s.

SETTING
A couch with a short table in front.

TIME
The present.

*Lights up on BARBARA, a woman in her mid-20s in basic millennial garb, sitting on the couch, holding a pregnancy test and staring at her iPhone. She looks deep in thought. From offstage a door slams and a voice calls out to her.*

ELI (*Offstage.*): Barbara? You here?

*BARBARA quickly puts the phone and test down, then starts to raise them again, then hides them away. It is very mechanical. She coughs and responds, overly loud.*

BARBARA: Yup! In the living room, Eli.

*ELI enters; he is the same age as her, with a messenger bag over his shoulder and wearing the same kind of generic, label-less clothes she wears.*

ELI: Hey, I tried to rush...

BARBARA (*Overlapping as he enters.*): I was just text...

*They stop, and then start again, saying the exact same thing.*

ELI: I tried to...

BARBARA: I was just...

*They stop, then laugh, but it's weirdly forced, as if they were both expected to laugh there. Eli sits down next to her, removing his messenger bag.*

ELI: You go, Barb.

BARBARA: No, there's... it's nothing to, uh, go, I was just, texting you, and... here you are.

ELI: Yeah. (*Pause.*) So?

BARBARA: So... (*Overly dramatic deep breath.*) I'm...

ELI: You're...?

BARBARA (*Nodding slowly*): I... I am.

ELI: You are?!

BARBARA: Yes. (*More enthusiastically.*) Yes, Eli!

ELI: Honey, oh my god!

> *He leans over to hug her; she flinches and it winds up being awkward, though she returns it.*

BARBARA: I tested twice.

ELI: Did you use one of those new... one of those... (*Pause, suddenly turning to the audience and with a complete shift in character.*) Line?

KAY (*Offstage, a beleaguered female growl.*): Oh for Christ's sake!

> *KAY storms onstage, preferably from the audience; she is older than the other two by about forty years, and she has a very distinctive personal style, like a turquoise Navajo robe and mismatched earrings or something. ELI and BARBARA—actually, DON and ANNE—scoot away from each other unconsciously, DON looking guilty and ANNE looks exasperated.*

KAY (*Cont.*): Don, what did we say yesterday?

ELI/DON: Uh...

KAY: <u>What</u> did we say? We said <u>today</u>, absolutely, positively, <u>no more</u> calling for lines!

DON: Well, but... what if I can't remember the line?

KAY: You have to! The festival opens tonight, we don't have any more <u>time</u>!

DON: But what if I <u>can't</u>?!

BARBARA/ANNE: Improvise, dumbass!

KAY (*Violently gesturing at Anne.*): You! Zip it! Do <u>not</u> give my actor a note, got it?

ANNE: But Kay—!

KAY: <u>Shut up</u>, Anne! (*Deep breath.*) I know. Okay? <u>I know</u>. It's my own damned fault for casting a couple. But you two have <u>got</u> to pull your heads out of your asses and get this shit together. Got it? (*Short beat.*) <u>Got it</u>?!

ANNE & DON: Yeah...

KAY (*Softening slightly.*): Look... I understand. I get it. (*Full-on Amanda Wingfield.*) When I dated Robert Goulet, it was absolute shit when we were fighting during a show—!

ANNE: You dated Robert Goulet?

DON (*Overlapping by a split-second.*): Who's Robert Goulet?

> *The women stare at DON, who does a weird little shrug and inches away from them.*

KAY (*Pushing on.*): You have to separate the play from reality. Do you understand that? It's like... the opposite of Method. Or Meisner. Or Chubbuck. Or... whateverthehell it doesn't matter, the point is, learn the lines. Learn the lines. Learn... the freakin'... lines.

ANNE & DON (*Finishing with her on the last part, nodding.*): Freakin'... lines.

KAY: Good. Yes. Okay. (*Deep breath.*) I need a Danish. Or chocolate. Or a chocolate-covered Danish. Just... run lines with each other. No emotion, remember what we talked about: the lines become integral, and then the emotion is added on after, like butter on a potato. Commence!

> *KAY exits out through the audience, leaving ANNE and DON alone. They don't look at each other, and stand and move away from one another.*

ANNE: Alright. Let's just... like she said, run lines. No emotion. Whenever you're ready.

DON/ELI: Okay. (*Deep breath, overwrought preparation, then, deadpan.*) Barbara. You here.

ANNE/BARBARA (*A little nod, then, deadpan.*): Yup. In the living room, Eli.

ELI: Hey, I tried to rush...

BARBARA (*Overlapping.*): I was just text...

ELI (*Short pause.*): I tried to...

BARBARA (*Short pause.*): I was just...

> *They stop, then laugh, both of them just saying the word "Ha" in monotone.*

ELI: You go Barb.

BARBARA: No, it's nothing... (*Pause.*) I was just texting you and... here you are.

ELI: Yeah. (*Pause.*) So.

BARBARA: So I'm...

ELI: You're…

BARBARA: I. I am.

ELI: You are.

BARBARA: Yes. Yes, Eli.

ELI: Honey. Oh my god—

*Instinctively he leans over to hug her; she flinches and he stops himself, breaking character.*

ELI/DON (*Cont.*): S-sorry.

ANNE (*Annoyed*): No, don't, just—go on.

*He takes a moment, breathes, and starts again, deadpan.*

ELI: Honey, oh my god.

ANNE/BARBARA (*Back to deadpan, too.*): I tested twice.

ELI: Did you use one of those new… GPS ones with email and… uh, and stuff.

BARBARA (*Trying to stay monotone, but getting frustrated.*): No. Those things were a fortune. Just the old-fashioned stick.

ELI: So that's why you've been off so lately. (*Beat.*) <u>So</u> off, lately. (*Beat.*) I'm sorry I didn't… (*Long pause, while BARBARA glares at him; then, suddenly clapping, excited.*) <u>two and two</u>! Put two and two together. (*Beat, seeing her look, back to deadpan.*) Well I mean we sort of did.

BARBARA (*Punching him, harder than she should.*): Stop. But. Do you want the baby.

ELI: Of course.

BARBARA: No. Think about it. Just really think. For a minute.

ELI: Okay. Well. It's scary.

BARBARA: Yeah.

ELI: We're only 25. There's a lot of debt ahead of us.

BARBARA: Keep going.

ELI: Car payments. Insurance. We'd have to start saving for college.

ANNE/BARBARA (*Beat; with inflection.*): Now? (*Beat; sighing in exasperation.*) Your line is—never mind. (*More annoyed than deadpan from now on.*) Now you see it.

ELI: So. You've been going through all of this in your head without me.

BARBARA: Basically.

ELI: Why.

BARBARA: Because I'm the one who knows. And you're so carefree and forgetful and I (*Briefly sarcastically.*) "love" that. And I wasn't sure if you wanted it. For real. The responsibility.

ELI/DON (*Annoyed with her attitude, less deadpan.*): Well, I do. It sounds flippant, I might as well say I plan to stay home during Lamaze class and... and eat snacks in the Waiting Room. But I want to know more. I want to... (*Long pause; out-of-character.*) Shit! I can never get this... (*Trying to get back in.*) I... I want—

ANNE/BARBARA (*Way less deadpan.*): I want you not to worry that <u>I'm</u> going—

ELI (*Stopping her with a curt gesture, abandoning the pretense of monotone.*): Yes, <u>thank you</u>; I want you not to worrythatI'mgoingtoworry. Yes. Got it.

BARBARA (*Really done with this charade.*): Okay. Okay then.

ELI: I love you Barb.

BARBARA: I love you too, Eli.

*He makes a weak kissing sound, and she makes a face. Frustrated, he throws his hands up.*

DON: Could you try, like, even a <u>little</u> bit, not to be so snippy?

ANNE: Why? Would it make you learn your lines any better?!

DON: I'm sorry, that's not all <u>my</u> fault, when we're supposed to hug you keep trying t—

ANNE: Damn it!! (*She puts her face in her hands and makes a frustrated groan.*) God, this is gonna be the worst ten minutes <u>ever</u>!

DON (*Pause; quietly.*): It's... it's weird, okay? I'm not used to... not... touching you, anymore. After all these years, and then, suddenly... not... being... (*Gesturing stupidly.*) Y'know.

ANNE (*Beat; arms crossed, rubbing her shoulders anxiously.*): Yeah. I know what you mean.

DON: You do?

ANNE: <u>Yeah</u>, it's... weird. Not being... <u>together</u>.

DON: Well...

ANNE: Well what?

DON: Why... aren't we?

ANNE: Excuse me?

DON: Why aren't we... together? Anymore?

ANNE: You know.

DON: No. No, I don't. You always think I know more than I do. I don't. (*Gesturing with frustration.*) I don't even know these lines!

ANNE (*Turning away, growing progressively more distraught.*): And whose fault is that?!

DON (*Throwing his hands up.*): Mine! I know, everything's my fault. I've made peace with that. I've accepted my role as the dumber half of us, and that's fine, but apparently I've done something so monumentally stupid that I no longer deserve even the courtesy of being talked to about it. I... look, I'm not afraid to admit it... I love you, and, if you don't love me anymore...

> ANNE *breaks down completely, sobbing loudly. DON doesn't even break stride.*

DON (*Cont.*): Aaaand you're crying. I've made you cry. By loving you. Or—Have I made you? How—What—what is going on; what's happening right now? Seriously, what did I miss?

> ANNE *abruptly turns and hugs him tightly, still sniffling. DON awkwardly pats her, then hugs her cautiously, and finally ANNE speaks.*

ANNE (*Genuinely.*): I'm sorry.

DON (*Beat.*) For...?

ANNE (*Releasing him.*): You dumbass. Can't you guess why this play is making me upset?

DON (*Beyond confused.*): Wait, so... it's the play that's making you upset?!

ANNE: No! I mean, yes! I mean—AHHH!! (*Taking a deep breath.*) I'm...

DON (*Not getting it.*): You're...?

ANNE (*Nodding slowly, gesturing to her stomach*): I... I am.

DON: You... (*An explosive realization.*) You are?!

ANNE (*Exasperated.*): Yes! Yes, Don!

DON/ELI (*Transitioning seamlessly.*): Honey, oh my god—!

*He hugs her, and she returns it, feeling relieved.*

ANNE/BARBARA (*Transitioning seamlessly.*): I tested twice.

ELI: Did you use one of those new ones with the... you know, GPS and email and the bells and whistles and stuff?

BARBARA (*Snorting.*): No. Those things were a fortune. Just, the old-fashioned stick.

ELI: So... that's why you've been so off lately! I'm sorry I didn't put two and two together. (*Beat; grinning stupidly.*) Well, I mean, we sort of did—

BARBARA (*Punching him playfully.*): Stop. But... (*Coming to it.*) Do you want the baby?

ELI (*Immediately.*): Of course!

BARBARA: No... think about it. Just, really think. For a minute.

ELI: Okay. Well... (*Thinking.*) It's... scary...

BARBARA: Uh, yeah.

ELI (*Eyes widening.*): I mean, we're only 25, there's a lot of debt ahead of us...

BARBARA: Keep going...

ELI: Car payments, insurance... and we'd have to start saving for college now...

BARBARA: Now you see it...

ELI (*Whistling.*): So, you've been going through all of this in your head without me?

BARBARA (*Glad it's out there.*): Basically.

ELI: Why??

BARBARA: Because... I'm the one who knows. And you're, so... carefree, and... forgetful... and... (*Honestly.*) I love that. And, I wasn't sure... if you wanted it. For real. The... responsibility.

ELI (*Thinking hard for a minute.*): Well... I do. Sounds so flippant, I know, I might as well be saying I plan to stay home during Lamaze class and eat chips in the Waiting Room, but... I want to know more. (*Pause.*) I want you not to worry that I'm going to worry.

BARBARA (*Hugging him tightly.*): Okay. Okay then.

ELI/DON: I love you Anne.

BARBARA/ANNE: I love you too, Don.

*They kiss, passionately. From the back of the audience KAY starts applauding, hurrying up onstage next to them. She has a chocolate-covered Danish in her mouth, which she takes out once she begins to speak. They break and look at her, dazed, not sure if they're the characters in the play or... the Characters in the Play.*

KAY: And <u>that</u> is how you do a freakin' play*!!* See? See?? You get it intrinsic, it sinks into your very <u>bones</u>, and <u>then</u> and <u>only</u> then will the play come to life. You have to make it the best ten minutes <u>ever</u>! You have to <u>live</u> the characters, and then you will <u>be</u> the characters. Genius. <u>Genius</u>. We're gonna win this thing for sure. (*Snapping her fingers.*) Alright kids, they're opening the house, let's get backstage, and I want you running lines again and again until your <u>lips</u> fall off. Make me <u>proud</u>, make me <u>happy</u>, let's win this thing for <u>us</u>... because God knows the <u>playwright</u> doesn't deserve it with this shit. Break legs, <u>merde, bona fortuna</u>!!

*She takes an enormous bite of Danish and exits, humming. ELI/DON and BARBARA/ANNE exchange a brief look, are about to speak to each other, and—*

*Blackout.*

END OF PLAY

## *2017 Runner Up*

# Always

### by

### Stephen Cooper

Directed by Louise Stinespring

Assistant Director, John Stinespring

with

Tom Aposporos as Edward

Andrea Dovner as Vivien

CHARACTERS
EDWARD, a man, 50 to 85, VIVIAN's husband.

VIVIAN, a woman, 50 to 85, EDWARD's wife.

SETTING
The set is a couch with a chair facing it. There is a small coffee table between the couch and chair where the tray with wine and cheese will be placed. The tray will have some small plates to hold the crackers and cheese. Offstage unseen is a kitchen where cheese and crackers are prepared.

TIME
The present.

*At lights up EDWARD sits in a chair facing the couch. A small coffee table is between the chair and couch. EDWARD is looking at a bottle of white wine and he has a corkscrew to open the bottle. VIVIAN is offstage, in the unseen kitchen, preparing a tray of cheese and crackers.*

EDWARD (*Loudly!*): I won't answer a crazy question like that!

VIVIAN (*Offstage.*): It's not crazy. In fact, it's quite sensible.

EDWARD: What's sensible to you is crazy to me!

*VIVIAN enters with tray with two wine glasses, cheese and crackers.*

VIVIAN: Unless we're together in some horrible car accident, one of us will go first. That's a simple fact.

*VIVIAN puts tray down on coffee table and sits on the couch.*

EDWARD: I don't want to discuss that "simple fact."

*EDWARD opens the wine while talking and pours two glasses of wine.*

Tonight I'm looking forward to some wine and cheese. I don't want to spoil it by thinking about that depressing question.

VIVIAN: It's not depressing. It's realistic. I'd expect a rational person like you to be realistic.

*EDWARD and VIVIAN pick up their wine glasses, and clink them together in a practiced way as though they have been doing this for years. As conversation continues they nibble on crackers and cheese, and sip wine which is occasionally refilled by EDWARD.*

EDWARD: Realism deals with real facts. Today we're alive. That's the fact. So let's enjoy this moment and leave that alone. I don't want to go there.

VIVIAN: All I asked is, "What would you do if I went first?"

EDWARD: "Went first?" Don't you mean "Died first?" If it wasn't a depressing question you wouldn't have to sanitize it with a euphemism.

VIVIAN: Okay. I'll ask it again... straight. What would you do if I died first? It's a realistic possibility to me.

EDWARD: It's hypothetical. The statistics are clear. Men die earlier... <u>before</u> women. That's why there are so many widows around here. And I'm older than you... I'll probably go first. So you don't have to worry about an answer.

VIVIAN: I'm not worried about the answer. I think you're worried about the question.

EDWARD: Why do you bring this up?

VIVIAN: I dunno. It just came to me. No special reason. Just curious.

EDWARD: Sorry, I can't satisfy your curiousity.

VIVIAN: I'm surprised you can't give me a simple answer. Something. Anything.

EDWARD: After grieving, I'll sell this place, move into a mobile home, eat take-out every meal, put on a lot of weight, die soon, and join you in heaven.

VIVIAN: An interesting scenario. But I wasn't expecting sarcasm. We always said it was better to plan for eventualities before they happened. This is talking about something ahead of time.

EDWARD: Pre-planning?

VIVIAN: Yeah. Since I wouldn't be around to see what happened... in case I "went first"... died first... I was just wondering, what would you do?

EDWARD: Okay... Here's the truth. I'll take care of the house... keep it clean the way you like... sweep every day... live here as long as possible... and then sell it and move into something smaller. Something small enough for one... And I will eat healthy... Like you.

VIVIAN: Much better. I don't like to think of you in a mobile home. Doesn't suit you. Too small. You belong in a house.

EDWARD: Now you can go happy. I'll stay in the house. (*EDWARD refills the glasses with wine, takes some cheese on a cracker, takes a bite, and then continues.*) And I will continue to enjoy wine and cheese on Friday afternoons.

VIVIAN: Alone?

EDWARD: With you.

VIVIAN: That misses the point. If I went first, you would be alone.

EDWARD: Mmmm. That's logical. Even if not realistic.

VIVIAN: So who would you have wine with?

EDWARD: Are you asking if I would have an affair?

VIVIAN: No. If I were... gone... before you... you'd be single. You can only have an "affair" if you're married.

EDWARD: Good point. I'm not experienced in affairs.

VIVIAN: I know you well enough to know you'd be unhappy being alone. That concerns me. Now's the time to think about possibilities.

EDWARD: What possibilities?

VIVIAN: Dating.

EDWARD: Dating? It's been a long time...

VIVIAN: I don't think so. We've been dating for a long time. It would just be with someone else.

EDWARD: Like who?

VIVIAN: I was thinking of girls.

EDWARD: At my age there wouldn't be any "girls." I think they'd be women. In fact, mature women.

VIVIAN: Of course. Women. And as you so clearly put it... "mature women." Anyway, if you were single, who would you date?

EDWARD: I wouldn't touch that question with a ten-foot pole.

VIVIAN: Why?

EDWARD: You're asking me what other women I find attractive. There's no good answer to that question.

VIVIAN: You embarrassed?

EDWARD: No. It's a loaded question. With implications.

VIVIAN: What implications?

EDWARD: If I said someone was attractive, some woman friend, some "mature woman friend"... some woman from a couple we know, then when we met them... or her... at some party, or if we went out to dinner with them... you would be jealous. You know... wondering...

VIVIAN: Wondering what?

EDWARD: Whether I found her attractive...or more attractive... than... which I wouldn't... so don't even go there. You know what I need? A drink. Something stronger.

VIVIAN: Eddie, you don't need anything stronger. This wine is lovely... you made a great find. (*Pause*.) How about this? If I died, would you consider seeing Marilyn?

EDWARD: Marilyn who?

VIVIAN: Marilyn Denhardt. From the bridge club.

EDWARD: Would you believe me if I said I never think about her?

VIVIAN: I wouldn't. Not for a second. She's the most attractive woman in the club.

EDWARD: Well, I don't.

VIVIAN: You never noticed her cleavage?

EDWARD: What?

VIVIAN: Her cleavage. The thing between her big breasts. Every man in the room stares at her when she walks around.

EDWARD: I don't stare.

VIVIAN: I don't mind. You're a man, aren't you?

EDWARD: I should tell you that there are two types of men in the world. I belong to the leg-man tribe... and you have beautiful legs.

VIVIAN: Oh, thank you, Eddie.

EDWARD: So I'm not swayed by Marilyn's body.

VIVIAN: So?

EDWARD: So... what?

VIVIAN: So would you date her?

EDWARD: She's married!

VIVIAN: I wasn't asking about adultery.

EDWARD: But with Ernie around, dating her would be adultery.

VIVIAN: Can't you think out of the box? If she became a widow, would you date her?

EDWARD: Are you planning to murder Ernie? I like him. I don't want him killed. Even if that made her a widow.

VIVIAN: I'm asking a fer-instance question. If she were a widow, would you be interested?

EDWARD: I don't think about Marilyn. And why the hell are you working to fix me up today? This whole discussion... and your question... is premature... and ridiculous.

VIVIAN: It's not ridiculous. If I were dead, I would worry about you being lonely.

EDWARD: If you were dead, you wouldn't have any worries. And besides, the kids are two hours away. They'll be here more than I need them. I won't be lonely.

VIVIAN: I wasn't talking about the kids. I'm talking about the fact that you don't have any of your own friends.

EDWARD: That's because I love being with you. And we've got lots of friends. I don't need other friends.

VIVIAN: That's my point. All our friends are our friends, not your friends. You don't have your own friends. I'm talking about you making new friends.

EDWARD: I'll make friends.

VIVIAN: You're inexperienced in friending. I'm trying to open your mind to new possibilities.

EDWARD: You've given me more possibilities than I need... or want.

VIVIAN: I'll suggest some other women that you could date. My preferred list. We're just imagining. That's all. You don't have to call anyone today. How about Robin Marks, or Jen Simons, or maybe Marge Williams?

EDWARD: Boy, that list came out pretty fast. You must have been working on this quite a bit.

VIVIAN: So?

EDWARD: So what?

VIVIAN: So who?

EDWARD: Oh. You want an answer?

VIVIAN: Yeah.

EDWARD: It's a good list... Yeah, they're all fine.

VIVIAN: So if I died, and you dated any of those women, you have my approval.

EDWARD: I'll remember the list. But that doesn't mean I would forget you. (*Pause.*) So what brings this discussion up?

VIVIAN: I guess it was going for my mammogram. Makes you think.

EDWARD: You've had mammograms before. I know mammograms make you nervous. But you never asked that question before.

VIVIAN: I guess I never thought about it before.

EDWARD: You've never had any problems. Everything they saw was minor. Nothing very serious.

VIVIAN: I'll be honest with you, Eddie. It's serious.

EDWARD: Serious?

VIVIAN: The doctor called. The radiologist saw something.

> EDWARD *gets up and sits down on the couch next to* VIVIAN *and puts his arms around her. He hugs her and talks softly.*

EDWARD: Oh, Viv, I'm so sorry that you have to go through this again. Callbacks can make anyone nervous. It worries me too. You've had cysts and...what are they...oh, calcifications and other stuff. Lots of things that turned out to be nothing. All benign.

VIVIAN: Stop it, Eddie! This time it's not benign! There's something growing. The oncologist went into detail. I can handle it. If you can. I need you to be realistic...

EDWARD: I am realistic. Yes, it's scary. (*Pause.*) You know I'll be with you all the way. Every visit.

VIVIAN: This could be my time.

EDWARD: I understand. I really do.

VIVIAN: That's what started me on all this... you know... life without me.

EDWARD: Let's concentrate on the medical stuff, not my future.

VIVIAN: It's real. We have to face it.

EDWARD: Don't worry about me. Let me worry about you. Let me take care of you.

VIVIAN: I will... if you'll accept my worrying about you.

EDWARD: Of course. Thank you for the list. I hope you don't mind if I don't use it right now. Or soon. And know that I love you and care about you. Always.

VIVIAN: And I love you...the same way. Always.

*EDWARD takes the bottle, fills the glasses once more, raises his glass. VIVIAN looks at EDWARD and takes her glass. They look at each other.*

EDWARD: Here's to more wine, many wonderful bottles, and many cheeses from around the world. And many delicious evenings together.

*They clink glasses together as they look at each other. They sip wine.*

VIVIAN: To many wonderful evenings. Yes.

EDWARD: Yes. Together. Always.

*Lights fade.*

*Blackout.*

### END OF PLAY

## *2017 Audience Favorite*

# I'm Dead When I Say I'm Dead

### by

### Ron Pantello

Directed by Louise Stinespring

Assistant Director, John Stinespring

with

Mitcheal Pearl as Barry

Kathryn Chesley as The Urn/Mother

CHARACTERS
BARRY, a man, 28, successful but unable to settle down, marry or have a family.

THE URN/MOTHER: An urn that's the voice of BARRY's mother. Can only be seen by the audience.

SETTING
BARRY's apartment, a typical New York City bachelor pad. The stage is set with a front door opening to a living room with furniture, a small kitchen with a table, chairs, and cabinets, and a closet.

TIME
The present.

>   *Lights up. BARRY enters the apartment dressed in a suit, tie undone clearly exhausted from the day. He is carrying an urn which he sits in the center of the kitchen table. He takes off his coat, putting it on the back of a dining room chair.*

BARRY (*Speaking to THE URN.*): I can't believe you. You choose to be cremated but rented a casket so everyone would think you were being buried like a normal person. Who cares what people think?

>   *BARRY moves to the cabinet taking out a bottle of vodka. He pours, goes to the refrigerator for ice then stirs the ice around the vodka. Takes a drink and faces THE URN.*

BARRY: And why in God's name leave the urn to me? My brother would have been a better choice... you like him better anyway. Aren't you afraid I'll lose you? What were you thinking? And I'm not keeping you on the mantel. (*Pointing at THE URN.*) You... in the closet.

>   *BARRY takes THE URN placing it in the closet. Shuts the door.*

BARRY (*Muttering to himself.*): I thought I was done with her.

THE URN (*Heard from the closet.*): You're never done with your mother.

BARRY: Shit!

THE URN: Open the door.

Shocked, BARRY stares at the closet in disbelief. Slowly moves toward the closet.

BARRY: It's really you?

THE URN: Yes, now open the door.

>   *BARRY slowly cracks open the door. As he peeps in then slams the door.*

BARRY: Don't tell me you're still here! What did I do to deserve this?

THE URN (*From the closet*): You and I have unfinished business Mr. Big Shot.

BARRY: What the hell does that mean?

THE URN: I can't leave until you fix yourself. Mothers never leave until their work is done. Frankly, you are still half baked. We have a lot to talk about. Open the door.

> BARRY slowly opens the door. He enters the closet then exits the closet with THE URN, moving to the kitchen table.

BARRY: I can't believe this.

> BARRY sits at the kitchen table. The mother exits the closet moving slightly UPSTAGE. BARRY, still in shock, picks up his drink and sips. Looking at and talking to THE URN.

BARRY (*Cont.*): What do you want?

THE URN: I want what all Jewish mothers want. Are you married? No. Do you date nice Jewish girls? No. Did you visit your mother? No. Need I go on.

BARRY: I see nothing has changed.

THE URN: Have some respect for the dead.

> The mother walks around the room. BARRY sits at the table looking at THE URN.

THE URN (*Cont.*): Now say you are sorry for speaking to your only mother like that.

BARRY: Sorry!... Wait, I can't believe I said I'm sorry to an urn. I take it back...

THE URN: Too late. I accept your long overdue apology. It's a start.

BARRY: I can't believe this is happening. I am not talking to an urn.

THE URN: Oh yes you are. I'm your mother, you have to listen to me. If not, I will haunt you for the rest of your days. Do you really want that?

BARRY: Trust me, I don't. Now what do you want?

THE URN: I want answers to some questions.

BARRY (*Thinking.*): If I answer your questions can I get my sanity back?

THE URN: Yes... well, maybe. Depending on your answers.

BARRY: Fine, gimme your best shot.

THE URN: Why didn't you call. Why Didn't you text, not even a tweet. One hundred and forty characters too many for your mother? Too busy big shot?

BARRY: But you're dead!

THE URN: Wrong answer. You're making this hard... just like I thought.

BARRY: Then what's the right answer?

THE URN: You're here with me. That's the right answer. Of course I had to die to get you to do the right thing.

BARRY: This is ridiculous...

THE URN: You never invited me to your home. I had to die to get invited over.

BARRY: I didn't invite you over. You inherited yourself over.

THE URN: Same thing. I'm here and not leaving. Deal with it.

BARRY (*Moaning.*): Ughhhhh.

THE URN: Say you're happy I left you my ashes.

BARRY: I'm happy.

THE URN: And I can live on your mantel.

BARRY: I'm happy to keep your ashes on the mantel. Next.

THE URN: We need to discuss your woman friend.

BARRY: You know this is going to end badly.

THE URN: No it's not. It's going to end when I say it ends. Your brother says you have a new girl.

BARRY: Not exactly. I'm just seeing someone.

THE URN: Someone must have a name.

BARRY: It's not serious. What's the difference?

THE URN: Your brother says her name is Cinnamon.

BARRY: It's a nickname.

THE URN: <u>No</u>... it's a spice... My son cannot date a spice.

BARRY: She's a fairly nice girl.

THE URN: <u>Fairly nice</u> doesn't cut it. Sounds like she's a gold digger.

BARRY: You don't know her.

THE URN: I know enough. What kind of Jewish girl is named after a spice?

BARRY: She's not Jewish.

THE URN: Let me answer using your vernacular... <u>no</u> <u>shit</u> she's not Jewish. I got rid of her.

BARRY: Just like that...

THE URN: Just like that. I told her to make herself useful, I told her to find a baker.

BARRY: What did you do?

THE URN: Lets just say she's toast. Now, we need to talk about your brother.

BARRY: What could possibly be wrong with Mr. Perfect?

THE URN: You need to be closer.

BARRY: Mom, he's married with three kids. Lives in the suburbs. We got nothing...

THE URN: You got blood, that's what you got.

BARRY: No more games. What's up?

THE URN: So... your brother wants to franchise his deli's. Of course he doesn't have a clue as to how to do that. You Mr. Smarty Pants financial guy knows.

BARRY: So you want me to...?

THE URN: Help your brother. Go into business with your brother. It will be good for everybody.

BARRY: He may not want my help.

THE URN: He wants your help. He just doesn't know how to ask his baby brother.

BARRY: How do you know that?

THE URN: God... you are stupid. I'm a mother, that's how I know. Can you just do this one little thing?

BARRY: If I do this will you leave?

THE URN: So now you want me to leave.

BARRY: Yes... No, I didn't mean it that way... what am I doing talking to a dead person?

THE URN: I'll tell you when I'm dead. Deal with it.

BARRY: I must be going crazy...

THE URN: You're fine, just confused. There's more.

BARRY (*Sarcastic.*): Great? What?

THE URN: Grandchildren.

BARRY: You have three. You adore them.

THE URN: I need more.

BARRY: You know he had a vasectomy...Three is just fine.

THE URN: So now you're telling me how many grandchildren I should have?

BARRY (*Becoming nervous.*): Suggesting, just suggesting.

THE URN: You're getting a little long in the tooth. So, maybe just two for you.

BARRY: I don't have a wife.

THE URN: So now you see the problem.

BARRY: You just got rid of Cinnamon.

THE URN: Of course. What did you expect? I don't want a little nutmeg or ginger grandchildren running around. What's a matter with you?

BARRY: Let me guess? You have some suggestions.

THE URN: Maybe one.

BARRY: Is your suggestion Jewish?

THE URN: Coincidentally she happens to be Jewish.

BARRY: Maybe I prefer non-Jewish girls.

THE URN: Now why would you prefer non-Jewish girls?

BARRY: Uh... have you been listening to this conversation?

THE URN: Don't be a schmuck. You are not marrying a Shiksa.

BARRY: You're dead. You can't make me do anything.

THE URN: Jewish mothers are never dead. I'm dead when I say I'm dead. (*Pause.*) Deal with it.

BARRY: I need another drink.

*BARRY gets up and makes another drink. Returns to the table.*

THE URN: You shouldn't drink so much. It clouds your judgment.

BARRY: Trust me, it couldn't be more clouded.

THE URN: So... before my heart attack I was talking to the Golds -

BARRY: I thought you didn't like the Irish.

THE URN: They're not Irish; they're Jews.

BARRY: They were born in Ireland.

THE URN: Don't confuse me. They're Jews.

BARRY: And?

THE URN: You know Maureen. You always liked her.

BARRY: Yes... but we never got together.

THE URN: That was just bad timing. Different friends, different colleges.

BARRY (*Pause.*): What did you do?

THE URN: I left you to Maureen in my will.

BARRY: That's the craziest thing I've ever heard.

THE URN: It's true.

BARRY: You don't leave people to other people in wills.

THE URN: It's all spelled out. And the will was sent to the Golds the moment I passed.

BARRY: So that's why they came to sit Shiva? To see what crazy people look like?

THE URN: Well somebody had to jump start your life. Now you know. I think you'll get a call.

BARRY: What if Maureen isn't interested?

THE URN: Then I'll need your second bedroom. You'll be stuck with me for eternity. Frankly, I'd much rather have a nice peaceful rest rather than worry about you. Now put me on the mantel where I can watch over you.

*BARRY picks up THE URN and walks to the mantel placing THE URN in the center. He starts to walk away. Stops. Walks back, kisses THE URN, a spot light appears on THE URN. Phone rings.*

BARRY: Hello... Oh, Maureen...

*BARRY turns to the mantel.*

THE URN: Ahaaaa.

*Light on THE URN dims, then lights dim.*

*Blackout.*

END OF PLAY

# A Big Wave

### by

## Connie Schindewolf

Directed by Bob Trisolini

with

Jenny Aldrich as Joann

Don Walker as Jack

CHARACTERS
JOANN, a 65ish woman, sarcastic, divorced, full of guilt.

JACK, a 65ish man, widower, understanding.

SETTING
On a beach, somewhere on the west coast of Florida about 7:30 a.m. There is a folding chair JOANN has brought.

TIME
Present

> As the curtain rises, JOANN is standing, looking out over the water (toward the audience). She has a forlorn look on her face as she searches with her eyes for something in the water. The sounds of the waves can be heard and then they fade as the dialogue starts. JACK is in the background with a backpack and carrying a clipboard and a small bucket. He turns and walks toward JOANN.

JACK: Seen any birds out yet?

JOANN: What? Are you from the newspaper? No comment. Just leave me alone.

JACK: I'm not a journalist. Just doing turtle work.

JOANN: Oh.

JACK: But I have seen you here every morning, know who you are... I mean what happened with your grandson.

JOANN: Everybody knows.

JACK: Ever seen a baby turtle? I'm going to release this one. He was late coming out of that nest back there. But, I can't if the birds are out. He wouldn't stand a chance.

JOANN: I've seen them. Cute. Birds aren't around yet.

JACK (*Bends down and tips bucket over so turtle can get out.*): Bye little guy. Good luck. Never get tired of watching that. New life, new beginnings. Look, now watch and his little head will come up for air. Look, there it is.

JOANN: Do they always come up for air?

JACK: Yeah, just sometimes the waves are too rough to see it.

JOANN: What chance does he have?

JACK: Not good. One in a thousand.

JOANN: Why bother?

JACK: Why not? Don't have anything better to do.

JOANN: People ask me why I'm still here… looking… waiting. Well, I don't have anything better to do either.

JACK: It has been ten days.

JOANN (*Sitting in her chair.*): You don't think I know that?

JACK: I just mean… I don't know what I mean. Sorry for your loss.

JOANN: You know how many people have said that?

JACK: I'm sure they meant it.

JOANN: Sorry, sorry, sorry. I'm so sick of that word, sorry, as if they could understand.

*Pause, then she rises quickly, looking out.*

JACK: What do you see?

JOANN: Something way out there.

JACK: I do see something, but I'm sure it's not a…

JOANN: A body? You can say that. I know what you're all thinking, that I'm crazy watching and waiting here where my Noah drowned.

JACK: Don't think you're crazy. I just don't think the body would wash up here. It'd be somewhere else by now. You know because of currents and things.

JOANN: I don't care. This is where he left and so this is where I wait. I don't care that the search went from rescue to recovery and now to nothing. I'm here.

JACK: Well, I'll wait with you then a few minutes.

JOANN: Go on and do your turtle work.

JACK: I only have about a quarter of a mile to go. Not much activity today so I'm ahead of schedule. That nest back there didn't disorient. That means turtles go in the wrong direction.

JOANN: Lived on this key long enough to know about the turtles.

JACK: Look at all the little tracks. Went straight to the water. Even under your chair.

JOANN: I got here just before daylight so I missed that.

JACK: Right before dawn... my favorite time of day, twilight. Just seems like the secrets of the universe about to be revealed. I always think about that movie, <u>City of Angels</u> with Nicholas Cage, when all the angels are standing on the beach waiting for dawn.

JOANN: You think there are angels on the beach?

JACK: I don't know.

JOANN: Look it's closer. What is it?

JACK: I can't tell. Could be anything. Stuff falls off boats all the time.

JOANN: I just can't make it out.

JACK: We find all kinds of things washed up when we're doing turtle work, buoys, crab traps, life jackets.

JOANN: He wasn't wearing one.

JACK: I'm sorry... I didn't...

JOANN: There you go with that word again, sorry. Well I'm the one who's sorry. Sorry that he wasn't wearing one, sorry that I thought he'd be safe just standing knee deep in water, sorry that I didn't see that huge wave coming, sorry that it knocked him down and pulled him out by the ankles, sorry that I couldn't get to him in time, sorry that it took the Coast Guard over 15 damn minutes to get here, sorry that my 7-year-old little Noah's head didn't bob up like that stupid turtle so I could see where to swim to, sorry that I just didn't keep on swimming out there and stay with him wherever he went!

JACK: But then you'd have died too.

JOANN: He's not dead until they find a body!

JACK: Sorry. I mean it's hard not to say that word. You couldn't have known that wave was coming or that there were rip currents out there. No one blames you.

JOANN: That's what my daughter says, "I don't blame you, Mom. It wasn't your fault." My fault? I was the one watching him that day. I'm the one who decided to take him to the beach. He didn't even have a swimsuit on, just shorts and a t-shirt wearing his new little sunglasses. I was so sure to put lots of sunscreen on him. "NeNe, you're the sunscreen witch," he'd say. Anything to protect my little Noah. I told him we weren't going in the water, just going to set up our chairs and enjoy the sun. "NeNe, can I get my feet wet?" I said, "Sure."

JOANN (*Cont.*): I closed my eyes for a second to take in the warmth of the sun on my body. When I opened them, he was knee deep. "Noah, come back here." He turned around to look at me with that oops-I've-been-bad little grin of his, and he couldn't have known the wave was coming. The last look on his face was one of terror as it drug him out, swallowing him up like a hungry fish. Isn't his name ironic? Noah from the Bible survived when the earth was covered with water, and my little Noah disappeared when standing knee deep in it.

JACK: I don't know what to say.

JOANN: Say nothing. I don't even know you, and I just told you the most personal story of my life.

JACK: I'm Jack. Now you know me.

JOANN: JoAnn. And you won't see me cry. The first five days that's all I did. Enough tears to raise the level of the Gulf of Mexico. Yeah, me and climate change, both raising the sea level.

JACK: So how long will you keep this vigil?

JOANN: As long as it takes.

JACK: For what?

JOANN: Answers. (*Looking out.*) It's getting closer. What is it? It's about the right size. It looks black.

JACK: That's the way the sun makes it look. I can't tell yet, but it's definitely coming in.

JOANN: There's something else about what happened.

JACK: What?

JOANN: My daughter knows though.

JACK: You don't have to tell me anything.

JOANN: I can't swim. Oh I can tread water a little.

JACK: Even a skilled swimmer might not have been able to…

JOANN: Save him? Might not? You see, if I could swim, I might have been able to save him.

JACK: If I'd have known CPR, I might have been able to save my wife.

JOANN: Oh, I'm sorry. Heart attack?

JACK: Yes.

JOANN: How did you get over that?

JACK: I just... went on.

JOANN (*Looking out.*): I'm going to wade out and get it.

JACK: No, whatever it is it could be full of barnacles and they're sharp. When it's close enough to tell what it is, I can get it.

*He takes his backpack off and puts it on the beach.*

JOANN: Ok. Maybe we should call someone.

JACK: JoAnn, it's not your Noah.

JOANN: You don't know that yet.

JACK: No. I don't.

JOANN: You know I sit here and I fantasize about what could have happened... why he hasn't been found. My favorite one is that he washed out very far but grabbed a hold of something and was able to stay afloat. A foreign couple on a boat pick him up, rescue him, but don't know English. Well, they couldn't have kids and they think this is a miracle, kind of like in the beginning of Superman, you know. They've got him, and someday Noah is going to call me, I'll pick it up, and he'll say, "NeNe, come get me."

JACK: That's an amazing story, but...

JOANN: Don't you tell me that's not possible!

JACK: Anything is possible.

JOANN: Thank you. It went under now. I can't see it! It was so close. No, there it is again!

JACK: Yes, I see it. It's not a...

JOANN: What? What is it? Tell me, damn it! What is it?

JACK: A frond. A palm frond. Just a branch of a palm tree.

JOANN: No.

JACK: Yes it is.

JOANN: I see, you're right. I should have known.

*JOANN sits, defeated. JACK gathers his stuff.*

JACK: I'm sorry, I mean...

JOANN: Forget it.

JACK: Want to walk with me the rest of the way? Can always use another pair of eyes to look for the tracks and things.

JOANN: No thank you. I belong here.

JACK: Well, I've got to get going. Bye.

JOANN: Goodbye.

JACK (*Walks a few steps and then steps back to her.*): You know we start the same time you come out here every day. Always need more people, especially now that some nests are disorienting and we have to count tracks and search for the babies. You might like that... saving babies.

JOANN: I don't know.

JACK (*Starts to go again but turns back.*): And we find lots of stuff washed up. Last week I found a pair of sunglasses.

JOANN: Kids sunglasses?

JACK: No, but I have found kids sunglasses before. You could join me tomorrow at 6:25. You park at the church and walk out to the beach access.

JOANN: Do you think there are angels on the beach?

JACK: Maybe there are. (*Pause.*) See you tomorrow?

JOANN: Maybe. Anything's possible.

*They smile, he turns and walks on, and JOANN looks after him and then out over the water.*

*Lights fade.*

*Blackout.*

### END OF PLAY

# Kennedy's Acolytes

by

Jack Gilhooley

Directed by Sara Logan

with

Nicole Cunningham as Eileen

Sally Fint as Deirdre

Johana Davila as Oona

CHARACTERS
DEIRDRE, a young Irish woman of 16 to 17.

OONA, a young Irish woman of 16 to 17.

EILEEN, a young Irish woman of 16 to 17.

SETTING
A basically empty town square with a bench and (perhaps) a streetlamp in rural Ireland.

TIME
The evening of November 22, 1963.

> *DEIDRE and OONA are heavily dressed and standing in the square. They never stray far from a trash can that gives off a fire's heat. They periodically warm their hands and their rear ends.*

DEIRDRE: How close did you get?

OONA: I could touch him.

DEIRDRE: So did ye?

OONA: Lord, no.

DEIRDRE: Why not?

OONA: I was afraid.

 DEIRDRE: Of Kennedy?

OONA: Course not. He had these big bruiser-type guards.

DEIRDRE: He didn't need them here. In the states, yeah. But not in Wexford. We're civilized over here. Except on the football pitch. Rumor has it that he'd move over here when his presidency was over. And why not? He'd be able to walk into any pub in the land. And without guards. The gents wouldn't let him buy a round. Lift a jar and have a bit of craic with the boyos. A game of darts or two. Then home for dinner with Jackie an' the wee ones. Little John-John would soon be old enough to join a football club. His da would've been a sponsor. Take the lads out after a match. Treat them to sweets an' such. Grand it would be, for sure.

OONA: Somehow I never saw that happening.

DEIRDRE: Why not? He could afford it. In that case ye should've reached out to him. He was shakin' hands with any bogtrotter who could reach him. Imagine the germs he musta picked up. (*Pause.*) You were close enough to nick his wallet.

OONA: I was frozen.

DEIRDRE: How could you freeze in June? If you were that close you coulda kissed him. If I was that close I'd've kissed him.

OONA: Deirdre!

DEIRDRE: That's what I'd've done. I'd've snogged John Fitzgerald Kennedy. Right in front of Jackie. He'd have savored it.

OONA: I'm sure Jackie would've panicked over that. Imagine, Deirdre Flanagan as JFK's teenaged mistress.

DEIRDRE: That's somethin' you could brag about to your grandkids… snoggin' the President of The United States.

OONA: I wasn't thinkin' about grandkids as President John F. Kennedy was approachin'. I was thinkin' I might wet myself. And I'd hardly tell my grandkids that I kissed the American president. They'd think there auld granny was a cheeky slag.

DEIRDRE: Well you are, sort of. (*Pause.*) Then you could tell them that you wet yourself.

OONA: I wouldn't tell them that even if I did. And I didn't.

DEIRDRE: Congratulations, Oona. Discipline is yer middle name. Y'know, you'll get nowhere in life bein' fearful.

OONA: Now it's too late. Geez, it was only last June. I'll never have another chance to touch Kennedy.

DEIRDRE: They'll probably have an open casket for the viewin'. You could fly over, get in line and touch him when you pass by. Kiss 'em even. No need for security, now.

OONA: I wouldn't touch a dead man.

DEIRDRE: Why? Death is not contagious.

OONA: Well, snoggin' seems to be contagious with you. You even kissed Gerald O'Malley behind the stables.

DEIRDRE: Where'd ye hear that?

OONA: Everybody saw it.

DEIRDRE: Who's everybody?

OONA: Mary Catherine Monaghan. And my sister.

DEIRDRE: That's everybody? (*Pause.*) For your information, He kissed me. It was not mutual. He snuck up on me. And it wasn't on the lips. If Gerald O'Malley had kissed me on the lips I'd have run home and washed my mouth out.

OONA: So it was a... well... a sneaky snoggin'. Would you have confessed it?

DEIRDRE: Course not. I was an innocent party. An what I confess is between me and the priest.

OONA: Did you enjoy it?

DEIRDRE (*Shrugs.*): I might've enjoyed it if it hadn't been Gerald. There was nothin' to confess.

OONA: What if it had been Billy Darby?

DEIRDRE: If it had been Billy I would <u>certainly</u> be goin' to confession on Saturday.

   *EILEEN enters.*

DEIRDRE (*Cont.*): H'lo, Eileen.

EILEEN: H'lo, mates.

OONA: Hey Eileen, did ya hear?

EILEEN: That Kathy Doyle is preggers? Big surprise.

OONA: Old news.

EILEEN: So she and Robbie Ryan are gettin' married. Not a bad deal for Kathy. She couldn'a done better on the up an' up. An' maybe the baby will look like him an' not like her. What more could a homely girl ask? Sometimes it's not such a bad idea to get yerself up the pole. Saves her from serving a sentence at the Magdalene Laundry.

DEIRDRE (*To EILEEN*): Kennedy's dead.

EILEEN: Yer kiddin'.

DEIRDRE: Shot to death.

EILEEN: Who done it?

DEIRDRE: They got a guy but he's only a suspect.

EILEEN: Bridie Keough musta done it. She never forgave Dermot for givin' her the boot and takin' up with Bridget O'Shea. An' Bridie's da is a hunter with plenty of rifles in the house.

OONA: G'wan, Bridie wouldn't harm a fly.

EILEEN: You dunno Bridie the way I know—

DEIRDRE: You two stop yer babblin'. We're not talkin' of <u>Dermot</u> Kennedy.

OONA: Course not. It's John Kennedy been murdered.

EILEEN: Lucky Dermot. Who's John Kennedy? That's Dermot's cousin from Cavan?

DEIRDRE: <u>Jack Kennedy, you nit</u>!

EILEEN (*Calmly.*): Oh, Jack Kennedy. Why didn't ye say so? Well, that's America for ye.

OONA: "That's America for ye." That's all you have to say?

EILEEN: Whataya want me to say?

OONA: The greatest man in the world is dead.

EILEEN: Don't gimmee that. I thought you girls figgered the pope is head man.

OONA: One or the other. Depends on who you talk to.

EILEEN: Ask me, why don'tcha? I'd vote for Gary Cooper. (*Pause.*) Oona, I know you travelled to Wexford to see him last summer. An' he looked like a movie star.

OONA: But not Gary Cooper. Is that what yer sayin'?

EILEEN: But "the greatest man in the world"?

OONA: You weren't there. You didn't feel the excitement. You couldn't have known.

EILEEN: True. I'm no fool. I watched it on telly at my sister's house. An' me da says he took orders from yer very same pope.

DEIRDRE: Did yer da figure that out drivin' his lorry?

EILEEN: There's nothin' shameful about drivin' a lorry. (*To OONA.*) Least he's not a butcher. (*To DEIRDRE.*) Or a postman.

OONA: (*To EILEEN.*) Spoken like a true atheist.

EILEEN: <u>Protestants aren't atheists</u>! <u>Take that back</u>!

OONA: <u>Make me</u>!

*They skirmish briefly. DEIRDRE intercedes.*

DEIRDRE: Enough. This is a solemn time.

*They desist. Suddenly, EILEEN starts to cry.*

OONA: There's her true colors. I hardly hit ya an' here comes the water works.

EILEEN: I'm not cryin' from you. I'm cryin for... Kennedy.

*DEIRDRE and OONA look to one another.*

DEIRDRE: You changed yer tune.

EILEEN: I knew he'd... been shot. I got outta the house cause I can't cry over Jack Kennedy at home. (*Pause.*) Give us a fag, Dee.

DEIRDRE: I stopped smokin'.

EILEEN: You just started smokin'. An' yer stoppin' already? That's dumb. You wanna be some kinda weird duck? Everybody smokes.

DEIRDRE: That's why I stopped. Plus, it stunts yer growth.

OONA: Well then, I'm glad I started at 13. I'm just the height I wanna be.

EILEEN: Sorry, Oona. I was way outta line at a time like this.

*They shake hands.*

EILEEN: An they just caught a guy. His name is Oswald.

DEIRDRE: Oswald? He musta been mad at the world with a name like Oswald. He shoulda killed his parents for naming him Oswald. Why take it out on Kennedy?

EILEEN: That's his last name.

OONA: Still, it's no reason to kill the president.

EILEEN: I gotta go home. Listen to the old man gloat. Crikey.

OONA: You just got here.

EILEEN: I tole ye'. I come out for a good cry.

DEIRDRE: Why doesn't yer da move to the North if he can't stand his Catholic neighbors?

EILEEN: He doesn't move north cause me mum wouldn't go with him. Nor would I.

OONA: And where else would ye find such lovely friends as us, eh Eileen?

EILEEN: Don't make me cry again, Oona.

*She smiles and as she exits...*

Slan (*Pronounced "slawn."*), girls.

OONA: Slan, Eileen.

DEIRDRE: Slan.

DEIRDRE: Don't listen to Sister Agatha. Prots aren't atheists.

OONA: I know. An' I never listen to Sister Aggie. If I ever thought about a religious vocation, she put the kibosh on it.

DEIRDRE: What's "kibosh?"

OONA: Figger it out. I'm goin'. The assassination will be all over the telly. Why can't they just let him rest in peace?

DEIRDRE: It's what people want. It'll be on for days to come. Me mum was sayin' a rosary when I left the house. I was about to ask what good that would possibly do now. But she's locked into tradition even if it makes no sense.

OONA: There's no mention of the rosary in The Bible.

DEIRDRE: You've never read The Bible.

OONA: So what. I have it on good authority.

DEIRDRE: What good authority?

OONA: My cousin Brendan is in the sem. Studyin' for the priesthood. He says that even the mass isn't in The Bible.

DEIRDRE: Some priest he'll make.

OONA: But I kept me gob shut with mum. Leave her to her habits. I'm goin' right to bed. Try to sleep. We'll get over this.

OONA: No, Dee. We'll never get over it. Slan.

DEIRDRE: Slan, Oona.

*DEIRDRE exits.*

OONA (*To herself.*): I shoulda reached out an' touched him.

*She stares straight ahead then exits, opposite.*

*Blackout.*

### END OF PLAY

# Secret's Out

## by

## Greg Burdick

Directed by Daniel Greene

with

Paul Mullen as Darnell

Mitcheal Pearl as Carlos

Nicole Cunningham as Gina

Olivia Yagy as Jashanna

CHARACTERS

GINA, Hispanic woman, 24, fashionable, sexy.

CARLOS, Hispanic man, 26, impeccably dressed.

DARNELL, black man, 47, a cab driver.

JASHANNA, young woman, 16, DARNELL's daughter, a cheerleader.

SETTING

A bench outside the Victoria's Secret store at Atlantic Terminal Mall, Brooklyn, NY.

TIME

Mid-afternoon, summer.

*Lights up on DARNELL sitting on a bench outside a Victoria's Secret store. A significant number of shopping bags lay at his feet. He fans himself in vain to combat the mall's broken air conditioning. CARLOS walks up with his arm wrapped around GINA.*

GINA: Pleeeeease? I really need one.

CARLOS: You have so many already.

GINA (*Playfully.*): C'mon, papi. I'll pick out something you'll really like...

CARLOS: Gina...

GINA: What if I promise... to give you a private fashion show later on?

*CARLOS shares a look with DARNELL.*

CARLOS: Not really sure how I could argue with that.

*He reaches into his pocket for his wallet, fishes out his credit card and gives it to her. GINA squeals, kisses him, and enters the store. CARLOS joins DARNELL on the bench.*

CARLOS: Women.

DARNELL: I'm sorry?

CARLOS: I said, "Women."

DARNELL: What about them?

CARLOS: Master manipulators.

DARNELL: You're just now discovering this? Good luck in life.

CARLOS: No. I know. I only meant...

DARNELL: And it didn't look like you were resisting too hard back there, but, then again, who could blame you? (*He looks after GINA.*)

CARLOS: It's true. She is beautiful.

DARNELL: I saw.

CARLOS: And smart too.

DARNELL: Smart enough to part you from your credit card.

CARLOS: I know. You're right. This place is a racket. Victoria's Secret.

DARNELL: The secret is the shit is overpriced.

CARLOS: That is no secret.

DARNELL: Oh, now don't complain too hard.

CARLOS: Why's that?

DARNELL: She's still interested in wearing that stuff. That'll change.

CARLOS: Don't tell me this.

DARNELL: Oh it'll happen. But it happens slowly. Real slowly. So slowly you won't notice it's happening until...

CARLOS: Until?

DARNELL: Until one day you'll see her make her intimate apparel decisions at Target. Or Wal-Mart.

CARLOS: You mean...?

DARNELL: The Value Pack.

CARLOS: Don't tell me this! Your lady wears the granny panties?

DARNELL: When the relationship gets familiar and comfortable, my friend, so does the underwear. The thrill is gone, baby. The thrill... is... gone.

CARLOS: Don't get me wrong. I appreciate what I've got here. With Gina. She usually insists I go in with her and watch her try it all on. She's not exactly shy.

DARNELL: You do realize this begs the question: Why are you sitting here talking to me?

CARLOS: I lose my mind in there. It's too much to take. Major-league overstimulation. When she pulls me into that dressing room, I...

DARNELL (*Grinning.*): Yeah...?

CARLOS: We... I end up spending a shit-ton more than I should.

DARNELL: For some dental floss and a sweatband, embroidered with the word "PINK!"

CARLOS: Right? It's so dumb. But I can't resist it. Last time, I nearly got thrown out.

DARNELL: What happened?

CARLOS: I caught myself staring, slack-jawed, at one of the employees changing outfits on a mannequin. Slipping that lace lower, and lower, and... (*He gets lost in the reverie.*) It's crazy, but it's one of the hottest things I've ever seen. I mean, the mannequins... they don't even have heads! Explain that! After it was over, I felt like I needed to pay just for watching. I can't go in there anymore. (*CARLOS gets a text message. He looks at his phone.*) See? I knew it. She's trying to lure me in.

DARNELL: She ask you to join her?

CARLOS: Not exactly... with words, but... here. Look.

DARNELL (*Eyes wide.*): Oh my dear Lord. Have mercy. How does she stay so...?

CARLOS: Zumba.

DARNELL: It's working. Put your damn phone away and get in there!

CARLOS: Told you. It's not a good idea. Best to just chill here, and let her do her thing.

*They wait.*

DARNELL: Can't exactly chill here. Ugh. This heat.

CARLOS: Air is on in all the stores. Must just be out in the mall building. I'm Carlos, by the way.

DARNELL: Darnell.

CARLOS: You'd probably be cooler inside the store, bro.

DARNELL: I can't be in there either.

CARLOS: Too hot for you too?

DARNELL: No. Just... awkward.

CARLOS: What do you mean?

DARNELL: You wouldn't understand.

CARLOS: Try me.

DARNELL: You're too young. You couldn't possibly-

CARLOS: So enlighten me.

DARNELL: Just wait until you have a daughter.

CARLOS: I've got three sisters-

DARNELL: Not the same. Totally different situation.

CARLOS: How old is...

DARNELL: Jashanna. Sixteen. She just turned this month. And her aunt, my well-intending sister, thought it'd be a great idea to give her a gift card here to celebrate. So now she's on a mission to fill up her dresser with lots of skimpy unmentionables.

CARLOS: Well, that's important for her, right?. To express herself sexually so that...

DARNELL: I'm not trying to hear this.

CARLOS: No, really. She's at an important point in her life. A time of self discovery.

DARNELL: Oh, I know. I'm not worried about that. It's the boys discovering her that concerns me.

CARLOS (*Laughs, knowingly.*): Any other kids?

DARNELL: Just my daughter. She's wonderful, but you know how men always seem to hope for a son? I'm starting to see the logic in that.

CARLOS: How so?

DARNELL: Well, with a son, you only have to worry about that one dick. With a daughter, you're worried about all of them.

CARLOS: I never thought about that.

DARNELL: Sure you have. You never thought about your sisters getting banged by... ?

CARLOS: Bro don't talk about my sisters.

DARNELL: See? You have thought about it.

CARLOS: Well yeah. I'm always looking out for them, if that's what you mean.

DARNELL: Exactly, man. Exactly. And this place...

CARLOS: Yeah?

DARNELL: The whole chain exists because of us. Men. I mean c'mon. You can bet it wasn't a woman behind Victoria's Secret. It had to have been some shrewd business guy. A man... who knew we're always thinking with the smaller head and not the larger one. And our women buy it all because they worry it's the only way they'll keep our attention. We've created the monster. Us.

*CARLOS web-searches on his phone.*

CARLOS: Shit, no way. You're right. "Businessman Roy Raymond opened the first Victoria's Secret store on June 12, 1977."

DARNELL: Your honor, I rest my case.

CARLOS: It says here that the inspiration for the company came one day when he was shopping for lingerie for his wife in a department store. He got stared down by the sales ladies, making him feel like a pervert for being there.

DARNELL: And there you have my reason for sitting on this bench.

CARLOS: You're a pervert?

DARNELL: No! Jesus. Would ya listen?

CARLOS: Well what then?

DARNELL: Picture it. I go in there with my sixteen year old daughter, all made up.... she's very mature looking for her age. She's fingering all of that stuff, saying "Daddy, do you like this one? Should I buy this Daddy? Oooh, Daddy, I want it, I want it!" What do you think the other customers are going to think of me?

CARLOS: I'm beginning to see your point.

DARNELL: And what's worse - synapses are firing in here... connections are being made inside my brain that should not be made! Got to compartmentalize! Compartmentalize! I can't see my daughter in that way! And she shouldn't see her dad seeing her in that way. I mean, think about it. What if you went in there with your sisters when the saleslady was working on that mannequin, slipping those panties down to the...

CARLOS: Okay, okay! I get it. I get it. We don't belong in there. We both just need to stay put. Right here. (*Pause.*) We are the monsters, aren't we?

*They are both fanning themselves now... sweating. JASHANNA exits the store, with lots of bags... a huge haul. She is followed by GINA, who carries one lonely little VS bag.*

JASHANNA: Okay Daddy. I'm ready.

CARLOS: Compartmentalize, bro. Compartmentalize.

GINA: Making friends, babe?

CARLOS: Huh? Oh yeah. (*He takes her bag.*)

GINA: Did you like the, uh...? (*She grins and twirls her phone.*)

CARLOS: Oh. Yeah. Totally.

DARNELL: Zumba, bro. Zumba.

GINA: Huh?

CARLOS: Hey! Oh, nothing, Gina. Let's get out of this heat. Take it easy, man.

DARNELL: You too, man. You too.

*They part in different directions. As they do, DARNELL trudges off behind JASHANNA, triumphant and CARLOS tosses GINA's purchase into the nearest trash can without her noticing. They walk off.*

*Lights dim.*

*Blackout.*

END OF PLAY

# The Call

## by

## Frank Motz

Directed by Bob Trisolini

with

Lilian Moore as Kimberly

Tony Boothby as Brett

Courtney Hawk as Caroline

CHARACTERS
KIMBERLY SANDEFORE, a woman, 40 to 60, Speaker of the House.

BRETT SANDEFORE, a man, 40 to 60, her husband.

CAROLINE, a woman, 40 to 60.

SETTING
A living room with a table CENTER, a couch LEFT and a chair RIGHT. There is a large clock sitting on the table.

TIME
The present.

*As lights go up, KIMBERLY is on her cell phone standing next to the table. BRETT enters right five seconds after she starts speaking. He stops and listens attentively.*

KIMBERLY: Congratulations, Mr. President-Elect... as Speaker of the House you can count on my help, but the position of my party is very different from your party and so... what?... what did you say... Larry, are you serious?... can your campaign people hear this?... well they are right, what you are suggesting is crazy... Larry, if you are bullshitting me... alright, alright...I believe you. Ten minutes! ... Give me ten minutes to consider my answer and call me back... because I need time to think about what you are asking me, you son of a bitch!... you promise not to speak to the media until we talk. Okay, ten minutes.

*She ends the call on her cell phone and holds it out and looks at it for a moment, taking in what she just heard and lays it carefully on the table.*

BRETT: Kim, what was that all about?

*KIMBERLY walks slowly to the couch, deep in thought.*

BRETT (*Cont.*): Kimberly Sandefore! This your husband, Brett, speaking!

*KIMBERLY stops and looks at him; he calms himself.*

What in the hell is going on?

KIMBERLY: I'm sorry. Let me sit down. I don't have a lot of time.

BRETT: I heard. Ten minutes.

KIMBERLY (*Looks at the clock*): Nine minutes.

*She goes to the couch and sits, she is deep in thought.*

BRETT: So?

KIMBERLY (*She continues to ponder as she responds to his questions.*): That was Larry.

BRETT: I figured.

KIMBERLY: He called to tell me he wants to work together.

BRETT: As the Speaker of the House from the opposing party, he should call you. Look, I'm just a college professor, but I've been married to you long enough to know how the conversation goes. You say congratulations and offer your help in any way you can, but remind him you two differ on every issue and he thanks you and says he wants to reach out to you and your party and find a way to bring the country together. Then you both announce to the press what you said to each other and after a respectable period of time, say two weeks, you both start verbally attacking each other and doing everything you can to block each other's initiatives.

KIMBERLY: It didn't go like that.

BRETT (*Serious, he goes over and sits down next to her.*): How did it go?

KIMBERLY (*Looks at him.*): Brett, he wants to try and change things. He says if I agree to partner with him, he wants to get back to our parties working together again. Sitting down and compromising and passing legislation to try and resolve issues like the national debt, the minimum wage, the immigration issue, all of it.

BRETT (*Concerned*): But you've always said you can't trust him?

KIMBERLY: I know.

BRETT: You said he's a partisan ideologue who would stab his mother in the back to make his position on an issue the law of the land.

KIMBERLY: He's probably said worse about me.

BRETT: So you're going to forget all that?

KIMBERLY: That's what he's asking me to do. (*She gets up and goes to the table and picks up the clock and looks at it.*) And I've got seven minutes to give him my answer. (*She puts the clock down.*) If I say no, he wants to promise each other we will never tell anyone we even considered it.

BRETT: And you believe him?

KIMBERLY (*Staring ahead and thinking.*): I do. (*Getting excited, she goes over and sits next to him.*) I do! I believe him, Brett! It was a Larry I never heard before. The tone of his voice. Everything! (*She looks out at the audience remembering the call.*) He got choked up suggesting it. The partisanship, the demonizing everyone in the other party, all of it. He wants to work together. He says if I'm willing, he is ready to risk everything.

BRETT (*Gets up and walks left, emotional*): Kimberly, Kimberly!

*He turns back to her.*

This goes against everything you have ever said to me. Everything you have built your career on. This wonderful life we both have! Look, I'm just the idealistic history professor that teaches young minds to believe in their dreams even though I know the real world will batter and bruise those dreams.

KIMBERLY: And what if the Speaker of the House and the President got together and decided to change that real world? What if you could show them evidence that two of the top government officials from different parties were working together to make the country better? What if you could tell them they can change their world to make it the way they think it should be and you <u>meant it</u>!

*BRETT gets up and starts to exit RIGHT.*

KIMBERLY (*Cont.*): Where are you going?

BRETT (*He stops and turns to her.*): To get you a sleeping pill.

KIMBERLY: What?!

BRETT: You're scaring me. You need to go to bed and go to sleep. I'll call and let him know you'll call tomorrow.

KIMBERLY (*She gets up and goes to him and puts her hands on his arms.*): Brett, I believe him. Maybe I shouldn't. Maybe it's the biggest mistake of my life. But doesn't somebody have to do something to change what's happened to all of us? It's like we're all on a treadmill and can't get off and it keeps going faster and faster. Weren't you just telling me how concerned you are about the essays your students are writing and their disgust and disappointment in the world they're supposed to become a part of?

*He breaks away and heads for the exit RIGHT, she stops him with her question.*

KIMBERLY (*Cont.*): Now where are you going?

BRETT (*He turns back to her again.*): To get you two sleeping pills.

KIMBERLY (*Looks at the clock.*): Brett, I have five minutes before he calls back.

*The doorbell rings.*

KIMBERLY (*Cont.*): That's Caroline. Let her in.

BRETT (*Intense.*): Are you going to say yes to that man?

KIMBERLY (*Emotional*): I don't know... I might.

BRETT (*Points to the door LEFT.*): Kim, I am getting ready to let the outside world in here in the form of the Senator from Georgia, the most viciously partisan politician I know. If you say to her what you have said to me, your career may be over.

KIMBERLY (*Angry.*): And what about Larry? He made the offer in front of all of his Caroline's! Do I leave him hanging out there by himself because he has the courage to say what we all know is true? (*Tender.*) Brett, I think this might be the most important moment of my life.

BRETT (*Equally tender.*): I think you may be right. (*He turns and heads RIGHT.*) I'll let her in. (*He stops and turns to her.*) Kim... I'm proud of you.

KIMBERLY: Thanks.

BRETT (*Goes to the door RIGHT and opens it.*): Caroline, come in.

   CAROLINE *barges past him and goes to* KIMBERLY.

BRETT (*Cont.*) I was just going to get some sleeping pills. Would you like one?

CAROLINE (*Turns to him in disgust.*): What?

BRETT (*As he exits LEFT.*): Never mind.

CAROLINE (*Frantic.*): Kim, we've got to get busy! We've got to get the word to our people! (*She begins walking around the stage looking out to the audience.*) It's payback time, baby! We are going to give them back exactly what they have given us these last eight years. We'll block everything they try to do!

KIMBERLY: And what about the country?

CAROLINE: (*Turns to KIMBERLY.*) What?

KIMBERLY: What happens to the country if we have four more years of nothing getting done? No laws passed? No problems solved? Not even an attempt to solve them.

CAROLINE: Kim, what's gotten into you? We're just doing to them what they have done to us. You know that.

KIMBERLY: Yes, I know. But something strange has happened. Larry called. He made me an offer. (*She looks at the clock.*) I have three minutes before he is going to call for his answer.

CAROLINE: What offer? What could that slimy, snake in the grass offer you?

KIMBERLY: He wants to bury all the partisan demonizing and work together to pass legislation to fix all these issues that we haven't done a thing to resolve. (*Goes to Caroline, sincere.*) Caroline, he really wants to try and work together and get all of our supporters to do the same, for the sake of our country.

CAROLINE (*Sincere.*): Kim?

KIMBERLY: Yes?

CAROLINE: Have you gone out of your fucking mind?

KIMBERLY: Maybe.

BRETT (*Enters with sleeping pills cupped in his hand.*): Okay, I got the sleeping pills right here. Who wants 'em?

CAROLINE (*Holds out her hand.*): Give me two.

BRETT (*Goes to her and gives her two.*): Coming right up! I knew they would come in handy. But, I didn't think it would be you.

CAROLINE (*Takes them and goes to KIMBERLY.*): They're not for me. Take these, Kim. And don't take that call. Let that lying, dirty bastard hang out to dry. Let him wonder what you are going to do and in the morning, kick him right between the thighs. Let him know this is going to be the most miserable four years of his life.

KIMBERLY: And the people of this country? What about them?

CAROLINE (*Turns to BRETT still cupping the pills in her hand.*): Brett, you're her husband! What do you think about all this?

BRETT (*Looks at KIMBERLY who looks at him.*): I think Kim has found something we lost along the way. And I am so glad she found it.

KIMBERLY: Really?

BRETT: Really.

CAROLINE: That's it! You are both out of your fucking minds! (*She goes to KIMBERLY.*) Why didn't Larry offer this when we had the oval office? I'll tell you why! Because they want to do this when they will get all the credit. They'll have the White House for the next twenty years! Kim, he is playing you for a sucker!

KIMBERLY: When did it all become... who gets the credit?

CAROLINE: The first thing we will do is remove you as Speaker. (*She places the pills on the floor, puts her foot on them and crushes them as she looks at KIMBERLY.*) Then we will crush you.

KIMBERLY (*Staring back, cannot believe what CAROLINE just said.*): Caroline? You would do that?

CAROLINE (*Serious.*): I would do that. All of us will do that.

KIMBERLY (*Points to the phone.*): That phone is going to ring any second. I think it's time for you to go.

CAROLINE (*As she exits.*): It's your funeral.

*Cell phone rings. They look at each other for a moment.*

BRETT: Madame Speaker, I believe that's for you.

*She goes over and picks up the phone.*

KIMBERLY: Yes, Mr. President Elect… Yes, I have an answer… (*Looks at BRETT and smiles and he smiles at her.*) Yes, yes, yes!… Me, too!… I agree! We have a lot to do!… (*Slower.*) Yes… yes… (*She looks out at the audience beaming.*) God Bless America.

*Lights dim.*

*Blackout.*

### END OF PLAY

# Wheelchair Chicken

by

Jason Cannon

Directed by Daniel Greene

with

Neil Levine as Roy

David Meyersburg as Whit

Jenny Aldrich as Shirley

CHARACTERS

ROY, a man, 70s to 80s, with thick, powerful arms, but who can take only a very few steps without having to sit down and must get around in a wheelchair.

WHIT, a man, 70s to 80s, bed-ridden. Roy's roommate.

SHIRLEY, a woman, 70s to 80s, gets around with a metal cane with tennis balls on the feet. Roy's girlfriend.

SETTING

ROY and WHIT's room in Rest Haven nursing home, which has two beds. ROY has a mirror that may be invisible so he faces the audience while painting his face.

TIME

The present, mid-morning.

> *Lights up as ROY stands before a mirror. WHIT lies in his bed. ROY has just finished shaving and is patting his face with aftershave.*

ROY: I've never lost!

WHIT: Yep.

ROY: <u>Never</u>. And I won't! Not today. Not never.

WHIT: Huh-uh.

ROY: You know why I've never lost and why I'll never lose?

> *WHIT has heard this many times before.*

WHIT (*Sighing.*): Arms.

ROY: Right, right, DAMN right. Arms! My legs are crap but I've never stopped working my arms.

WHIT: BIG arms.

ROY: Damn right. (*ROY moves slowly and with difficulty to his wheelchair and sits down as he speaks.*) Only thing bigger'n my arms are my damn balls, in't that right Whit?

WHIT: That's right, Roy.

ROY: <u>Damn</u> balls. You know my trick, my secret, the reason I always win and always will?

WHIT (*Needling, disrupting the ritual.*): Extreme halitosis?

ROY: YES, I lean back and... what? (*ROY glares at WHIT; decides to let it pass.*) Haw. Haw haw, Whit, yooooouuu... (*ROY spins adeptly in his wheelchair, leans back, brandishing the stirrups like weapons.*) No! I get goin', faster'n poop through a goose, big arms slammin' these wheels, and then at the last second, when they're deciding whether or not to bail out, I leeeeean back—still goin' full speed mind you!—and aim these metal damn stirrups right at their knees! THAT'S my trick, my secret weapon!

WHIT: Not so much a secret anymore now.

ROY: Doesn't matter. Cuz no one else in Rest Haven can balance <u>backwards</u> while zippin' <u>forwards</u>! Oh god, Whit, <u>god</u>, the way their eyes bulge in terror as I... (*He makes whooshing, slashing, zinging sounds as he spins around.*) There's nothin' like it. And when...

WHIT (*To shut ROY up; family is a sore spot.*): My boy's comin' tomorrow.

*Silence. ROY rolls around aimlessly; perhaps he mutters softly to himself. Then...*

ROY (*Chuckling.*): Remember I put Wilson back in rehab? Cracked his shin wiiiiide open...

WHIT: When's <u>your</u> boy comin', Roy?

*Beat.*

ROY: <u>Wide</u> open. To the damn <u>bone</u>. No one's dared to stay in against me since! (*Pause. He rolls around.*) Go to hell.

WHIT: Bringin' my grandson. Just like last week. Just like next.

ROY: If you're still breathin' next week.

WHIT: Yep. (*Pause. Satisfied.*) Yep.

*Silence. WHIT lays still, looking at the ceiling or maybe his eyes are closed. ROY sits, fuming. Suddenly he whirls around the room in his wheelchair.*

ROY: My boy's busy. REAL busy. New important job.

WHIT: Uh-huh.

ROY: And my granddaughter was sick, she's gettin' better, she was sick...

WHIT: For three months?

ROY: Damn three months! Three damn months, I don't care. (*Beat.*) Your boy's gettin' fat.

WHIT: Yep. (*Pause.*) I wish I could eat steak again.

*Silence.*

ROY (*Muttering.*) Busy important job. That's my boy.

*ROY stands painfully and hobbles back to the mirror. He pulls a tube of colored lipstick from his pocket, and starts applying it to his face, under his eyes like a football player, maybe across his forehead in some sort of violent pattern, or filling in his eyelids. He looks ridiculous yet also aggressive, like an attempt at a horror movie monster/villain. After a few moments of precise lipstick work...*

WHIT: That fake face paint doesn't scare anyone.

ROY: Fierce. (*Carefully drawing on his face.*) Sharp.

WHIT: Uh-huh.

*SHIRLEY enters brightly.*

SHIRLEY: G'morning Whit!

WHIT: Shirley.

SHIRLEY: Roy, angel, I've got great news! (*She sees him painting his face.*) Oh no. Roy. Roy no.

ROY: Don't start Shirl.

SHIRLEY: Whit, is it a game day??

WHIT: 'fraid so.

SHIRLEY: ROY.

ROY: Damn Shirley leave it!

SHIRLEY: Who's gonna pay for your macho lunacy this time, Roy? Is it Glen?

ROY: Doesn't matter who, I'm gonna win.

SHIRLEY: And is that my [*insert favorite weird name of lipstick shade*]?! Roy, you gotta stop this! You know Nurse Collins is just looking for any excuse. She's gonna kick you out of Rest Haven, if you don't kill yourself first. Your boy will have to move you somewhere else.

WHIT (*Warning.*): Hup.

ROY (*He points at her with the lipstick.*): You don't talk about my boy! He's busy!

SHIRLEY: Roy, angel, I'm sorry, I know, but listen...

ROY: Why should I listen to you?? You're only even with me cuz I put your old flame in traction. I won you a pretty penny that day, didn't I? You bet on the right horse _that_ day, didn't you? Well, sweetheart, you can bet on me again today. (*As he speaks he finishes his face, caps the lipstick and puts it back in his pocket, and moves back to his wheelchair, sitting down carefully.*) I don't care who it is, I've never lost, and damn you for telling me to stop when you were the biggest game day bettor of all of 'em!

SHIRLEY: I know I was, Roy, but I've stopped and now you've got to stop! The attendants are on high alert. They're sick of all the broken bones. There's even a rumor Nurse Collins has installed cameras in the ceiling so she can get enough evidence to take away your wheelchair.

WHIT (*Under his breath.*): Aw hell, Shirley.

ROY: Take away my... ?! (*An awful, awful, _awful_ silence.*) Now both of you listen up. I'm gonna keep on playing wheelchair chicken until I drop dead, you get me? Until I'm smashed to a pulp or have a heart attack, I don't care, I'm slammin' my arms against these wheels and streakin' down that hallway as long as I draw breath!

SHIRLEY: Roy, angel, if you play today... you and me are through.

*ROY is stunned. WHIT whistles softly through his teeth.*

ROY: Shirl... !

SHIRLEY: No. _No_ Roy. I can't. I can't take it anymore. I won't!

ROY: You just don't get it, Shirl!

SHIRLEY: What don't I get, Roy? Please, I really would like to know! What is it? _What_?

ROY: It's the only good thing I have left in my life! (*Stunned beat. Then in a torrent...*) My son never... And I haven't seen my granddaughter since... The food is mushy crap, I'm not allowed beer but I still piss six times a night, showering is now a team damn sport and not in a good way, speaking of which and no offense sweetheart but my pecker hasn't been hard in seven damn _years_, and wheelchair chicken is the _only_ thing tellin' me I'm still _alive_, the only thing provin' my heart still beats! When Glen or Wilson or whoever sees me comin' at 'em full throttle, knowin' I don't care, that I'll go all the way, and I see 'em bail out, divin' like chickens...!

SHIRLEY (*Pause.*): Roy...

ROY: ...that tells me I'm actually still a _man_.

*Silence. SHIRLEY carefully approaches ROY, touches him gently. He starts to crumple under her touch, but suddenly goes rigid. He growls and spins away with a flourish.*

ROY: Wish me damn luck! (*Silence.*) Alright.

*ROY exits, zipping adroitly out the door. SHIRLEY shuffles to the door, looking out after ROY, tracking him down the hall.*

SHIRLEY: Whit. I don't understand. He's risking everything. It just doesn't <u>figure</u>.

*From down the hall we hear cheering, the excited voices of Rest Haven's bettors, bookies, and wheelchair chicken fans. Perhaps we hear ROY's name chanted a few times.*

SHIRLEY: Tell me something?

WHIT: Hmm?

SHIRLEY: If he hadn't shattered both your kneecaps in your last match, would *you* still be playing?

*WHIT looks at her.*

WHIT: Some things don't figure, Shirley. Some things just <u>are</u>.

*SHIRLEY snorts, not knowing whether to laugh or cry. Then she sighs heavily.*

SHIRLEY: They're here.

WHIT: Huh?

SHIRLEY: Roy's son and granddaughter. They're here. That's what I was coming to tell him.

WHIT: Oh! (*Beat.*) Oh man.

*The crash of metal and a sudden and ongoing chorus of screams and shrieks is heard offstage. SHIRLEY looks out the door and gasps.*

WHIT: Roy?

SHIRLEY: Oh no. Oh god no.

*SHIRLEY's knees buckle, her hand goes to her chest, and she seems to stumble. Sudden blackout. The horrified shrieking fades as… Lights come back up. ROY is in bed, looking at the ceiling, face clean. WHIT is in bed, looking at the ceiling. WHIT looks at ROY. Looks back at the ceiling. Silence.*

WHIT: She's gonna be OK. (*Pause.*) Shirley told me she was gonna be ok.

*Pause.*

ROY: I was so focused on Glen. I didn't even see her run out, she was just so small. But... she's also gotten so big.

*Beat.*

WHIT: You only busted one of her shins. The other is barely scratched. You turned in time. All her friends will sign her cast. It'll be off in no time. Your granddaughter's gonna be just fine.

*ROY chokes a bit. Gags a bit. Clears his throat.*

WHIT (*Looking at ROY, gently.*): Your boy ever gonna come back?

*Pause.*

ROY: Nurse Collins... she... she took away my...

WHIT: Yeah. Yeah I know, buddy.

*Pause. They both look at the ceiling.*

ROY: My boy. My granddaughter. They came.

WHIT: Mm-hmm.

ROY: They came.

WHIT: They sure did, buddy.

*Pause. Then ROY begins to weep silently, and repeats and repeats into the blackout...*

ROY: I'm not a chicken. I'm a man. I'm a man. I'm a man. I'm a man. I'm a man. I'm a man...

*Lights dim.*

*Blackout.*

## END OF PLAY

# *Student Play Festival Winner 2017*

# Amazing Grace

## by

## Luke Valadie

Directed by Preston Boyd

with

Chuck Conlon as Smith

James Kassees as Newton

Letherio Jones as Slave

Tami Vaughn as Wife/Assistant

CHARACTERS
SMITH, a man, 40s.

NEWTON, a man, 20s.

SLAVE, a black man, 20s to 40s.

WIFE/ASSISTANT, a woman, 40s.

SETTING
SMITH's office.

TIME
The 1740s.

> *The hymn* Amazing Grace *plays.*
>
> *Lights up on SMITH and NEWTON.*

SMITH: My last captain, you know, earned two thousand pounds on this same voyage. More than he had earned on all of his previous voyages combined.

NEWTON: Two thousand? In the matter of a year?

SMITH: Yes, two thousand. He's taken some time off now to live with his family. He may never need to do a voyage again. The point is, John…

NEWTON: Yes?

SMITH: I need you to do this for me. From here to Africa to pick up the slaves, then to the Caribbean, and back again. One year's voyage, and you'll be a rich man. I don't see how anyone in his right mind could possibly turn this down.

NEWTON: Hold on a minute. My musical compositions have come a long way recently. They may one day be as lucrative as this deal you're offering.

SMITH: Not that hobby, again? Get over it, man! This is a man's work I'm offering, respectable work. Do you really hope to make your living as a singing harlot?

NEWTON (*Shaking his head at insults.*): But the route's dangerous. You know that. And at some point I'd like to start a family, settle down, buy some of my own slaves.

SMITH: This is the perfect opportunity to get that started!

NEWTON: It's a lot of money, I'll grant you that. But the risk… the risk is real, Smith.

SMITH: Come on, man, you're a skilled captain. You'll have no trouble. It's a single trip. I'll provide the ship and the crew. Give me one year.

NEWTON (*Sarcastically.*): Oh, only a year.

SMITH: After this voyage you'll have everything you need to start a family and buy some slaves.

NEWTON: I suppose that's true...

SMITH: That's exactly what my last captain did. Think of his prosperity!

*Pause, as NEWTON contemplates.*

NEWTON: God, I don't know...

SMITH: Don't think about the risk. Think of the profits.

NEWTON: Two thousand, you said?

SMITH: Indeed.

NEWTON: That's a significant sum, no doubt, but does it account for the danger? I think not. Twenty five hundred and I'm in. You've told me the value of the cargo, so I know you can spare an extra five hundred.

SMITH (*Thinks for a moment*): I suppose that's fair. Twenty five hundred it is.

NEWTON (*Smiles, then with bravado.*): Alright, it's a deal then.

SMITH (*Extending hand for hand shake, then speaking as they shake hands.*) Fantastic! Believe me, John, you'll be glad you didn't pass up this opportunity. It's unlike any of the piddling voyages you've done in the past. This is real business, and soon you'll have real wealth.

NEWTON: You're right. I welcome the opportunity.

*SLAVE walks in carrying tray of tea. As he begins to walk up to the men, he from comes behind NEWTON.*

SMITH: Good. Good.

NEWTON: Thanks for offering such irresistible profits. And you were right. No man in his right mind could have said no.

SMITH: Well, Newton, I know you well enough. And every man has a price.

*NEWTON stands, smiling.*

NEWTON. I'll be in touch next week so we can work out the details.

*NEWTON turns around, runs into SLAVE, gets tea all over him.*

SLAVE: I'm so sorry, sir! Let me get that for you...

NEWTON: Enough! Get away from me, you useless piece of filth!

*SLAVE backs away, looks very guilty.*

SMITH: You imbecile! Can you do nothing right? (*Turning to John.*) John, I apologize for this clumsy lout.

SLAVE: Really, sir, let me help...

NEWTON: No! I told you to get away!

SMITH: Listen to the man! Did you not hear him the first time?

SLAVE: I'm sorry, I'm so sorry...

SMITH: John, can I offer you a new shirt?

NEWTON: No, no. It's not your fault.. But if this were my slave, he'd receive a good whipping! (*He spits on SLAVE's shoe.*)

*SLAVE exits.*

SMITH: I assure you that he'll receive a just punishment, and you won't have to cast your eyes upon him again.

NEWTON: Very well. (*Dabbing himself with cloth.*) Next week, then.

*After NEWTON exits, SMITH shakes his head, then sits behind his desk. Lights go down, then back up to show the passage of time. SMITH sits at his desk, writing, then his assistant enters with a sense of urgency.*

ASSISTANT: Sir! Sir! I come with news of the voyage.

SMITH: Ah, Newton's journey? Good news, I presume? (*Putting down his pen.*) Have they arrived in the Caribbean?

*The ASSISTANT looks away and doesn't respond at first.*

SMITH (*Cont.*): Well, go on, what is it?

ASSISTANT: There was a storm, sir... a bad one.

SMITH: And?

ASSISTANT: Newton was on the second leg of his trip from Africa to the Caribbean, less than a hundred miles from port. The ship, it was... it was utterly destroyed. All the cargo lost.

SMITH: And my crew?

ASSISTANT: I'm not sure, but I presume that all were lost as well.

SMITH: Is this some sick joke that Newton asked you to play on me?

ASSISTANT (*After a long pause.*): No, sir, I'm afraid not.

SMITH: But he ranked among the finest captains to sail beneath the British flag. How could he have possibly lost all of my cargo and crew?

ASSISTANT: I honestly don't know, sir.

SMITH: And what of Newton? Did he go down with the ship?

ASSISTANT: No, sir. He... he was picked up by a passing Navy vessel. From the report I received, Newton was drowning when one of the slaves pulled him from the wreckage. The slave drowned shortly afterwards. As for Newton, he's on his way back to London.

SMITH: If he'd been a true captain, he would've finished the job or drowned himself. Clearly, I misjudged the man. Bring him to me as soon as he arrives!

ASSISTANT: Yes, sir. Anything else?

SMITH (*Standing, then speaking mostly to himself as he paces.*): His reputation was impeccable. How... how could he have done this to me?

ASSISTANT: I... I don't know, sir.

SMITH (*Still pacing.*): Of course you don't know. I wasn't asking you, you fool! Do you have any idea how much capital was on that ship? (*Disconsolate.*) Half of everything I owned... half.

*SMITH sits and buries his head in his hands.*

ASSISTANT: I'm at a loss for words, sir.

SMITH: Then be gone from my sight.

*Lights go down, then back up to show the passage of time. SMITH sits at his desk, when NEWTON enters, head down, hoping to avert SMITH's glare.*

SMITH: Look up at me, man, and make an account of yourself.

NEWTON: The storm, it... it came upon us without warning. The voyage had gone perfectly up until that point. We got to Africa without a hitch, then we....

*NEWTON looks away, defeated, guilty.*

SMITH: Stop your stammering and get to the bloody point!

NEWTON: After we picked up the slaves, and set out for the Caribbean...

SMITH: Yes? And then?

NEWTON: Despite our efforts, we couldn't get the sails down in time after the storm broke.

*NEWTON looks visibly distressed.*

SMITH (*Impatiently.*): And?

NEWTON (*After hesitating.*) The slaves, your crew, they... they all perished. (*Now visibly upset.*) Except for the nameless slave who pulled me from the wreckage. (*He looks up.*) He saved my life, my worthless, <u>wretched</u> life.

SMITH: How could you have failed me, Newton? You know how much capital was invested in that ship and cargo!

NEWTON: Do you not think I did everything in my power? The storm was simply too much.

SMITH: You're an expert captain. You should have done more—or you should've gone down with my ship.

NEWTON: I fully intended to do so, then I was saved. Oh, how I wish that slave had let me be. By God, the torment... Believe me, every single waking moment since that ship began to break in two, since I heard the screams of drowning men, I... I....

SMITH: If you weren't man enough for the job, you shouldn't have taken it.

NEWTON: So, that's how it is. You begged me to take the journey, and now you... you treat me as if it's all <u>my</u> fault, like I had any control over the storm. Is that it?

SMITH (*After a long pause.*): God, Newton, think of all I've lost.

NEWTON: How do you think I feel? Hundreds of men died under my watch! <u>My</u> watch. My God, can't you understand?

SMITH: Oh, get over it, man.

NEWTON (*Growling.*): Get over it? Just like that, huh? Am I simply to forget the hundreds of souls from Africa who now lie at the bottom of the Atlantic? Who died just so that we could line our pockets with gold?

SMITH: That's the business we're in! That's how we earn our daily bread. If you're not up for it, you should have never taken the job.

NEWTON: That may be your way of life, but I'm through with it.

SMITH: To hell you are! You owe me another journey, but this time you'll be an assistant captain with a pittance for your pay. You ruined my last voyage, John. You're not out of the woods.

*SLAVE enters room. He looks to SMITH, then NEWTON.*

SLAVE: Tea, sir?

SMITH (*Looking at SLAVE.*): Be gone, you worthless wretch.

NEWTON: Stop it, Smith. (*To SLAVE.*) Are you the one who spilled tea on me last time I was here?

*SLAVE puts his head down and nods.*

NEWTON: I want to apologize for behavior that day. I... I...

SMITH: What? Now you apologize to slaves? Have you lost all respect for yourself? (*Looks at SLAVE.*) Go on! Get out of here!

NEWTON (*Standing.*): Stop! Do you not understand? Ever since the wreck, I've regretted every last moment of my life beforehand.

SMITH: By God, John. Cease this madness immediately.

NEWTON: Not until you show your slave the respect that he deserves.

SMITH: What the hell has gotten into you, man? He's a slave!

NEWTON: It's because of a slave that I'm even standing here. And I won't have you disgrace him or any of his lot in my presence!

SMITH (*Slowly rising.*): You've gone insane, haven't you?

NEWTON: That shipwreck taught me more than anything else in my life. I was a blind man, groping in the darkness. But no more.

SMITH: Leave now, John!

NEWTON: Not until we strike another bargain.

SMITH: Over what?

NEWTON: Your slave. I want to purchase his freedom. Name your price.

SMITH: (*Still laughing.*) Well, John, he's not for sale. One failed voyage and you turn into something disgusting and shameful? I really expected more from you. You could have been one of my greatest sailors. I could have made you rich...

NEWTON (*Interrupting.*): To hell with being rich!

SMITH: But you failed, and now look what you are.

NEWTON: You think I give a damn about the money? None of that matters, Smith.

SMITH: Oh, is that so? I seem to remember you being swayed by money alone!

NEWTON: No longer! Everything you've ever worked for has been built on others' suffering!

SMITH: Is this a joke? I thought you had more sense than that!

NEWTON: And I thought you had some decency about you! Now name the price for this man's freedom!

SMITH: Get out of my sight and go to hell.

NEWTON: Too late, Smith. I've already been there.

*Lights dim.*

*Blackout.*

END OF PLAY

# Rights and Permissions

A Big Wave ©2017 by Connie Schindewolf. Reprinted by permission of Connie Schindewolf. For performance rights, contact Connie Schindewolf (allmyturtles52@msn.com).

A Bottle of Vodka ©2014 by Connie Schindewolf. Reprinted by permission of Connie Schindewolf. For performance rights, contact Connie Schindewolf (allmyturtles52@msn.com).

A Tender Moment ©2016 by Frank Motz. Reprinted by permission of Frank Motz. For performance rights, contact Frank Motz (fmotz@neo.rr.com).

Always ©2017 by Stephen Cooper. Reprinted by permission of Stephen Cooper. For performance rights, contact Stephen Cooper (cooper@umich.edu).

Amazing Grace ©2017 by Luke Valadie. Reprinted by permission of Luke Valadie. For performance rights, contact Theatre Odyssey (theatreodyssey@gmail.com).

As Long as the Moon Shines ©2015 by Julien Freij. Reprinted by permission of Julien Freij. For performance rights, contact Theatre Odyssey (theatreodyssey@gmail.com).

Brothers in Arms ©2016 by Julien Freij. Reprinted by permission of Julien Freij. For performance rights, contact Theatre Odyssey (theatreodyssey@gmail.com).

Call These Delicate Creatures Ours, and Not Their Appetites ©2016 by Peter A. Balaskas. Reprinted by permission of Peter A. Balaskas. For performance rights, contact Peter A. Balaskas (exmachinapab@aol.com).

Chopping Celery ©2016 by Connie Schindewolf. Reprinted by permission of Connie Schindewolf. For performance rights, contact Connie Schindewolf (allmyturtles52@msn.com).

Clarinet Licks ©2016 by Fredric Sirasky. Reprinted by permission of Fredric Sirasky. For performance rights, contact Theatre Odyssey (theatreodyssey@gmail.com).

Elevate My Life ©2014 by Joseph Grosso. Reprinted by permission of Joseph Grosso. For performance rights, contact Theatre Odyssey (joseph_grosso@rocketmail.com).

Dream On, Merry May ©2015 by Bernard Yanelli. Reprinted by permission of Bernard Yanelli. For performance rights, contact Bernard Yanelli (bernard.yanelli@gmail.com).

Fancy Seeing You Here ©2014 by Marvin Albert. Reprinted by permission of Marvin Albert. For performance rights, contact Marvin Albert (gerrimarvin@comcast.net).

For Art's Sake ©2014 by Bernard Yanelli. Reprinted by permission of Bernard Yanelli. For performance rights, contact Bernard Yanelli (bernard.yanelli@gmail.com).

Hands ©2016 by Sylvia Reed. Reprinted by permission of Sylvia Reed. For performance rights, contact Sylvia Reed (sylviareedw@gmail.com).

High School Reunion ©2015 by Arthur Keyser. Reprinted by permission of Arthur Keyser. For performance rights, contact Art Senior Theatre Resource Center (www.seniortheatre.com).

I'll Be Home for Christmas ©2014 by Dale E. Moore. Reprinted by permission of Dale E. Moore. For performance rights, contact Dale E. Moore (demor37@yahoo.com).

I'm Dead When I Say I'm Dead ©2017 by Ron Pantello. Reprinted by permission of Ron Pantello. For performance rights, contact Ron Pantello (rgp123s@aol.com).

# Rights and Permissions (Continued)

It's Time to Move ©2015 by Ron Pantello. Reprinted by permission of Ron Pantello. For performance rights, contact Ron Pantello (rgp123s@aol.com).

Just Fooling ©2014 by Verna Safran. Reprinted by permission of Verna Safran. For performance rights, contact Michael Tomasson (michael.tomasson@gmail.com).

Kennedy's Acolytes ©2017 by Jack Gilhooley. Reprinted by permission of Jack Gilhooley. For performance rights, contact Jack Gilhooley (jackgilhooley@tampabay.rr.com).

Miss O'Hara, I Have a Confession to Make ©2016 by Bernard Yanelli. Reprinted by permission of Bernard Yanelli. For performance rights, contact Bernard Yanelli (bernard.yanelli@gmail.com).

Nimby ©2015 by Robert Kinast. Reprinted by permission of Robert Kinast. For performance rights, contact Robert Kinast (rkinast@aol.com).

School for Wives ©2014 by Arthur Keyser. Reprinted by permission of Arthur Keyser. For performance rights, contact Art Senior Theatre Resource Center (www.seniortheatre.com).

Secret's Out ©2017 by Greg Burdick. Reprinted by permission of Greg Burdick. For performance rights, contact Greg Burdick (gdburdick@gmail.com).

Silences ©2016 by Mark E Leib. Reprinted by permission of Mark E. Leib. For performance rights, contact Mark E. Leib (meleib48@gmail.com).

Smart Bra ©2014 by Sylvia Reed. Reprinted by permission of Sylvia Reed. For performance rights, contact Sylvia Reed (sylviareedw@gmail.com).

The Best Ten Minutes Ever ©2017 by Dylan Jones. Reprinted by permission of Dylan Jones. For performance rights, contact Theatre Odyssey (theatreodyssey@gmail.com).

The Call ©2017 by Frank Motz. Reprinted by permission of Frank Motz. For performance rights, contact Frank Motz (fmotz@neo.rr.com).

The Clown ©2016 by Larry Hamm. Reprinted by permission of Larry Hamm. For performance rights, contact Larry Hamm (larry@larryhamm.com).

The Coward ©2015 by Dylan Jones. Reprinted by permission of Dylan Jones. For performance rights, contact Theatre Odyssey (theatreodyssey@gmail.com).

The Dancing Lessons ©2015 by Connie Schindewolf. Reprinted by permission of Connie Schindewolf. For performance rights, contact Connie Schindewolf (allmyturtles52@msn.com).

The Locket ©2015 by Mark E Leib. Reprinted by permission of Mark E. Leib. For performance rights, contact Mark E. Leib (meleib48@gmail.com).

Visiting Grandpa ©2014 by Ron Pantello. Reprinted by permission of Ron Pantello. For performance rights, contact Ron Pantello (rgp123s@aol.com).

Wheelchair Chicken ©2017 by Jason Cannon. Reprinted by permission of Jason Cannon. For performance rights, contact Jason Cannon (citizencannon@gmail.com).

Why ©2015 by Marvin Albert. Reprinted by permission of Marvin Albert. For performance rights, contact Marvin Albert (gerrimarvin@comcast.net).

# ALSO FROM NIGEL PUBLISHING

Founded in 2006 to promote the efforts of playwrights and actors on the Gulf Coast of Florida, Theatre Odyssey is preparing for its 13th Ten-Minute Play Festival in 2018, having premiered over 150 plays, many of which have enjoyed later productions throughout the United States. This volume represents the third in a series, each volume covering four years of the Festival.

## Theatre Odyssey Ten-Minute Play Festival
### Volume One: 2006—2009

Volume One covers those plays from the first four years of the Festival and includes winners Claws and Effect (by Michael Phelan), Preconception (by Larry Hamm), and Stormy (by Walton Beacham).

TO PURCHASE VOLUME ONE CONTACT Theatre Odyssey at www.theatreodyssey.org or theatreodyssey@gmail.com

## Theatre Odyssey Ten-Minute Play Festival
### Volume Two: 2010—2013

Volume Two covers those plays from the second four years of the Festival and includes winners The Silence (by Connie Schindewolf), The Ordinance (by Paul Argentini), Confessions à Deux (by Stephen Cooper), and A Little Help (by Bernard Yanelli).

TO PURCHASE VOLUME TWO CONTACT Theatre Odyssey at www.theatreodyssey.org or theatreodyssey@gmail.com

## Available through Amazon, Barnes & Noble, Target and other National Booksellers

www.ingramcontent.com/pod-product-compliance
Lightning Source LLC
Chambersburg PA
CBHW060113170426
43198CB00010B/876